The C++ Primer
A Gentle Introduction to C++

M. T. Skinner

 **Silicon Press**
Summit New Jersey USA

 **Prentice Hall**
New York London Toronto Sydney Tokyo Singapore

First published in the USA by Silicon Press, 25 Beverly Road,
Summit, New Jersey 07901, USA, and co-published for sale outside
North America by Prentice Hall, Campus 400, Maylands Avenue, Hemel
Hempstead, Hertfordshire HP2 7EZ, England, a division of
Simon Schuster International Group, and Silicon Press.

Printed in Great Britain by Redwood Books, Trowbridge, Wiltshire

---

Library of Congress Cataloging-in-Publication Data

Skinner, M. T.
    The C++ primer: a gentle introduction to C++ / M. T. Skinner.
        p.   cm.
    Includes bibliographical references (p.   ) and index.
    ISBN 0-13-088501-0: $40.00
    1. C++ (Computer program language)   I. Title
[QA76.73.C153S56   1992b]
005.13´3--dc20   92-29100
                                                          CIP

British Library Cataloguing in Publication Data

A catalogue record for this book is available from the British Library.

ISBN 0-13-088501-0 (pbk)

---

5 96 95

CONTENTS

PREFACE

A programming language is the "user interface" with which the programmer (user) instructs the computer what actions are to be performed. A computer "program" is a series of instructions in a programming language to accomplish a task. A "general purpose" programming language is one that can be used for writing programs for a variety of application (problem) domains. On the other hand, a specialized programming language can only be used for a specific application domain.

C++ is a general purpose programming language designed by Bjarne Stroustrup [1991] of AT&T Bell Laboratories.[1] C++ is the successor to the very popular C programming language [Kernighan & Ritchie 1989]. Although C++ is based on C, it is not just a new version of C! C++ is a new generation programming language.

C++ provides a variety of facilities such as those for

- defining constants and variables,
- variable initialization,
- assignment,
- expression specification,
- conditional execution,
- loops,
- function definitions and calls,
- data abstraction,
- multiple inheritance,
- passing arguments by reference,
- initialization,
- automating cleanup,
- operator and function overloading,
- type conversions, and

---

1. Square brackets are used to cite references to works, listed in the Bibliography, where readers can find detailed information.

- writing templates.

Besides improving upon C by providing facilities for better type checking such as "function prototypes", C++ provides facilities for "object-oriented" programming. In object-oriented programming, the focus of the program is the data, i.e., the objects, in the program. In conventional programming, the focus of the program is the data manipulation code. Object-oriented programming is now recognized as a powerful programming technique that supports code reuse and that can lead to the development of modular and extensible programs.

The primary facilities which make a programming language into an object-oriented programming language are those for data abstraction and inheritance. These facilities allow programmers to write applications using concepts and notations natural to the application domain. For example, data abstraction allows programmers to elegantly model application domain objects such as input/output devices, robots, and employees. And inheritance allows the preservation of relationships between object types that are related to each other, e.g., employees and managers.

1. ABOUT THIS BOOK

This book is an introduction to C++. Although no prior programming knowledge is required, such knowledge will be a definite plus in reading this book and learning C++ quickly. The material in this book is based on the book titled *The Advanced C++ Book* [Skinner 1992].

C++ provides many facilities for writing clear and succinct programs. In this book, I will discuss only those C++ facilities that give programmers most of the power and benefits of using C++. I will avoid discussing in detail the esoteric facilities of C++, which are meant primarily for advanced programmers. After a quick introduction to C++, I will discuss the following C++ topics in detail:

- Basics
- Types
- Operators and expressions
- Statements
- Functions
- Arrays
- Pointers
- Structures
- Classes
- Members
- Inheritance
- Friends
- Type conversions
- Overloading
- Stream input/output

- Templates
- Variable argument functions
- Preprocessor
- C++ libraries

The book contains numerous examples, which have been tested. When a C++ header file or a source file contains five or more lines, then line numbers are printed in the left margin besides the code shown. These numbers are printed for ease of reference; they are not part of the C++ code.

A diskette containing the source code for the examples presented in the book is available from Silicon Press. Names of the files containing the code of the example programs are specified in the text for two reasons:

- Ease of reference, because C++ files often include other files.

- To locate the examples on the diskette.

2. C++ VERSION DESCRIBED IN THIS BOOK

C++ is a language that has been evolving to meet the needs of its users. The version of C++ described in this book is the latest version of C++ [Stroustrup 1991; Ellis & Stroustrup 1990]. This version of C++, which is being used as the basis for the ANSI standardization of C++, is an enhanced version of the original C++ as described in the book titled *The C++ Programming Language* [Stroustrup 1986].

3. FONT CONVENTION

I will use `typewriter` font to show C++ code (program fragments). Within the C++ code, if an item is not actual code, but is instead an item representing code to be filled in, then I will use *italic* font. Also, I will use *italic* font for items in the C++ code shown and for C++ keywords when referring to them in the text.

4. ACKNOWLEDGMENTS

I am grateful to Dick Diffenderfer and to the anonymous reviewers for their comments. I am very appreciative of and indebted to Silicon Press for encouraging me to write this book.

M. T. Skinner

Chapter 1
INTRODUCTION

Programming is the discipline of writing a sequence of instructions, called a "program", to control a computer. Computer instructions are often called "statements." Some statements are called "declarations" or "definitions", because their main role is to specify information. Other statements are called "executable" statements, because they make the computer perform (execute) actions.

Often, for ease of use, multiple statements that perform a single task are bundled together and given one name. In most programming languages this bundling is done by using the "function" facility. A function (that is, the instructions represented by it) is executed by simply "calling" the function. A function can also return a value, that is, the result of its execution.

A program is much like a cooking recipe. If the recipe is correct and we follow it to the letter, then the result will be as claimed for the recipe. Similarly, if the program is written correctly, then the computer (which always follows instructions to the letter) will do what we expect.

Computers typically understand programs written in a very "low-level" language called "machine code." A machine code instruction is a series of 0s and 1s. Programs for the early computers were written in machine code. Unfortunately, humans find machine code very hard to read and understand. Consequently, computer scientists developed "high-level" programming languages, which are intended for human use. They also developed "compilers" (translators) that convert programs written in high-level programming languages to machine code programs.

Compilers are themselves programs. Most of the early compilers, and many of the present day compilers, belong to the "batch" category in that they are "invoked" to translate the program after the program has been written. The program is itself written with the help of an "editor" and then saved in a "file". The editor does not know about programming language rules; as a result, it cannot flag errors in the program. The compiler flags errors in the program and these must be corrected using the editor.

The class of errors flagged by the compiler are called "syntactic" or "compile-time" errors. There is another class of errors called "run-time" errors, which are the result of inappropriate instructions in the program. Such errors can be detected only when the program is run. Fixing compile-time errors is routine. Fixing run-time errors can be difficult, because these errors often do not manifest themselves at the "erroneous" instructions. Instead their effects become visible at some later, possibly much later, point in the execution of the program.

The newer generation of compilers, as exemplified by the Borland C++ compiler, offer an integrated interactive environment in which the compiler

1. assists the programmer to write the program,
2. detects syntax errors as the program is entered,
3. provides facilities to "run" the program, and
4. helps locate run-time errors (with a "debugger").

Regardless of whether the compiler is of the batch or of the interactive variety, compiling is a two-stage process: first the program is written and then it is translated. Another category of translation programs is an "interpreter" which gives the programmer the view that computers understand a high-level programming language such as C++. Interpreters execute program instructions as soon as they read them. Consequently, errors (particular run-time errors) are detected at an early stage in the program development process. However, program execution using an interpreter is slow compared to the execution of the compiled version of the same program.

1. WRITING PROGRAMS IN C++

C++ programs, especially large ones, tend to be object-oriented in that the programs focus on "data objects." This style of programming is called "object-oriented" programming. The purpose of an "object-oriented" program is to establish (setup or create) the objects and then manipulate them.

An excellent way of learning programming is to write programs. In this section, I will show you two simple programs, explain what they do, and how they do it. The first program focuses on printing output. The second one illustrates the three important functions of a program: input, followed by computation, and then output. The programming facilities used in these examples will be discussed in detail in the coming chapters.

1.1 PRINTING OUTPUT

We will write a simple program that prints the following lines on the monitor screen:

```
Hello Programmer!
Welcome to the World of C++!
```

The C++ program that prints these two lines is (file *hello.cpp*)

```
#include <iostream.h>
int main()
{
    cout << "Hello Programmer!" << endl;
    cout << "Welcome to the World of C++!" << endl;
}
```

The program is stored in the file *hello.cpp*, which is called the source file. Line 1 is a C++ "preprocessor" *include* instruction, which includes all the "declarations" necessary to use the input/output facilities. Before an item is used in C++, it must be "defined" or "declared." A C++ item "definition" tells the C++ compiler exactly what the item is, how it should be used and, if appropriate, C++ instructions to be executed when the item is used. An item "declaration" simply informs the C++ compiler how the item will be used. Item declarations are used routinely, because the item definition may be given later in the source file or it may be given in a separate source file. Files that contain only declarations are called "header" files.

The C++ compiler actually consists of two parts: a "preprocessor" and the actual compiler. The preprocessor, as its name implies, processes the program before the compiler. It only processes lines that begin with the # character. In this program there is only one such line, the *#include* instruction. The effect of the above *#include* instruction is to bring into the C++ program the contents of the header file *iostream.h*. This file contains the declarations for the facilities that are used for writing output or for reading data. The angle brackets surrounding the header file name tell the C++ to look for the specified header file in "standard" places.

The definition of the *main* function starts with line 2 and has the form

```
int main()
{
    body
}
```

main is the name of the function. Each program must have a *main* function, which is the function executed first. C++ requires specification of the *main* function to construct a complete program. Normally, functions must be explicitly called from within the program. The distinguished *main* function is an exception – it is "called" by the operating system, e.g., MS-DOS[TM] or UNIX[TM], to begin execution.

Line 2 (the first line of the function definition) specifies that we are now defining a "function" named *main*, the left curly brace in line 3 signals the beginning of the body of *main* and the right curly brace in line 6 signals the end of the body.

The first line of the definition of function *main* contains a pair of parentheses (right after the identifier *main*). This "empty" pair indicates that *main* will not accept any values such as numbers or strings before beginning program execution. Such values are called "arguments" and they are supplied by the caller of a function (which in case of *main* is the operating system). To be precise, we should have declared *main* as

```
int main(void)
{
    body
}
```

where "identifier" (word) *void* indicates that *main* does not accept any arguments. This identifier is a special word in C++ and can only be used as specified by C++. For historical reasons (the C ancestry of C++), this identifier is omitted.

The actual output is produced as a result of executing the two instructions in the body of the *main* function:

```
cout << "Hello Programmer!" << endl;
cout << "Welcome to the World of C++!" << endl;
```

Each of these lines of C++ code prints a text string followed by the new-line character. Note that the text to be output is enclosed within quotes. *cout* refers to the monitor. Actually, to be precise, *cout* is the name of the "output stream" that refers to the monitor. Output is written to output streams and input is read from "input streams." The character pair << is an output stream "operator" (just as the character + is the arithmetic addition operator). Operator << sends its right operand (the value on the right) to the stream specified by the left operand (the value on the left). It then returns the stream as its result.

Each of the above two lines is a C++ statement. Except for executable statements that end with a curly brace, all other statements must be terminated by a semicolon. (Statements enclosed within curly braces are called "compound" statements.)

The above two output instructions could have also been written as

```
cout << "Hello Programmer!";
cout << endl;
cout << "Welcome to the World of C++!";
cout << endl;
```

endl is the name of a special function called a "manipulator" function. The effect of using it with the <<, as shown above, is to print a new-line character.

Unlike in languages such as BASIC, in C++ we cannot tell the compiler or the interpreter to simply execute the two output statements (lines 4-5 in the program shown above) to produce the desired output. These statements must be encapsulated within a *main* program.

1.1.1 FILE NAMING CONVENTION Files containing C++ programs are called "source" files. Many C++ compilers require that C++ source files names must have an appropriate "suffix" such as *.c* or *.cpp*. For example, UNIX system C++ compilers require C++ source files to have the *.c* suffix. MS-DOS® system C++ compilers, such as the Zortech and Borland C++ compilers, require C++ source files to have the suffix *.cpp* so that the compiler can distinguish them from C source files, which must have the *.c* suffix. C++ source files can also be given the *.c* suffix, but then a C++ compiler must be notified, using a compiler "option," that the source file with a *.c* suffix actually contains a C++ program. To avoid confusion, we will simply use the *.cpp* suffix for C++ source files.

Files that contain only declarations are called "header" files. By convention, the suffix *.h* is used for the names of header files.

1.1.2 RUNNING THE PROGRAM The two desired lines (the program "output") are printed when the program is run. But before the program can be run, it must be compiled. With the Borland C++ compiler,[1] the above program is compiled as[2]

```
bcc hello.cpp
```

or as

```
bcc hello
```

In the latter case, the C++ compiler looks for a file named *hello.cpp* to compile (translate). The result of the C++ compiler are two files:

1. *hello.obj*: machine code translation of the C++ program in *hello.cpp*.

2. *hello.exe*: "executable" version of *hello.obj*, which can be executed by the computer. *hello.exe* is the same as *hello.obj*, but it has been "linked" (combined) with other programs (stored in libraries) that are necessary to make the program executable.

The program is executed (run) by typing

---

1. The Turbo C++ compiler is another C++ compiler marketed by Borland.
2. The operating system prompt characters are not shown.

```
hello.exe
```

or simply

```
hello
```

and it prints

```
Hello Programmer!
Welcome to the World of C++!
```

On UNIX systems, C++ source files are typically expected to have the suffix *.c*. Assuming that the name *CC* refers to the C++ compiler, file *hello.c* can be compiled and linked with the command

```
CC hello.c
```

This produces an executable file named *a.out*, which can then be made to run (execute) by typing

```
a.out
```

UNIX programmers can, of course, give the executable file a name more mnemonic than the default name *a.out*. For example, the C++ compiler can be instructed to name the executable file *hello* using the option *-o* as follows:

```
CC -ohello hello.c
```

The resulting executable program can be executed by typing

```
hello
```

1.2 COMPUTING ROOTS OF A QUADRATIC EQUATION

We will now write a program to compute the roots of a quadratic equation of the form

$$y = ax^2 + bx + c$$

The roots of the above quadratic equation are

$$x_1 = \frac{-b + \sqrt{b^2 - 4ac}}{2a}$$

$$x_2 = \frac{-b - \sqrt{b^2 - 4ac}}{2a}$$

The equation shown above will not be a quadratic equation if coefficient a is zero; in such a case the equation is said to be a "linear" equation. The above formulas cannot be used to compute roots of linear equations. Using these formulas in such cases will result in a "division-by-zero" error which will cause the program to terminate "abnormally."

The roots of the above quadratic equation will be complex values if the expression

$$b^2 - 4ac$$

is negative. In this case, we will not compute the roots.

If this problem seems too mathematical, do not worry. Our focus is not on the mathematics of quadratic equations; instead, we are interested in just using the above formulas to compute the roots of a quadratic equation.

The program to compute the roots of a quadratic equation is more complicated than the previous program because it does much more than just print two lines of text. The quadratic equation roots program reads user-supplied data, three items at a time, computes the roots of the quadratic equation, and then prints the roots. The program then repeats the whole process until the input is "exhausted" (finished).

It is usually a good idea to try and informally describe what the program does in English (mixed with programming notation) before writing it in pure C++. The quadratic equation roots program can be described in English-like notation as follows:

```
while  (there is more input, read it)  {
       if  (the roots are complex)
             print an error message and restart the loop ;
       compute and print the roots ;
}
```

The *while* statement specifies a "loop", which executes its body (the statements within the curly braces) as long as the condition *there is more input* is true. The *if* conditional statement executes the statement associated with it, that is, *print an error message and restart the loop* only in cases when its condition *the roots are complex* holds (is true). We will discuss the semantics of these statements in detail in Chapter 5.

We have written the above description not in ordinary English, but in a combination of English and C++ statements (*while* and *if*), and placed different items on different lines with different indentations. Such a descriptive language is often called "pseudo code." Pseudo code descriptions are easier to understand than C++ (or other programming language descriptions) and they are more precise than ordinary English descriptions. However, these descriptions are less precise than C++ programs and therefore cannot be used as programs.

Here is the C++ version of the roots program (file *roots.cpp*):

```
    #include <iostream.h>
    #include <math.h>
    int main()
    {
5       float a, b, c, x1, x2, tmp;
        while (cin >> a >> b >> c) {
            if (a == 0) {
                cerr << "Error! First coeff is 0!";
                cerr << endl;
10              continue;
            }
            if ((tmp = b*b - 4*a*c) < 0) {
                cerr << "Error! Coeff ";
                cerr << a << ", " << b << ", " << c;
15              cerr << " have complex roots" << endl;
                continue;
            }
            tmp = sqrt(tmp);
            x1 = (-b+tmp)/(2*a);
20          x2 = (-b-tmp)/(2*a);
            cout << "Coeff = " << a << ", " << b << ", " << c;
            cout << "; Roots = " << x1 << ", " << x2 << endl;
        }
    }
```

As mentioned earlier, this program is more complicated than the first one. Do not despair if you find this program a bit too complicated — we shall discuss this program in detail.

The first two lines

```
#include <iostream.h>
#include <math.h>
```

include the header files for the input/output facilities (file *iostream.h*) and the declarations of the math facilities (file *math.h*), respectively. These files include the declarations of many facilities besides the ones we will use. We do not need to worry about the specific contents of these files. We simply include them as specified in the descriptions of the input/output and the math facilities (discussed later in detail).

Then, as before, comes the *main* function definition (lines 4-24), which has the form:

```
int main()
{
    body
}
```

This time the *main* function contains a variable definition statement, followed by a *while* statement, which contains a whole lot of other statements. The variable definition statement (line 5)

```
float a, b, c, x1, x2, tmp;
```

defines (specifies) the identifiers *a*, *b*, *c*, *x1*, *x2*, and *tmp*. Identifiers are names. There are special rules for constructing identifiers, which we will discuss in the next chapter. These identifiers name locations in the computer memory which will hold floating-point values (specified by the keyword *float*). We have not assigned any values to these identifiers as yet. The value associated with an identifier, or simply the value of an identifier, can vary. Such identifiers are called "variables." To be more precise, the above identifiers are *float* or floating-point variables. The value assigned to a variable can be changed at any time.

After the definition statement comes the *while* statement (lines 6-23), which in this case has the form

```
while (expression) {
    statements (this is the loop body)
}
```

The *while* statement is a "loop" statement, because as long as the condition denoted by *expression* evaluates to "true" (which in C++ means a non-zero value), the *while* statement repeatedly executes the statements in its body. An "expression" in its simplest form consists of a value such as a number or a string, or an identifier. More complicated expressions can be built using operators and functions.

The *while* expression in this example

```
cin >> a >> b >> c
```

reads three values as input from the keyboard (denoted by *cin*). The person running the program must supply the input values, which are "assigned" to the variables *a*, *b*, and *c*. The input operator >> assigns the first value to the variable *a*, the second value to variable *b*, and the third value to *c*.

Variable *cin*, whose definition is contained in the standard header file *iostream.h*, is by default associated with the standard input stream, that is, the keyboard. Therefore, unless the user of our roots program does something special (we shall see examples of this later), our program will expect the user to supply input by entering values at the keyboard.

The above expression is equivalent to the expression

```
cin >> a, cin >> b, cin >> c
```

where the three input subexpressions are combined by using commas to form a big expression. The value of each of these expressions is the value returned by the input operation, which is the value of the input stream variable *cin*, that is, the input stream itself.

The value of the combined expression is the value of the expression following the last comma, that is, the value returned by the last input operation, which is the input stream *cin*. The *while* statement examines the state of the stream to determine whether or not to continue. The input stream value "evaluates" (using some special rules) to true if operator >> did not encounter the end of input (or any other error) when attempting to read a value; otherwise, it evaluates to "false."

As a result, the *while* statement continues executing the statements in its body as long as >> is able to successfully read values from the input.

The *while* loop body

```
if (a == 0) {
    cerr << "Error! First coeff is 0!";
    cout << endl;
    continue;
}
if ((tmp = b*b - 4*a*c) < 0) {
    cerr << "Error! Coeff ";
    cerr << a << ", " << b << ", " << c;
    cerr << " have complex roots" << endl;
    continue;
}
tmp = sqrt(tmp);
x1 = (-b+tmp)/(2*a);
x2 = (-b-tmp)/(2*a);
cout << "Coeff = " << a << ", " << b << ", " << c;
cout << "; Roots = " << x1 << ", " << x2 << endl;
```

consists of

1. two *if* statements (and its body) followed by

2. three "assignment" statements (each has the assignment operator which is denoted by the = symbol; assignment statements are used to assign values to variables) and

3. two output statements.

The first *if* statement checks to see whether or not coefficient *a* is zero. If it is zero, then the roots cannot be computed because we cannot divide by zero (this division is required in the formulas shown for computing the roots). Both *if* statements have the form

```
if (expression) {
    true-alternative
}
```

The body of the *if* statement, denoted by *true-alternative*, is executed only if the specified *expression* evaluates to true, that is, if the expression

```
a == 0
```

evaluates to true. If the *if* expression is true, i.e., if *a* is equal to zero, then the statements specified by the *true-alternative* are executed.

```
cerr << "Error! First coeff is 0!";
cerr << endl;
continue;
```

The first two statements simply write output to the monitor. Like stream *cout*, the error stream *cerr* is associated with the monitor. Output redirection (discussed later) can be used to associate these streams with different files or the same file (on MS-DOS, only stream *cout* can be associated with a file). Writing error messages to *cerr* and writing ordinary output to *cout*, in conjunction with "output redirection", makes it possible to separate error messages from normal output. Output redirection is discussed later.

The effect of the *continue* statement

```
continue;
```

is to skip the remaining statements in the loop body and to continue the next iteration (execution of the loop body) of the enclosing loop (the *while* loop in our example).

The second *if* statement checks to see whether the quadratic equation has complex roots or real roots. The body of the *if* statement, denoted by *true-alternative*, is executed only if the specified *expression* evaluates to true, that is, if the expression

```
(tmp = b*b - 4*a*c) < 0
```

evaluates to true. This expression is evaluated by first computing the value of the expression

```
b*b - 4*a*c
```

and assigning it to the variable *tmp*. The value of the expression

```
tmp = b*b - 4*a*c
```

which is simply the value of the variable *tmp*, is then compared with 0.

```
(tmp = b*b - 4*a*c) < 0
```

If the value is less than 0, then the *if* expression evaluates to true, indicating that the quadratic equation has complex roots. Parentheses are used in the expression to specify the order in which the components of the expression are to be evaluated. If the *if* expression is true, then the statements specified by the *true-alternative* are executed:

```
cerr << "Error! Coeff ";
cerr << a << ", " << b << ", " << c;
cerr << " have complex roots" << endl;
continue;
```

The second output statement writes the values of the variables *a*, *b*, and *c* to the monitor.

Following the two *if* statements is the remainder of the *while* loop body, that is, the five statements

```
tmp = sqrt(tmp);
x1 = (-b+tmp)/(2*a);
x2 = (-b-tmp)/(2*a);
cout << "Coeff = " << a << ", " << b << ", " << c;
cout << "; Roots = " << x1 << ", " << x2 << endl;
```

The first three statements are assignment statements and the fourth and fifth statements are output statements (we have seen several of these). The first assignment statement takes the value of *tmp*, calculates its square root (by calling a C++ function), and makes this value the new value of *tmp*. The next two assignment statements compute the roots of the quadratic equation and assign these roots in the variables *x1* and *x2*. The last two statements print the coefficients along with appropriate explanatory text on the monitor.

1.2.1 COMPILING AND RUNNING THE PROGRAM The above program can be compiled and linked to form an executable program as follows with the Borland C++ compiler:

```
bcc roots
```

The Borland C++ compiler translates this program to machine code, loads the appropriate library facilities, combines them with the program and puts the resulting code in the file *roots.exe*. This program can be executed (made to run) by typing

```
roots
```

The program then waits for input. In this "interactive" mode, the user must supply the input by entering appropriate values at the keyboard. On MS-DOS systems, the end of input is indicated by typing ^Z (control-Z) followed by a carriage return, while on UNIX systems the end of input is indicated by typing ^D (control-D).

Here is a sample interactive session (on MS-DOS):

```
roots
1 4 4
Coeff = 1, 4, 4; Roots = -2, -2
1 -4 4
Coeff = 1, -4, 4; Roots = 2, 2
^Z
```

After each set of coefficients entered by the user, the program prints the results.

Input is typically made available to a program by the operating system (e.g., MS-DOS or UNIX systems) on a line-by-line basis and not as it is entered. In other words, input is transmitted to the program only after the user presses "enter." (Pressing enter moves the cursor to the next line on the monitor screen.) This gives the user a chance to backspace and correct input before it is transmitted to the program. For example, in the above interactive session, input is not made available to the program by MS-DOS after the user has entered the first coefficient, or the second and third coefficients, but only after the user has pressed enter following the third coefficient.

Instead of entering the data interactively every time, the programmer can store the coefficients in a file using a screen editor or word processor (the data must be in clear text form) and instruct the program to take the data from that file. Suppose we store the above coefficients in the file *roots.in*. Program *roots* can be made to read the data from this file and print the results on the screen as follows:

```
roots <roots.in
Coeff = 1, 4, 4; Roots = -2, -2
Coeff = 1, -4, 4; Roots = 2, 2
```

Using the MS-DOS or UNIX operator < to specify the file from which input is to be read is called "input redirection." Operator < is called the input redirection operator.

Similarly, the output of the above program can be stored in a file, say *roots.out*, by using the MS-DOS or UNIX output redirection operator > :

```
roots <roots.in >roots.out
```

2. PROGRAM TERMINATION

C++ programs can terminate by completing execution of the *main* function (by reaching the right curly brace delimiting the body of *main*), by calling function *exit*, or by executing the *return* statement in the *main* function. Function *exit* must be called explicitly if a value is to be returned to the environment, that is, to an operating system such as MS-DOS or UNIX. The integer value returned to the operating system is specified as the argument of the *exit* function call, for example,

```
exit(0);
```

The value returned is used to indicate whether or not the program completed execution successfully. By convention, *exit* is called with a zero argument to indicate successful (normal) termination and with a non-zero argument to indicate error (abnormal) termination. The program status information can be used by other programs at the DOS or UNIX level to take appropriate actions.

If the *main* function terminates by completing its body or by executing the *return* statement, then function *exit* is called automatically. However, in this case the argument with which function *exit* is called is unspecified and the value returned by the program to the environment is meaningless.

3. EXERCISE

1. Write in English (or pseudo code) a program to

    a. sort a list of numbers;
    b. compute the largest of 5 numbers.

Chapter 2

BASICS

In this chapter, I will discuss the basic ingredients of a C++ program: the characters that can be used in constructing a program, rules for constructing identifiers (names of entities in a program) and how literal values are specified. But first, I will discuss the font conventions used in this book.

1. FONT CONVENTION

The `typewriter` font is used to show program code. Within program code, *italic* font is used to describe general concepts, which must be replaced by specific items. The presence of items in *italic* font within code means that the code is not complete C++ code.

Italic font, when used for items embedded within the normal text, specifies that the items are from the code being or are words that have a special meaning for C++.

2. CHARACTER SET

The C++ character set is the set of characters that can be used for constructing C++ programs and for communicating with the environment, that is, for program input and output.

The C++ character set consists of the following characters:

1. Upper- and lower-case letters.

2. Digits 0 through 9.

3. The space character plus the following additional characters:

    > ! % ^ & * ( ) − + = { } | ˜ [ ] \ ; ' : < > ? , . / #

C++ also provides a special notation for specifying some non-printing characters and the characters ', "", ?, and \, which have a special meaning in C++ (this notation allows these characters to be printed like ordinary characters):

description	character	denotation
null	NUL	\0
new line	NL (LF)	\n
horizontal tab	HT	\t
vertical tab	VT	\t
backspace	BS	\b
carriage return	CR	\r
form feed	FF	\f
alert	BEL	\a
backslash	\	\\
question mark	?	\?
single quote	'	\'
double quote	"	\"
octal number	*ooo*	*ooo*
hex number	*hhh*	\x*hhh*

The backslash character is used to suppress the special role played by some characters in C++. For example, string constants are delimited by the double quote character (discussed later). To include the double quote character in a string, the denotation "\" " is used.

Arbitrary characters can be denoted as "*ddd*" where *ddd* stands for one to three octal digits specifying the internal encoding of the character. Alternatively, the hexadecimal notation "\x*hhh*" can be used. This notation is used especially for specifying control characters and other non-printing characters. For example, the escape character *esc* is denoted as \033 (assuming that the compiler uses the ASCII encoding for the escape character).

3. IDENTIFIERS

"Identifiers" are symbolic names given to entities in C++ programs. We have seen several examples of identifiers already. For example, in the program

```
#include <iostream.h>
int main()
{
    cout << "Hello Programmer!" << endl;
    cout << "Welcome to the World of C++!" << endl;
}
```

identifier *main* is the name of a function and *cout* is the name of the output stream (the monitor by default).

The rules for constructing identifiers are as follows:

1. An identifier is an arbitrary long sequence of letters and digits.

2. The first character of the identifier must be a letter.

3. The underscore character _ is treated like a letter.

4. Identifiers beginning with two underscores are reserved for internal use by the C++ compiler.

5. C++ is case sensitive. Upper- and lower-case letters are treated as different characters.

6. Some identifiers are designated as "keywords" and cannot be used as the names of "user-defined" entities (complete list is given below).

Note that some C++ compilers may ignore the trailing characters in long identifiers. For example, only the first 31 characters may be considered to be significant.

Here are examples of legal identifiers:

```
i
pi
temp
sum12
max_sales
RetailIncome
_i
```

And now here are examples of illegal identifiers:

```
12
1stMonth
Jan Sales
__index
new
```

These identifiers are invalid for the following reasons:

1. *12* and *1stMonth* begin with a digit instead of a letter.

2. *Jan Sales* contains a blank (space) character.

3. *__index* begins with two underscores.

4. *new* is a keyword (see below).

3.1 KEYWORDS

Here is a list of the C++ identifiers, which are designated as keywords, because they have a special meaning in C++ programs:

asm	double	new	switch
auto	else	operator	template
break	enum	private	this
case	extern	protected	throw
catch	float	public	try
char	for	register	union
class	friend	return	typedef
const	goto	short	unsigned
continue	if	signed	virtual
default	inline	sizeof	void
delete	int	static	volatile
do	long	struct	while

As an example of a keyword, consider the following C++ statement, which makes *x* positive if it is negative initially:

```
if (x < 0)
    x = -x;
```

Identifier *if* is a keyword. When the C++ compiler sees the *if* keyword, it knows that it should now expect to find the *if* conditional statement. Incidentally, the above statement is executed as follows:

> If the original value of *x* is less than 0, then *x* is assigned the negative of its original value; otherwise, no action is performed.

4. CONSTANTS (LITERAL VALUES)

C++ allows programmers to express the following different kinds of constants (literal values):

1. *Integer constants* (*whole numbers*) are simply sequences of digits. For example,

```
44
0
```

Negative integer constants are preceded by a minus sign:

```
-31
-100
```

C++ allows programmers to specify very large constants, which are called long (double-precision) integer constants. Such constants are specified by placing the letter *l* (or *L*) at the end of an integer-constant, for example,

```
33L
-101L
```

Constants can also be specified in "octal" or "hexadecimal" notation instead of in decimal notation. A leading 0 indicates an octal constant and a leading 0x or 0X indicates a hexadecimal (hex) constant.

2. *Real (floating-point) constants.* Some examples are

```
0.0
3.1416
```

Negative floating-point constants are preceded by a minus sign:

```
-99.0
```

By default, floating-point constants are interpreted as double-precision constants. C++ also allows programmers to specify ordinary (single-precision) floating-point constants and extra long double-precision constants. Ordinary (single-precision) floating-point constants are specified by using the suffix f (or F) and long double-precision constants are specified using the suffix l (or L). Some examples are

```
32.0f
32.0F
3.1416l
3.1416L
```

The letter e (or E) is used to specify the exponent of floating-point constants written in the scientific notation: Some examples are

```
10E4
1.0E-2
1e5
```

These constants denote the values 100000, 0.01, and 100000, respectively.

3. *Character constants*:

```
'a'
'z'
```

4. *String constants* are character sequences enclosed in double quotes:

```
"Hello World"
"Enter Data Values:"
"1993"
"Were you born before 1980?"
```

5. COMMENTS

A "comment" is text in a program that is meant for the human reader and not for the C++ compiler. Comments are given in programs to make them more self explanatory.

In C++ there are two ways of writing comments:

1. The character pair `/*` is used to specify the beginning of a comment and the character pair `*/` is used to specify its end.

2. The character pair `//` also specifies the beginning of a comment; such a comment is automatically terminated by the end of a line.

Here is a version of the roots computing program (from the first chapter) that is "annotated" with comments (file *rootsc.cpp*):

```
     #include <iostream.h>
     #include <math.h>
     /*****************************************************/
     /*                  PROGRAM TO COMPUTE                */
 5   /*                     ROOTS OF                       */
     /*                  QUADRATIC EQUATIONS               */
     /*                  y = a*x*x + b*x + c               */
     /*****************************************************/
     int main()
10   {
         float a, b, c, //the coefficients
               x1, x2,  //the roots
               tmp;     //temporary variable
         int n;

15
         while (cin >> a >> b >> c){ //read input if present
             if (a == 0) {
                 cerr << "Error! First coeff is 0!";
                 cerr << endl;
20               continue;
             }
             if ((tmp = b*b - 4*a*c) < 0) { //complex roots?
                 cerr << "Error! Coeff ";
                 cerr << a << ", " << b << ", " << c;
25               cerr << " have complex roots" << endl;
                 continue;
             }
             tmp = sqrt(tmp);
             x1 = (-b+tmp)/(2*a);
30           x2 = (-b-tmp)/(2*a);
             cout <<"Coeff = " << a << ", " << b << ", " << c;
             cout <<"; Roots = " << x1 << ", " << x2 << endl;
         }
     }
```

6. EXERCISES

1. What is an identifier?

2. What is the difference between a variable and a constant?

3. Describe in English, as precisely as you can, how you will sort a list of numbers in increasing order. Then sort the following numbers using your sorting recipe: 5 0 -4 5 22

Chapter 3
TYPES AND OBJECTS

Programs manipulate data, which can be numbers, strings, or values of other types. A data "type" in a programming language specifies a set of legal values and the operations that can be performed on these values. Types are used to specify the kinds of values that can be associated with program entities such as constant identifiers, variables, and functions (discussed later).

C++ requires that the programmer explicitly specify the type of the values that can be associated with each program entity. Once specified, the type of a program entity cannot be changed in the program. The C++ compiler uses the type information to ensure that inappropriate values are not associated with program entities. One implication of requiring programmers to specify the types explicitly in a program is that values of different types cannot be associated with the same program entity.

1. BASIC TYPES

C++ provides the programmer with a set of predefined (built-in) data types, which are called the "fundamental" types. The fundamental types provided by C++ are the character, integer, and floating-point types. These three types come in a variety of flavors. We will only discuss the important ones in this book.

The programmer can in a straightforward manner define additional new types, called "enumeration" types, by listing the values of each such type. The basic types in C++ are the fundamental types plus the enumeration types.

The character, integer, and enumeration types are collectively called the *integral* types. The integral and floating-point types are together called the *arithmetic* types.

A programmer can use the basic types directly to specify the types of program entities. The basic types can also be used to construct complex or composite types, which can then be used to specify the types of program entities. Note that composite types can be also be used, along with the basic types, to construct new complex types.

1.1 CHARACTER

The character type is denoted by the identifier *char*. Here are examples illustrating the use of type *char* to declare and define program entities:

```
char c;
const char delim = ':';
char upper(char);
```

The above code defines *c* to be a character variable, *delim* to be a constant identifier whose value is the character :, and *upper* as a function that takes a *char* value and returns a *char* value.

Here is a trivial program illustrating the use of type *char* (file *upper.cpp*):

```
       #include <iostream.h>
       #include <ctype.h>
       int main()
       {
5          char c;
           cout << "Type 1 character and then enter: ";
           cin >> c;
           c = toupper(c);
           cout << c << endl;
10     }
```

The program reads a character from input and prints its upper-case version. The first line includes the declarations of the stream input/output facilities. The second line includes the prototype (that is, function declaration) of the C++ function *toupper*, which is used to convert a character to upper case (if the character is not a lower-case character, then it does not perform any conversion). Remember that all facilities referenced in a C++ program must be declared or defined before they are referenced.

Chapter 16 describes all the C++ functions. These functions are stored in the "standard C++ library." Any standard library functions used in a C++ program are automatically "linked" (joined) to the C++ program by the C++ compiler.

The character to be converted to upper case is "passed" (sent) to function *toupper* as an "argument." *c* is declared as a variable of type *char*. The program prompts the user for a single character, reads the character, converts it to upper case, and then prints the upper-case version (followed by a new line).

The above program is compiled as

```
bcc upper
```

which produces the executable program *upper.exe*. This program is executed by typing

```
upper
```

Here is a sample interaction of this program with the user:

```
Type 1 character and then enter: e
E
```

Type *char* is typically implemented using one "byte" (8 bits) of the computer memory. Internally, values of type *char* are stored as integers. As a result, the *char* type is sometimes used to store small integer values, that is, as a very small integer type.

1.2 ENUMERATION TYPES

An enumeration type is a type whose values are identifiers. Enumeration types are declared as

enum *type-name* { *list-of-identifiers* }

As an example, consider the enumeration type *trafficLight* that may be used in a program to control traffic:

```
enum trafficLight {red, yellow, green};
```

Type *trafficLight* has three values (denoting colors): *red*, *yellow*, and *green*. These are the only values that can be associated with an object of type *trafficLight*.

The following program fragment (incomplete program) illustrates the use of the enumeration type *trafficLight* to select the appropriate code for execution:

```
trafficLight t = red;
    ...
switch (t) {
case red: ...
        break;
case yellow: ...
        break;
case green: ...
        break;
}
```

Identifier *t* is declared as a variable of type *trafficLight* and it is initially given the value *red*. Any of the values *red*, *yellow* and *green* can be associated with variable *t*. The value of *t* can be changed in the program as appropriate.

The four ellipses (...) in the above program fragment represent code that is not specified here and is not relevant to our discussion. In a complete program these ellipses must be replaced by actual code. The "*switch*" statement is a multi-way branch statement. Execution of this statement proceeds as follows: depending upon the value of t, the statements (denoted by the ellipsis) following the appropriate label are executed. The *break* statement following each ellipsis causes program execution to "break" out of the *switch* statement, which completes execution of the *switch* statement.

1.3 INTEGER

C++ provides three integer types that can store integers of different sizes:

1. Small integer type *short int* (or just *short*).

2. Normal integer type *int*.

3. Extra precision integer type *long int* (or just *long*).

As mentioned earlier, type *char* is often used as a very small integer type.

C++ guarantees only that the largest number that can be stored using an object of type *int* will be greater than or equal to the largest number that can be stored using an object of type *short*. Similarly, the largest number that can be stored using an object of type *long* will be greater than or equal to the largest number that can be stored using an object of type *int*. The above relationships can also be specified as

$largest(char) \leq largest(short) \leq largest(int) \leq largest(long)$

The storage required for objects of these types has the following relationship:

$storage(char) \leq storage(short) \leq storage(int) \leq storage(long)$

Here are examples of variables defined using the integer types:

```
short month;
int i;
long total;
```

month, *i*, and *total* are defined as variables of type *short*, *int*, and *long* respectively. We will primarily use type *int* in our programs.

To illustrate the use of the integer types, here is a simple program that reads two integers and prints the larger of the two values (file *max2.cpp*):

```
     #include <iostream.h>
     int main()
     {
         int a, b;
5        cin >> a >> b;
         if (a > b)
             cout << a << endl;
         else
             cout << b << endl;
10   }
```

Line 4 defines *a* and *b* as integer variables. Line 5 reads two integers (determined from the types of *a* and *b*) from the terminal and assigns their values to *a* and *b*. Line 6 is the beginning of an *"if"* conditional execution statement. If the condition

```
a > b
```

is true, that is, if *a* is greater than *b*, then the next statement (line 7) is executed, which prints the value of *a*. Otherwise, if the above condition is false (*a* is smaller than or equal *b*), then the statement following the *"else"* clause (line 9) is executed, which prints the value of *b*.

This program can be compiled using the Borland C++ compiler as

```
bcc max2
```

The above program can be executed by typing *max2*. The program then silently waits for the user to type two numbers. Unlike *upper*, *max2* does not prompt the user for input. Such "silent" programs are often used when the program input is being generated by another program.

Here is a sample interaction with *max2*:

```
max2
22 11
11
```

1.4 FLOATING-POINT

C++ provides three floating-point types of different precisions:

1. Normal floating-point type *float*.

2. Double precision floating-point type *double*.

3. Extra long double precision floating-point type *long double*.

We will mainly use the types *float* and *double* in our programs.

Here are examples of variables defined using the integer types:

```
float price;
double small;
long double epsilon;
```

price, *small*, and *epsilon* are defined as variables of type *float*, *double*, and *long double* respectively.

As an example illustrating the use of floating-point types, here is a program that computes the sine of a value. The input value for the program must be in degrees (file *sin.cpp*):

```
   #include <iostream.h>
   #include <math.h>
   int main()
   {
5      const float pi = 3.1416;
       double angle, sine;
       cout << "Type angle and then enter: ";
       cin >> angle;
       sine = sin(angle*pi/180.0);
10     cout << "Sine is " << sine << endl;
   }
```

We will use the C++ math function *sin* to compute the sine. The second line includes the header file *math.h* which contains the prototype of function *sin*. Lines 5 and 6, that is,

```
const float pi = 3.1416;
double angle, sine;
```

define *pi* as a constant identifier, which denotes the value 3.1416, and *angle* and *sine* as variables of type *double*.

The next two lines

```
cout << "Type angle and then enter: ";
cin >> angle;
```

prompt the user for the input angle and this value is read and stored in the variable *angle*.

Next, the sine of the value input is computed by calling the C++ function *sin*. This function is not called with the value input directly, because this value is in degrees and *sin* expects its argument to be in radians. Consequently, this value is first converted to radians and then passed to *sin*. (If you are uncomfortable about radians, do not worry. As I said earlier, our focus is not mathematics, but programming. Simply assume that you have been told how to compute radians from degrees.)

The result returned by function *sin* is stored in variable *sine*:

```
sine = sin(angle*pi/180.0);
```

Finally, the sine is printed using the statement

```
cout << "Sine is " << sine << endl;
```

Here are two sample interactions with program *sin*:

```
sin
Type angle and then enter: 90
1

sin
Type angle and then enter: 30
0.500001
```

2. MORE TYPES

In this chapter, we have discussed only the simple types. C++ allows users to define unsigned variants of the character and integer types. It also has the empty type, and provides the user facilities to define new types.

2.1 UNSIGNED TYPES

We have not discussed the "unsigned" variants of the character integer types. We will not be using unsigned types in this book. But it is worth mentioning them for completeness as they are used by some of the C++ library functions.

Unsigned types are declared by using the "type" qualifier *unsigned* when declaring objects. For example,

```
unsigned char c;
unsigned int q;
```

Unsigned types are often used when it is necessary to manipulate the "internal" (computer) representation of an integer as a bit pattern. The sign bit of *unsigned* integers is not treated as a special bit, which means that unsigned integers can also be used to hold larger positive integers.

2.2 EMPTY TYPE

The empty type *void* is primarily used for specifying

1. functions that do not return values and

2. *void* pointers, which refer to objects whose type is not known.

We shall be seeing examples of such functions and pointers in later chapters.

2.3 DERIVED (COMPLEX) TYPES

Derived (complex) types are types constructed using the basic types and other derived types. The derived types that can be constructed in C++ are arrays, functions, pointers, references, classes, structures and unions. These types will be discussed in detail in later chapters.

3. OBJECTS

A C++ "object" is a region of storage. Associated with objects are properties such as names and types. A name can be an identifier or an expression such as *p where *p* is a pointer. Besides objects, other C++ program components also have names, for example, functions, types, class members and labels. Names are declared and/or defined. As explained in Chapter 5, declarations are used to specify object properties, but they do not allocate storage for the object. Definitions are like declarations, but they also allocate storage.

Constant identifiers are symbolic names associated with constant objects. The initial value given to a constant object cannot be changed. Variables are identifiers associated with objects whose values can be changed. Both constant identifiers and variables must be declared/defined before they can be referenced.

4. TYPE DEFINITIONS

The *typedef* statement can be used to associate an identifier with a type. This statement is usually used to give symbolic names to types to facilitate program readability, and as a convenient abbreviation for complicated types. The *typedef* statement has the form

`typedef` *type-specification declarator;*

A type specification can be a type name such as one of the predefined type names, a type name defined using the *typedef* statement, or one of the other types discussed later in the book.

In its simplest form, a declarator is an identifier. In such a case, the effect of the *typedef* statement is to define this identifier as a new type name representing the type specified by *type-specification*. We will not formally describe all the possible forms of a declarator. Instead, the examples in this book will give you an idea of the different types of declarators. For complete details, see the definition of the C++ in *The C++ Programming Language* [Stroustrup 1991].

Here are examples of type definitions:

```
typedef float Kilograms;
typedef int Matrix[10][10];
typedef int Hour;
typedef char *Name;
```

These *typedef* statements define identifier

1. *Kilograms* as a synonym for the predefined type *float*,

2. *Matrix* as a synonym for a 2-dimensional array with 10 integer elements in each dimension (an array is a "data structure" that holds multiple values of the same type; arrays are discussed Chapter 7),

3. *Month* as a synonym for *int*, and

4. *Name* as a synonym for pointer to *char* (a pointer is a value that tells you the "address" or the "location" of another object).

These synonyms can now be used much like the predefined types to declare or define program entities. Here are examples of variable definitions using the types defined with the *typedef* statements:

```
Kilograms weight;
Matrix chart;
Month m;
Name first;
```

These definitions define

1. *weight* as a variable of type *Kilograms* (*float*),

2. *chart* as a variable of type *Matrix* (2-dimensional array with 10 integer elements in each dimension),

3. *m* as a variable of type *Month* (*int*), and

4. *first* as a variable of type *Name* (*char* pointer).

The above variables could also have been equivalently defined without using the *typedef* identifiers as follows:

```
float weight;
int chart[10][10];
int m;
char *first;
```

Here is a modified version of the sine program shown above that uses a *typedef* statement (file *sint.cpp*):

```
      #include <iostream.h>
      #include <math.h>
      int main()
      {
  5       typedef double Degrees;
          const float pi = 3.1416;
          double sine;
          Degrees angle;

 10       cout << "Type angle and then enter: ";
          cin >> angle;
          sine = sin(angle*pi/180.0);
          cout << "Sine is " << sine << endl;
      }
```

In this example, using the *typedef* statement to define a new type *Degrees* and using *Degrees* to define *angle* enhances the readability of the program. Although the resulting enhancement may seem insignificant in this small program, such uses of the *typedef* statement in large programs can improve program readability significantly.

5. EXERCISES

1. Write a program *lower*, which is like program *upper* except that it converts a letter from upper case to lower case. The header file *ctype.h* contains the declaration of a function *tolower*, which converts a character from upper case to lower case.

2. Write a program *min2*, which is like program *max2* except that it prints the smaller of the two values.

Chapter 4
OPERATORS AND EXPRESSIONS

C++ has many operators. These operators have rich semantics, which makes it possible to write small and compact C++ programs. Operators, along with literal values and identifiers, are used to construct and denote "complex" (non-simple) values called "expressions." Most of the C++ operators are used like operators in mathematics to construct expressions. In fact, some operators, like + and −, which represent addition and subtraction, correspond to the mathematical operators denoted by the same symbols.

Here is an example of an expression with straightforward semantics:

```
a + 3 * c
```

The value of this expression is computed by first evaluating the "subexpression" in which operator * denotes multiplication

```
3 * c
```

and then adding the result of this subexpression to the value of a. The constant 3 is the "left operand" of operator * and identifier c is its "right operand."

Expressions are evaluated in C++ according to the rules and semantics of the operators as specified by C++. Expression evaluation is controlled by the "precedence" of the operators and the manner in which they "associate with each other", that is, their "associativity." A table summarizing the precedence and associativity of all the C++ operators is given later.

An operator with a higher precedence is applied before one with a lower precedence. If there are several operators with equal precedence in an expression, then the leftmost such operator is applied first, provided these operators have left-to-right associativity; otherwise, the rightmost operator is applied first. Note that C++ operators with the same precedence also have the same associativity.

To be more specific, we will now look at some examples. In C++, the multiplication operator * has a higher precedence than the addition operator +. As a result, when computing the value of the expression

```
2 + 3 * 6
```

the subexpression

```
3 * 6
```

is evaluated first. It is replaced by its result in the original expression, that is,

```
2 + 18
```

which evaluates to 20.

Both the division and multiplication operators in C++ have the same precedence and they associate from left to right. Consequently, when computing the value of the expression

```
4 / 2 * 6
```

the subexpression

```
4 / 2
```

is evaluated first and it is replaced by its result in the original expression:

```
2 * 6
```

This expression evaluates to 12.

Parentheses can be used to change the order of expression evaluation by explicitly specifying the grouping of subexpressions. In the presence of parentheses, the innermost expression with parentheses is evaluated first according to the rules of operator precedence and associativity. For example, to ensure that multiplication in the above expression is performed before the division, it should be written as

```
4 / (2 * 6)
```

1. OPERATORS

C++ operators can take one, two, or three operands; such operators are called unary, binary, and ternary operators, respectively. Operators are like functions – they perform computation on their operands. The notations used for invoking various kinds of operators is different from that used for invoking functions, which is called the "functional" notation. By and large, the notation used for invoking C++ operators corresponds to the notation used in mathematics.

In C++ a variety of operations other than those involving "computation" are also implemented using operators. For example, the pair of parentheses in a function call such as

```
sin(angle)
```

is considered as an operator. We shall not discuss such operators in this chapter except to state their precedence and associativity. We will discuss these operators and the operations performed by them in later chapters as and when required.

In this section we will discuss some of the predefined operators in C++. As we shall see later, C++ allows users to extend these operators by allowing additional semantics to be associated with these operators.

1.1 ARITHMETIC OPERATORS

The arithmetic operators fall into two categories: additive and multiplicative operators. Each operator within this class has the same precedence and associativity. The multiplicative operators have a higher precedence than the additive operators, that is, in the absence of parentheses, the subexpressions containing them are evaluated first.

The additive arithmetic operators are

operator	name	type	associativity
+	addition	binary	left-to-right
-	subtraction	binary	left-to-right

The multiplicative arithmetic operators are

operator	name	type	associativity
*	multiplication	binary	left-to-right
/	division	binary	left-to-right
%	remainder	binary	left-to-right

The remainder operator should only be used with integer values.

The following constant identifier and variable definitions with initial values are used in the examples that follow:

```
const int n = 8;
int a = 36;
float y = 36.0;
```

Here are examples of expressions:

1. Expression

   ```
   a / 5
   ```

   evaluates to 7 but the expression

```
a / 5.0
```

evaluates to 7.2, because its divisor is a floating point value.

2. Expression

```
7 % 5
```

evaluates to 2 but the expression

```
7 % 5.0
```

is illegal, because its right operand is a floating-point value.

3. Expression

```
a + y / 4
```

evaluates to 40.5 (36 + 4.5). If one of the operands of an operator is a
floating-point value, then the other operand is, if appropriate, automatically
converted to a floating-point value. Arithmetic operand conversions rules
are described below in detail.

4. The above expression with a and y interchanged

```
y + a / 4
```

evaluates to 40 (36 + 4). Note that integer division produces an integer
(the fractional part is thrown away).

We will now take a look at a slightly bigger example that illustrates the use of
these operators. As mentioned in Chapter 1, the roots of the quadratic equation

$$y = ax^2 + bx + c$$

are given by the expressions

$$\frac{-b + \sqrt{b^2 - 4ac}}{2a}$$

$$\frac{-b - \sqrt{b^2 - 4ac}}{2a}$$

These expressions are written in C++ as

```
(-b+sqrt(b*b - 4*a*c))/(2*a);
```

and

```
(-b-sqrt(b*b - 4*a*c))/(2*a);
```

where *a*, *b*, and *c* are floating-point variables of type *float* and *sqrt* is the C++ standard library function that computes the square root of its argument.

Let us just consider in detail the first of the two C++ expressions. Two pairs of parentheses are used for grouping subexpressions to force evaluation of the expression in a specific order (the third pair belongs to the *sqrt* function call). Had the above C++ expression been written (incorrectly) without these two grouping parentheses pairs, say as

```
-b+sqrt(b*b - 4*a*c)/2*a;
```

then this C++ expression would be evaluated by

1. first computing the square root (the argument of the *sqrt* function is evaluated first and then the function is called), then
2. dividing the result by 2 and then multiplying it by *a*, and finally
3. adding the result of the multiplication to minus *b*.

Division and multiplication are performed before addition because their operations have a higher precedence. Division is performed before multiplication because the division operator appears before (to the left of) the multiplication operator.

In other words, the above C++ expression will have the value

$$-b + \frac{\sqrt{b^2-4ac}}{2}a$$

This is wrong, because the last *a* should be in the denominator multiplying the 2. The correct value is (as shown above)

$$\frac{-b +\sqrt{b^2-4ac}}{2a}$$

1.2 COMPARISON OPERATORS

The comparison operators are used for determining whether or not two values are equal:

operator	name	type	associativity
==	equality	binary	left-to-right
!=	inequality	binary	left-to-right

The equality and inequality operators return zero to indicate false and one to indicate true. These operators apply to only the basic types and pointers (the latter are discussed in Chapter 7).

As an example illustrating the use of the inequality operator, consider the following program that computes the sum of all the numbers given to it as input until it encounters a zero (file *end.cpp*):

```
   #include <iostream.h>
   int main()
   {
       int x, total = 0;
5      cin >> x;
       while (x != 0) {
           total = total + x;
           cin >> x;
       }
10     cout << "Total = " << total << endl;
   }
```

In this program, x and *total* are defined as integer variables. *total* is initialized to zero. The first input value is assigned to variable x. Then the program executes the following loop (lines 6-9):

```
while (x != 0) {
    total = total + x;
    cin >> x;
}
```

This loop executes the two statements in its body as long as x is not zero:

1. If x is not zero, go to step (2); otherwise, terminate the loop and go to the statement following the loop (line 10).

2. Add x to *total* (actually, the semantics of the addition statement are to first add the values of x and *total* and then make this be the new value of variable *total*).

3. Read and store the next input value in x.

4. Go to step (1).

The statement following the loop (line 10; see the complete program above) prints the total of the input values.

1.3 RELATIONAL OPERATORS

The relational operators shown below are used for comparing values to determine whether one value is smaller or larger than another value:

operator	name	type	associativity
<	less than	binary	left-to-right
<=	less than or equal to	binary	left-to-right
>=	greater than or equal to	binary	left-to-right
>	greater than	binary	left-to-right

Each relational operator returns zero to indicate false and one to indicate true.

To illustrate the semantics of these operators, we will use the following definition of a:

```
int a = 36;
```

Here are examples of expressions that illustrate the relational operators:

1. Expression

   ```
   a <= 36
   ```

   evaluates to true (the value returned is 1).

2. Expression

   ```
   a < 36
   ```

   evaluates to false (the value returned is 0).

3. Expression

   ```
   a > 36
   ```

   evaluates to false (the value returned is 0).

4. Expression

   ```
   a >= 36
   ```

   evaluates to true (the value returned is 1).

Suppose we have input data of the following form

$$n\ a_1\ a_2\ a_3\ a_4\ a_5\ ...$$

We will now write a program to compute the sum of the first n non-zero positive values from the list of numbers $a_1, a_2, ...,$ supplied as input (file *total.cpp*):

```
      #include <iostream.h>
      int main()
      {
          int n, i = 0;
5         int x, total = 0;

          cin >> n;
          while (i < n) {
              cin >> x;
10            if (x > 0) {
                  total = total + x;
                  i++;
              }
          }
15        cout << "Total of first " << n;
          cout << " positive values is ";
          cout << total << endl;
      }
```

The *while* loop (lines 8-14) is executed as long as i is less than n. i is initially zero (line 4); it is incremented (increased by 1; line 12) in the body of the loop. The loop body will be executed n times, because when i becomes equal to n then the expression

```
i < n
```

will become false and the loop will stop executing.

In the *while* loop, a value is read from input and stored in x (line 9). This value is added to *total* only if x is greater than zero by using the following *if* statement:

```
if (x > 0) {
    total = total + x;
    i++;
}
```

This *if* statement will execute its body (the statements within curly braces) only if x is greater than 0. The first statement in the body of the *if* statement increases the value of *total* by x and the next statement uses the increment operator ++ (explained later) to increase the value of i by one.

1.4 LOGICAL OPERATORS

The logical operators operate on the truth values "true" and "false." C++ operators returning logical values return one to indicate true and zero to indicate false. On the other hand, C++ operators accepting logical values as operands treat non-zero values as true and zero as false.

The C++ logical operators correspond to the mathematical Boolean operators:

operator	name	type	associativity
&&	logical and	binary	left-to-right
||	logical or	binary	left-to-right
!	logical not	unary	right-to-left

The semantics of the operators && and || are explained in the following tables:

||	false	true
false	false	true
true	true	true

&&	false	true
false	false	false
true	false	true

The true and false values in the first columns and in the first rows of the above tables represent the left and right operands, respectively.

The unary operator ! returns true if its operand evaluates to false and it returns false if its operand evaluates to true.

An important thing to note is that the operators && and || evaluate their second operand only if it is not possible to determine the result based on the value of the first operand. Specifically, && evaluates its second operand only if its first operand evaluates to false; || evaluates its second operand only if its first operand evaluates to true.

Now for examples:

1. Expression

   ```
   !3
   ```

   evaluates to zero.

2. The expression

   ```
   4.0 < 3.0 && 6
   ```

   evaluates to 1. Relational operators have a higher precedence than logical operators (see precedence table below).

3. Suppose that variables *a*, *b*, and *c* have been defined and initialized as follows:

   ```
   int a = 1, b = 2, c = 3;
   ```

   Then the expression

```
c < b && b < a
```

evaluates to false.

The above expression is not equivalent to the following expression

```
c < b < a
```

This expression evaluates to true because subexpression

```
c < b
```

evaluates to zero (false) and this is less than the value of *a* (which is one).

1.5 INCREMENT AND DECREMENT OPERATORS

These operators are used to increment or decrement their operands (which must be variables) by one:

operator	name	type	associativity
+ +	increment	unary prefix	right-to-left
--	decrement	unary prefix	right-to-left
+ +	increment	unary suffix	right-to-left
--	decrement	unary suffix	right-to-left

Now for examples. The suffix increment operator in the expression

```
a++
```

and the prefix increment operator in the expression

```
++a
```

both increase the value of *a* by one.

Similarly, the suffix decrement operator in the expression

```
a--
```

and the prefix decrement operator in the expression

```
--a
```

both decrease the value of *a* by one.

Both the suffix and prefix increment operators increase the value of their operand by one. The difference between them is in the value yielded by the operators. The value of the expression

++a

is the value of *a* after *a* has been incremented. On the other hand, the value of
the expression

a++

is the value of *a* before *a* is incremented.

The difference between the prefix and suffix decrement operators is similar.

1.6 SIZEOF OPERATOR

The *sizeof* operator is used to determine the memory space required, in bytes, for
an object or objects of a specific type:

operator	name	type	associativity
sizeof	size of object/type	unary	left-to-right

The following program prints the storage required for objects of the integer types
char,[1] *short*, *int*, and *long*, and for variable *a*, which is of type *long double* (file
size.cpp):

```
#include <iostream.h>
int main()
{
    long double a;

    cout << "size of char = " << sizeof(char) << endl;
    cout << "size of short = " << sizeof(short) << endl;
    cout << "size of int = " << sizeof(int) << endl;
    cout << "size of long = " << sizeof(long) << endl;
    cout << "size of a = " << sizeof(a) << endl;
}
```

The output of compiling and running this program is

```
size of char = 1
size of short = 2
size of int = 2
size of long = 4
size of a = 10
```

---

1. As mentioned in Chapter 3, the *char* type is sometimes used as a small integer type.

The units of the above numbers are bytes. It is interesting to note that objects of type *short* and *int* are allocated the same amount of memory space by the Borland C++ compiler. This means that there will be no difference between the precision and the storage allocated for objects of type *short* and *int*. Allocating the same amount of storage for both objects of type *short* and *int* is consistent with C++ semantics, because C++ requires only that the following three relationships hold:

```
sizeof(char) <= sizeof(short)
sizeof(short) <= sizeof(int)
sizeof(int) <= sizeof(long)
```

Instead of determining the storage required for storing variable *a*, we could have simply determined the storage required for objects of type *long double*. However, sometimes it is more convenient to determine the space required for an object instead of the space required for its type. This way, the type of an object can be changed without requiring any change to the operand of the *sizeof* operator.

Strictly speaking, the parentheses are not necessary when the operand of the *sizeof* operator is an expression.

1.7 CONDITIONAL OPERATOR

The conditional operator ?: takes three operands: if the value of the first operand is non-zero (true) then the result of the conditional operation is the value of the second operand; otherwise, the result is the value of the third operand:

operator	name	type	associativity
?:	conditional evaluation	ternary	right-to-left

Here are examples illustrating the use of the conditional operator:

1. Expression

    ```
    a ? a : - a
    ```

    yields the absolute value of *a*. If *a* is positive, then the value returned by the ?: operator is *a*; otherwise, the value returned is –*a*.

2. Expression

    ```
    a > b ? a : b
    ```

    yields the larger of *a* and *b* as its result. More specifically, if *a* is greater than *b*, then the value returned by the conditional operator ?: is *a*; otherwise, the value returned is *b*.

1.8 BIT OPERATORS

Each object is stored internally as a sequence of bits. The bit operators are intended for manipulating the bit representation. C++ provides operators for left and right shifting the bits in a word and for taking the bitwise *and*, *or*, and *exclusive or* of two operands. Typically, bit operations are used by system programmers to interface with the hardware and by programmers using bits instead of whole integers to minimize storage use. For details about bit operators, please see *The C++ Programming Language* [Stroustrup 1991].

1.9 COMMA OPERATOR

The comma operator is used to combine two expressions into one. The value returned by the comma operator is the value of its right operand:

operator	name	type	associativity
,	comma operator	binary	left-to-right

As an example, consider the comma expression

```
i, j
```

Both operands are evaluated, but the value of the expression is the value of *j*. In this example, it is unnecessary to evaluate the first operand. But this evaluation is a must because in some cases evaluating an expression changes the values of variables as illustrated by the following comma expression:

```
i++, j
```

Evaluating the first operand increments the value of *i* by 1.

Please note that the comma is also used in C++ in many other contexts as an item separator, for example, it is used to separate the arguments of a function call. In such cases, parentheses may have to be used to ensure that the comma is interpreted as the comma operator.

1.10 ASSIGNMENT OPERATORS

Assignment operators are used to assign values to objects. C++ has several assignment operators. These operators can be classified into two categories: simple assignment and compound assignment. The simple assignment operator (there is only one) assigns the value of its right operand to its left operand. The compound assignment operators operate on the left and right operands (the operation performed depends upon the compound assignment operator) and assign the resulting value to the left operand.

Here are the assignment operators:

operator	name	type	associativity
=	assignment	binary	right-to-left
+ =	compound assignment (addition)	binary	right-to-left
- =	compound assignment (subtraction)	binary	right-to-left
* =	compound assignment (multiplication)	binary	right-to-left
/ =	compound assignment (division)	binary	right-to-left
% =	compound assignment (remainder)	binary	right-to-left
< < =	compound assignment (left-shift)	binary	right-to-left
> > =	compound assignment (right-shift)	binary	right-to-left
& =	compound assignment (bitwise-and)	binary	right-to-left
^ =	compound assignment (bitwise-excl.-or)	binary	right-to-left
| =	compound assignment (bitwise-or)	binary	right-to-left

All the assignment operators have the same precedence.

The (simple) assignment operation has the form

variable = expression

The effect of the assignment operation is to assign (store) the value of *expression* to (in) the object identified by *variable*. This value becomes the new value of *variable*. This is also the value returned as the result of the assignment operation.

Although the assignment operation can be used as a subexpression within a larger expression, typically it is converted to a stand-alone statement (C+ + instruction) by appending a semicolon:

variable = expression;

The value returned by the assignment operator is *discarded* when the assignment expression is converted to a statement.

Before we look at examples of assignment, here are some comments:

1. The general form of the assignment operation is

    expression-identifying-an-object = value

    The left hand expression must identify an object. Otherwise, C+ + will flag an error.

2. We will not discuss the compound assignment operators that operate on the bit representation. For details about bit operators, please see *The C+ + Programming Language* [Stroustrup 1991].

3. The symbol = when used in a constant or variable declaration does not denote assignment. It denotes the initialization operation whose semantics are quite different from those of assignment, although in the simple

examples we have seen they seem to have equivalent semantics.

The following examples illustrate the use of the assignment operator;

```
a = 5;
max = x > y ? x : y;
i = j = 0;
```

As a result of these assignments,

1. *a* is assigned the value 5.

2. *max* is assigned the result of the conditional expression whose value is the larger of the values of *x* and *y*.

3. *i* is assigned the result of the assignment expression

    ```
    j = 0
    ```

    which is zero. This example illustrates that multiple variables can be assigned a value in the same statement.

Now here are examples illustrating the compound assignment operators;

```
i *= j;
i += j*a;
x *= i-a;
```

These statements are equivalent to the following statements that use the simple assignment operator:

```
i = i*j;
i = i+j*a;
x = x * (i-a);
```

Parentheses are used in the last statement to ensure that the subtraction takes place before the multiplication. As mentioned earlier, the multiplication operator has a higher precedence than the subtraction operator.

1.11 OPERATOR PRECEDENCE & ASSOCIATIVITY SUMMARY

All operators, including those not discussed above, are listed in this summary section for the sake of completeness.

Here is a summary of all the C++ operators in order of decreasing precedence. Unless otherwise specified, the operators associate from left to right:

category	operators	comments
scope	::	scope resolution
postfix	() [] -> . ++ --	
unary	! ~ + - ++ -- * & sizeof new delete	right-to-left
pointer-to-member	->* .*	
cast	(*type*)	right-to-left association
multiplication	* / %	
addition	+ -	
bit shift	<< >>	
relational	< <= > >=	
equality	== !=	
bit and	&	
bit incl. or	^	
bit excl. or	|	
logical and	&&	
logical or	||	
conditional	?:	right-to-left association
assignment	= += -= *= /= %= >>= <<= &= ^= |=	right-to-left association
comma		

As mentioned earlier, operators with higher precedence are evaluated first within an expression. For example, because the multiplication operator has a higher precedence than the addition operator, the expression

```
5 + 6 * 5
```

evaluates to 35 and not to 55. To force the addition to take place before the multiplication, parentheses can be used to explicitly specify the order of expression evaluation:

```
(5 + 6) * 5
```

This expression will evaluate to 55.

If an expression contains operators with the same precedence, then their associativity determines which operator is applied first. For example,

```
8/4*2
```

evaluates to 4 and not 1, because it is evaluated as

`(8/4)*2`

and not as

`8/(4*2)`

The multiplication and division operators have the same precedence and they have left-to-right associativity. As a result, the left most operator is applied first.

1.12 ARITHMETIC OPERAND CONVERSIONS

Operands of C++ operator are converted to the types specified according to the following set of rules, called the "arithmetic conversions", which are performed as follows:

1. If one operand is a *long double*, then the other is converted to *long double*.
2. Else, if one operand is a *double*, then the other is converted to *double*.
3. Else, if one operand is a *float*, then the other is converted to *float*.
4. Operands of type *char* and *short int* are converted to *int*. Then, provided the operand types are appropriate for the operator, the following conversions are performed:

   i. If one operand is of type *long int* and the second operand is of type *unsigned int*, then the second operand is converted to *long int* (in case the second operand type does not fit in a *long int*, then both are converted to *unsigned long int*).
   ii. Else, if one operand is a *long int*, then the other is converted to *long int*.
   iii. Else, if one operand is of type *unsigned int*, then the other is converted to *unsigned int*.
   iv. Else, both operands must be *int*s.

Suppose as an example, that *i* and *a* are defined as follows:

```
int i;
double a;
```

Then before the expression

`i + a`

is evaluated, the value of *i* is converted to a *double*, and then the addition is performed. The result of the addition has the type *double*.

2. EXPRESSIONS

As mentioned before, expressions are values constructed by using operators, other values, and identifiers. In general, the value of a C++ expression can only be determined at run time, that is, by executing the statements of the program preceding the expression and then "evaluating" the expression using the values currently associated with the identifiers in the expression.

There is a special class of expressions called "constant expressions." The values of such expressions can be determined without running the program, that is, at compile time. Operands in constant expressions can only be constant values, constant identifiers initialized to integer constant expressions, and *sizeof* expressions.

To illustrate constant expressions, I will first define *a* and *b* as constant identifiers:

```
const int a = 2;
const int b = 2*a;
```

Here now are examples of constant expressions:

```
2+3
sizeof(int)*2
a+b
a*sizeof(float)
```

3. EXPLICIT CONVERSIONS

Expressions of one type can be converted to expressions of other types by using the "cast" operator. For example, the value of a variable *d* of type *double* can be converted to an *int* as follows:

```
(int) d
```

Type casting is necessary in cases where a value of a specific type is required. For example, suppose that *i* and *j* are variables of type *int* and *a* is a variable of type *float* defined as follows:

```
int i = 6, j = 4;
float a;
```

Then after the assignment

```
a = i/j;
```

a will have the value 1, because that is the result of the dividing *i* by *j*. Integer division is used when both operands of the division operator are of integer types. In integer division, the remainder is thrown away.

To avoid losing the remainder, floating-point division must be used. Floating-point division is used when at least one of the operands is of a floating-point type. For example, we can use a cast to convert one of the operands of the division operator to type *float*:

```
a = ((float) i)/j;
```

Note that the right operand of the division operator will automatically be converted to a value of type *float* according to the arithmetic conversion rules described above. The result of the above division will be 1.5; this is the value that will be assigned to *a*.

Casts are used for converting between the fundamental types, pointers and integers, between different pointer types, between different reference types, and as explicitly defined by the user (see Chapter 8).

4. EXERCISES

1. Are the following expressions equivalent?

    ```
    a+3*b
    ```

    •

    ```
    3*b+a
    ```

    •

    ```
    (3*b)+a
    ```

    •

    ```
    3*(b+a)
    ```

    Explain why.

2. What is the value of this expression:

    ```
    a < b ? a : b
    ```

3. What are arithmetic conversion rules? When are they used?

4. What are casts and when are they used?

Chapter 5
STATEMENTS

A C++ program consists of a set of one or more files with each file containing a sequence of statements. C++ statements can be three kinds: declarations, definitions, and control statements. "Declarations" and "definitions" specify object properties such as type and "storage class." Definitions, in addition to specifying object properties, allocate storage for the object in memory. Declarations and definitions are not really necessary because a compiler can analyze how an object is used and use this information to deduce the object type and other object properties. Nevertheless, C++ requires programmers to declare or define an object before they reference the object because this facilitates error checking and allows the compiler to generate more efficient code.

"Control" statements represent code that manipulates objects in a program. These statements change the values of objects, examine object values and perform actions based on these values, perform actions repeatedly, and so on.

1. DECLARATIONS AND DEFINITIONS

C++ declaration and definitions have the form (simplified version)

type-specification declarator

A type specification can be a type name such as one of the predefined type names, a user-defined type name defined using the *typedef* statement, or one of the other types discussed later in the book.

As mentioned earlier, in its simplest form, a declarator is an identifier. In such a case, this identifier is defined as a program object with the characteristics specified in the declaration or definition. We will not formally describe all the possible forms of a declarator. Instead, the examples in this book will give you an idea of the different types of declarators. For complete details, see the definition of the C++ in *The C++ Programming Language* [Stroustrup 1991].

The general form of the declaration/definition statement is

type-qualifiers   storage-class   type   declarators-with-optional-initial-values ;

type-qualifiers are items that qualify the type. An example of a type qualifier is *const*, which specifies the type to be a "constant type"; values of objects of such a type cannot be changed. The *storage-class* is specified to alter the default "scope" and "lifetime" (longevity) of objects.

The general form of a declaration/definition differs from the simple form in that it allows the

1. specification of a type qualifier;

2. specification of the storage class;

3. declaration or definition of multiple objects in one statement; and

4. the specification of initial values for the objects.

1.1 DECLARATIONS VERSUS DEFINITIONS

Declarations "associate" a name with a program component and specify its properties. Definitions are like declarations except that they also allocate storage for an object. A declaration is a definition unless any of the following items is true:

1. The function body is not specified.

2. The keyword *extern* is present and a function body or an initial value is not specified.

3. A *static* data member of a class or a class name is being declared.

We have not discussed items (2) and (3) as yet; we will discuss all the above items later in detail.

1.2 CONSTANT IDENTIFIERS

Constant identifiers are symbolic names associated with constants (literals). Values associated with constant identifiers cannot be changed. We have already seen several examples of constant declarations. Here are some more:

```
const int m = 24, n = 36
const float pi = 3.1416;
const float a[5] = {1, 2, 3, 4, 5};
```

const is a type qualifier that specifies that the object being declared is a constant identifier. We informally use the phrase "constant identifier" to refer to an identifier whose type has been qualified to be "*const*."

The above declarations specify

1. *m* and *n* to be identifiers of type *const int* (constant integers) with the values 24 and 36, respectively,

2. *pi* as an identifier of type *const float* with the value 3.1416, and

3. *a* as a identifier of type *const array of float* with 5 elements; these elements are initialized to the values 1, 2, 3, 4, and 5, respectively (see Chapter 7 for a discussion of arrays).

Constant identifiers are typically initialized in their declarations. Constant identifiers cannot be initialized using the assignment operator. Note that the symbol = used in the above declarations does not denote the assignment operator; it simply separates the identifier from its initial value.

1.3 VARIABLES

Variables are identifiers with which values are associated and these values can be changed at any time. We have already seen several examples of variable definitions. Nevertheless, here are some more examples of variable definitions:

```
int i;
int m = 0, n = 32;
char *p;
char **pp;
double sales[12];
```

The effect of these definitions is to define

a. *i* a variable of type *int*,
b. *m* and *n* as variables of type *int* that have been initialized to 0 and 32, respectively,
c. *p* as a "*char* pointer" variable that refers to a character object,
d. *pp* as a "pointer" variable that refers to an object of type "pointer to *char*", and
e. *sales* as an "array" variable that has 12 components.

The last three definitions illustrate declarators that are more than simple identifiers. These declarators define objects of types that we have not seen so far. A "pointer" variable contains the "address" (location in computer memory) of an object. The address tells us where the object is located. An "array" variable is a composite object containing multiple component objects of the same type. We will discuss the above types in detail in later chapters.

Variables can also be declared (as opposed to being defined). A variable declaration allows the variable to be referenced before its definition is encountered. The definition of such a variable can be and typically is in another source file. Note that code for a *single* C++ program can be contained in *multiple* source files.

Here is an example of a variable declaration:

```
extern int a;
```

The keyword *extern* specifies that *a* will be defined elsewhere, later in the file containing this declaration or in another file that will be "linked" with this file to produce a complete program.

1.3.1 INITIAL VALUES An object must be initialized before its value is used; otherwise, the object value will be "garbage." Objects can be initialized in a variety of ways. For example, objects can be initialized

1. when they are defined,

2. by using the assignment operator, or

3. by using the input operator >>.

We have already seen all these initialization methods. The particular method used depends upon the application.

2. EXPRESSION STATEMENT

Any C++ expression can be converted into a statement by appending a semicolon to it:

expression;

Two examples of such statements are

```
a++;
```

which increments the value of variable *a* by one and

```
x1 = (-b+tmp)/(2*a);
```

which assigns a value to the variable *x1*.

Variable "assignment" statements have the form

var = value;

where *var* and *value* are both expressions. Expression *var* must refer to some object. Often *var* is simply an identifier. The types of expressions *var* and *value* must be "compatible", that is, their types should be identical or it should be possible to convert *value* to the type of *var*. For example, consider the following code:

```
float a;
...
a = 1;
```

The type of *a* is *float*. The value being assigned to *a* is the integer 1. Therefore, before 1 can be assigned to *a*, it must be converted to an equivalent *float* value, that is, 1.0f. This conversion is as specified by the arithmetic conversion rules (see Chapter 4). C++ knows how to convert integers to floating-point values. Had C++ not been able to perform such a conversion, then C++ would have "flagged" this assignment as erroneous.

It is important to note that C++ has assignment operators, but "technically speaking" it does not have an assignment statement (as in most languages). An assignment statement is simply a special case of an expression statement in which an assignment expression is converted to a statement by appending a semicolon. Informally, we will refer to such a statement as an assignment statement.

3. COMPOUND OR BLOCK STATEMENT

One or more C++ statements can be combined into a single "logical" statement by enclosing them in curly braces:

{ *statement-list* }

Such a logical statement is called a "compound" statement or a "block."

Blocks are typically used when

1. the C++ syntax requires a single statement, but where we need to specify multiple statements, and

2. to restrict the scope and lifetime of variables.

C++ syntax, for example, requires that the body of the *while* (loop) statement be a single statement. If the *while* loop body consists of multiple statements, then these statements must be enclosed within curly braces to convert them into one logical statement. This was exactly what we did in the *while* statement of the quadratic roots example discussed in Chapter 1:

```
     #include <iostream.h>
     #include <math.h>
     int main()
     {
5        float a, b, c, x1, x2, tmp;
         while (cin >> a >> b >> c) {
            if (a == 0) {
                cerr << "Error! First coeff is 0!";
                cerr << endl;
10               continue;
            }
            if ((tmp = b*b - 4*a*c) < 0) {
                cerr << "Error! Coeff ";
                cerr << a << ", " << b << ", " << c;
15               cerr << " have complex roots" << endl;
                continue;
            }
            tmp = sqrt(tmp);
            x1 = (-b+tmp)/(2*a);
20           x2 = (-b-tmp)/(2*a);
            cout << "Coeff = " << a << ", " << b << ", " << c;
            cout << "; Roots = " << x1 << ", " << x2 << endl;
         }
     }
```

The scope of variables declared in a block is local to the block and their lifetime extends from just after their definition to the end of the block. For example, consider the block in the following code:

```
...
{
    float tmp = a;
    a = b;
    b = tmp;
}
...
```

The code shown above exchanges the values of variables *a* and *b* (which must have been declared global to the block). Variable *tmp* is not needed after the values are exchanged (that is, after the values have been swapped). By declaring *tmp* within a block, we know it will only exist for the duration of the block (until the right curly brace). *tmp* will automatically be "deallocated" (destroyed) at the end of the block.

4. CONDITIONAL EXECUTION

C++ provides facilities for "conditional" execution. These facilities are used when the execution of some code (one or more statements) must depend upon the value of an expression. There are two statements in C++ that support conditional execution: the "two-way" *if* statement and the "multi-way" *switch* statement.

4.1 IF STATEMENT

The *if* statement comes in two flavors: with and without the *else* clause. Let us first look at the *if* statement without the *else* clause. This version of the *if* statement has the form

```
if (expression)
    statement
```

The code represented by *statement* in the *if* statement is called the "true" alternative, because it is executed only if *expression* evaluates to true (a non-zero value). If *expression* evaluates to false (zero), then the effect of this *if* statement is to do nothing (except for evaluating *expression*). Note that C++ considers non-zero values to denote true and zero to denote false.

Here is an example, illustrating the *if* statement, which sets variable x to its absolute value:

```
if (x < 0)
    x = -x;
```

The true alternative in this *if* statement

```
x = -x;
```

is executed only if the expression

```
x < 0
```

evaluates to true, that is, when x is less than 0. In this case x is set to the negative of its original value. If x is positive to start with, then the true alternative is not executed and x is not changed. Either way, the end result of executing this *if* statement is to ensure that x is set to the absolute of its original value.

We could alternatively have written this statement as

```
if (x < 0) x = -x;
```

This is a stylistic choice; C++ does not care. Except for simple *if* statements, the first choice is preferable from the program readability point of view.

The *if* statement with the *else* clause has the form

```
if (expression)
     statement
               1
else
     statement
               2
```

If *expression* evaluates to true, then the code represented by *statement₁*, called
the "true" alternative, is executed; otherwise, the code represented by *statement₂*,
called the "false" alternative, is executed.

Here is an example of the *if* statement with the *else* clause:

```
if (a < b)
    max = b;
else
    max = a;
```

Execution of this *if* statement sets variable *max* to the largest of the values of the
two variables *a* and *b*.

The following *if* statement

```
if (x < 0)
    x = -x;
```

which was shown previously, could also have been written using the *else* clause as

```
if (x < 0)
    x = -x;
else
    ;
```

In this case, the *else* clause consists of the *null* statement which does nothing
(discussed later). Consequently, no purpose is served in giving the *else* clause.

4.2 SWITCH STATEMENT

The *switch* statement is a generalization of the *if* statement: it allows
programmers to specify multi-way branching instead of two-way branching. As
an illustration of the syntax and semantics of the *switch* statement, consider the
following example:

```
     char action;
     float amount;
     long account;
     ...
 5   switch (action) {
     case 'b': balance(account); break;
     case 'd': deposit(amount, account); break;
     case 'w': withdraw(amount, account); break;
     case 's': summary(account); break;
10   default:  error(account);
     }
```

This *switch* statement is executed as follows:

1. Evaluate the *switch* expression *action*, which produces a value of type *char* (a character).

2. Each *case* labels specifies a *switch* statement alternative. If the value of the *switch* expression matches any of the *case* labels, then that alternative is executed. For example, if *action* evaluates to the character 'd', then the statements in the alternative marked with this character as its label, that is, the two statements (a semicolon terminates a statement)

   ```
   deposit(amount, account); break;
   ```

   are executed. The first statement is a call to the function *deposit* (we shall discuss functions in detail in the next chapter). Executing the second statement

   ```
   break;
   ```

   completes execution of the *switch* statement and the execution of the program then continues from after the *switch* statement.

3. If the value of the *switch* expression does not match any of the *case* labels, then the statement with the label *default* is executed.

The general form of the *switch* statement is

```
switch (expression) {
case label₁: statements₁; break;
...
case labelₙ: statementsₙ; break;
default: statementsₙ₊₁;
}
```

The *case* labels are constant expressions. No two *case* labels should evaluate to the same value.

The *switch* statement is executed as follows:

1. First, the *switch* expression is evaluated.

2. The value of this expression is then compared with the values of the *case* labels.

3.   a.   If there is a *case* label whose value is equal to that of the *switch* expression, then the alternative with this label, that is, the statements following this label, are executed.

      b.   Otherwise, if there is no such *case* label and the *default* label has been specified, then the *default* alternative will be executed.

This completes execution of the *switch* statement.

C++ does not require the programmer to give *break* statements in the *switch* statement as shown above. The *break* statements ensure that the *switch* statement will terminate after executing an alternative. Otherwise, instead of executing the statements following the *switch* statement, statements of the next alternative, if any, will be executed.

5. LOOPS

C++ provides three kinds of "loop" statements for repeatedly executing a set of statements, called the "loop body." The three loop statements are the *for*, the *while*, and the *do-while* statements. Although the three C++ loop statements provide equivalent functionality, they represent different "looping paradigms" (styles of expressing repeated execution).

5.1 FOR STATEMENT

The *for* statement repeatedly executes its body based using the following paradigm:

1. Declare and/or initialize variables that will be used in the loop.

2. Evaluate the loop expression.

3. If the loop expression evaluates to true, then execute the loop body and go to step 4; otherwise, terminate the loop.

4. Update the loop variables and go to step 2.

As an example of the *for* statement, consider the following program, which prints the squares of the numbers from 1 to 10:

```
#include <iostream.h>
int main()
{
    cout << "i" << '\t' << "i*i" << endl;
    for (int i = 1; i <= 10;   i++)
        cout << i << '\t' << i*i << endl;
}
```

The output of this program is

```
i      i*i
1      1
2      4
3      9
4      16
5      25
6      36
7      49
8      64
9      81
10     100
```

The *for* statement in the above program executes as follows:

1. Initialize variable *i* to 0.

2. Check if *i* is less than or equal to 10. If *i* is less than 10, then perform step 3; otherwise, execution of the *for* loop is complete.

3. Execute the print statement (the body of the *for* statement):

    ```
    cout << i << ' ' << i*i << endl;
    ```

    This statement prints the value of *i* followed by a tab (denoted by \t), the square of *i*, and a new line.

4. Increment *i* by 1, which is specified by the expression

    ```
    i++
    ```

    in the first line of the *for* statement.

5. Go to step 2.

Variable *i* is called the "loop" variable because its value depends upon how many times the loop has been executed. In this example, *i* is declared in the *for* loop header (first line of the *for* statement). We could have also written this program with the loop variable defined separately (before the *for* statement):

```
#include <iostream.h>
int main()
{
    int i;
    cout << "i" << '\t' << "i*i" << endl;
    for (i = 1; i <= 10;  i++)
        cout << i << '\t' << i*i << endl;
}
```

The general form of the *for* statement is[1]

for (*initializing-statement*$_{opt}$ *condition*$_{opt}$; *expression*$_{opt}$)
    statement

The *for* statement executes as follows:

1. The *initializing-statement* is executed first.

2. The loop *condition* is then evaluated. If it is false, then execution of the *for* loop is terminated (the statement following the *for* statement is executed). If the *condition* is true, then the *for* loop body (denoted by *statement*) is executed.

3. The loop "increment" *expression* is evaluated next. Typically, evaluation of this expression changes the value of one or more operands in the loop *condition*.

4. Go to step 2.

Any of the components in the *for* loop header can be omitted. If the loop condition is omitted, then it is assumed to be true. Consider, as an example, the following code "skeleton":

```
for (;;)
    ...
```

All the three components of the *for* loop header have been ómitted. As a result, the loop body denoted by ... will be executed "forever" unless the loop body contains a statement, such as a *break* or *return* statement (discussed later), to "exit" (terminate) the *for* loop.

---

1. In C++ [Stroustrup 1991], the *opt* subscript is used to indicate an optional item. An alternative notation, used in programming languages, is to enclose the optional item in square brackets.

The body of the *for* loop can only be a single statement. If the loop body consists of multiple statements, then these statements must combined into a single logical statement by using curly braces. As an example, consider the following program that computes the squares of the numbers supplied by the user:

```
#include <iostream.h>
int main()
{
    float a;
    for (;;) {
        cout << ':';
        cin >> a;
        cout << '\t' << a*a << endl;
    }
}
```

The program prints a colon and then waits for the user to enter the number whose square is to be computed. The program prints the square and then waits for the next number.

Here is a sample user interaction with this program:

```
:4
        16
:4.5
        20.25
:11
        121
:11.5
        132.25
:13
        169
:^C
```

This program is interesting for several reasons:

1. It is an example of a *for* loop that does not terminate; this means that the program does not terminate by itself. It must be terminated by explicitly "killing" it or "interrupting" it by typing control-C (^C), that is, by simultaneously pressing both the "control" and C keys.

2. The loop body consists of several statements, which have been combined into a single logical statement by using curly braces.

3. The program prints a colon to let the user know it is waiting for input. Reading user input is as simple as printing output. We simply use a different operator.

5.2 WHILE STATEMENT

The *while* statement repeatedly executes its body based on the following paradigm:

1. Evaluate the loop expression.

2. If the loop expression evaluates to true, then execute the loop body and go to step 1; otherwise, terminate the loop.

The *while* loop differs from the *for* loop in that facilities to initialize loop variables and update them are not provided as part of the *while* statement. Variables used in the loop expression must be initialized before the loop, and they must be updated within the loop body.

The *while* statement has the form

```
while (condition)
     statement
```

The body of the *while* loop, which is denoted by *statement*, is executed repeatedly as long as the specified condition is true.

As an example of the *while* loop, we will rewrite the program to print the squares of the numbers from 1 to 10:

```
    #include <iostream.h>
    int main()
    {
        cout << "i" << '\t' << "i*i" << endl;
5       int i = 1;
        while (i <= 10) {
            cout << i << '\t' << i*i << endl;
            i++;
        }
10  }
```

Note that the loop variable *i* is now incremented in the loop body (in the *for* statement *i* was incremented in the *for* header).

Instead of incrementing the loop variable *i* in the body of the *while* loop, we can increment it in the *while* condition itself. This requires starting with *i* equal to zero:

```
#include <iostream.h>
int main()
{
    cout << "i" << '\t' << "i*i" << endl;
    int i = 0;
    while (i++ <= 10)
        cout << i << '\t' << i*i << endl;
}
```

5.3 DO–WHILE STATEMENT

The *do-while* statement repeatedly executes its body based on the following paradigm:

1. Execute the loop body.

2. Evaluate the loop expression.

3. If the loop expression evaluates to true, then go to step 1; otherwise, terminate the loop.

The *do-while* statement is similar to the *while* statement except that the loop condition is evaluated after, instead of before, each execution of the loop body.

The *do-while* statement has the form

```
do
     statement
while (condition);
```

The body of the *do-while* loop, which is denoted by *statement*, is executed once and then repeatedly as long as the specified condition is true. Unlike the *while* loop, the *do-while* executes its body at least once.

Using the *do-while* loop, the program to compute the squares of the first ten numbers can be written as

```
     #include <iostream.h>
     int main()
     {
         cout << "i" << '\t' << "i*i" << endl;
5        int i = 1;
         do {
             cout << i << '\t' << i*i << endl;
             i++;
         }
10       while (i < 10);
     }
```

Note that the loop condition is different from that in the *while* loop version.

6. JUMP STATEMENTS

C++ provides several statements that cause a jump from one statement to another. We have already seen one statement: the *break* statement. It was used in the *switch* statement to jump to the statement following the *switch* statement after executing an alternative.

6.1 BREAK STATEMENT

The *break* statement

```
break;
```

is used to exit from the innermost *switch* or loop statement.

Here is skeleton code illustrating the use of a *break* statement to terminate a *for* statement:

```
for(...) {
    if (expression) {
        ...
        break;
    }
    ...
}
```

The *break* statement is executed conditionally, that is, when the *if* expression evaluates to true. The effect of the *break* statement is to cause an exit from the loop. The statement following the loop, if any, is then executed.

6.2 CONTINUE STATEMENT

The *continue* statement

```
continue;
```

is used to start the next execution of the innermost loop body containing it (provided the loop conditions are satisfied).

Here is skeleton code showing how a *continue* statement can be used to continue the next execution of the loop (without the loop body being executed completely):

```
for(...) {
    if (expression) {
        ...
        continue;
    }
    ...
}
```

Execution of the *continue* statement depends upon the value of the *if* expression. The effect of executing the *continue* statement is to immediately try and start the next execution of the loop body, that is the next "iteration." Of course, the next iteration will be performed only if the *for* condition is satisfied.

6.3 GOTO STATEMENT

The *goto* statement

```
goto identifier;
```

is used to transfer control to a statement with the label *identifier*. Any statement, including the null statement can be labeled as follows:

identifier: *statement*

Here is example code illustrating the use of a *goto* statement:

```
int x;
...
while(cin >> x) {
    if (x < 0) {
        ...
        goto negative;
    }
    ...
    continue;
    negative: cout << "negative value " << x;
}
```

If x (the value read from input), is negative, then the above program code jumps to the statement labeled *negative*, prints a message on the screen, and then goes on to execute the next iteration. If x is positive, then the code shown will eventually execute the *continue* statement, which makes the *while* loop start the next iteration.

6.4 RETURN STATEMENT

The *return* statement is used to terminate execution of a function and to return a function value. Please refer to Chapter 6 for details.

7. NULL STATEMENT

The *null* statement is a "no-op", that is, it does not do anything. It consists of just a semicolon:

```
;
```

The *null* statement is used when the C++ syntax requires a statement, but where, from a programming viewpoint, we do not need to specify any action.

As an example, consider the following program that reads a sequence of integers until it encounters a negative integer. The program prints the negative number and terminates (file *null.cpp*):

```
#include <iostream.h>
int main()
{
    int x = 0;
    while (cin >> x, x >= 0)
        ;
    cout << "First Negative Number = " << x << endl;
}
```

The expression controlling the execution of *while* loop is the comma expression

```
cin >> x, x >= 0
```

whose left operand assigns the next input value to x, and the right operand compares the newly assigned value with 0. The value of the comma expression is the value of this comparison. Thus the *while* statement executes until a negative value is encountered. There is no need for the loop to have a body. We simply use the null statement.

There is one problem with this program. If no negative value is encountered in the input, then this program will not terminate. We must also therefore check for the end of input. We can do this by simply incorporating the input stream *cin* as part of the right operand of the comma operator:

```
cin >> x, (x >= 0) && cin
```

In C++, when a stream variable such as *cin* is evaluated as part of a logical expression, then it evaluates to true provided no problem was encountered by the last stream operation; otherwise, it evaluates to false. Specifically, in our example, if the last input operation (denoted by >>) on stream *cin* encounters the end of input, then *cin* will evaluate to false. This means that the right operand of the comma operator

```
(x >= 0) && cin
```

will evaluate to false, which will cause the *while* loop to terminate.

Note that the precedence of the input operator >> is greater than that of the comma operator, which has the lowest precedence of all the operators. The left operand of the logical *and* operator && is enclosed within parentheses because the precedence of the relational operator >= is greater than that of the logical *and* operator.

Here is the above program modified to terminate upon encountering the end of input:

```
#include <iostream.h>
int main()
{
    int x = 0;
    while (cin >> x, x >= 0)
        ;
    cout << "First Negative Number = " << x << endl;
}
```

Note that the *while* loop can now terminate for two reasons: upon encountering a negative value or upon reaching the end of input. Consequently, the statement printing information about the negative value is made conditional to ensure that it is executed only if *x* is negative.

8. EXERCISES

1. The following *if* statement sets variable *max* to the largest of the two variables *a* and *b*:

```
if (a < b)
    max = b;
else
    max = a;
```

Two alternative ways of accomplishing the same task are

```
if (a <= b)
    max = b;
else
    max = a;
```

and

```
max = a;
if (a < b)
    max = b;
```

Compare and contrast these three solutions.

2. Write (and test) a program to convert temperature in Fahrenheit to temperature in Celsius. The conversion formula is

```
c = (f-32)*5.0/9.0
```

where c is the temperature in Fahrenheit and f is the temperature in Celsius.

3. Explain how the following expression will be evaluated

```
cin >> x, (x >= 0) && cin
```

if the parentheses enclosing the left operand of operator && are removed.

4. Why does C++ provide three different kinds of loop statements? Would one suffice? Which one? Justify your answer.

Chapter 6
FUNCTIONS

"Functions" are used for bundling multiple statements that perform a single task into one logical program component. These statements are executed by "calling" the function. The items supplied in a function call are called "arguments." For example, $x+y$ and *epsilon* are the arguments of the call to function *Sqrt*[1] that is embedded in the following assignment statement:

```
m = Sqrt(x+y, epsilon);
```

Suppose that function *Sqrt* is defined as

```
double Sqrt(double x, double accuracy)
{
    ...
}
```

The "parameters" of function *Sqrt* are x and *accuracy*. Parameters are the counterparts of the arguments within a function definition.

Information is passed to a function by means of arguments in the function call, and is returned to the "caller" from the function as the function result (using the *return* statement) and by updating the arguments. A correspondence is established between the arguments in the function call and the parameters specified in the function definition. Consequently, within the function body, information sent by the caller can be accessed using function parameters. Information can also be exchanged between the caller and the function by using global variables.

---

1. As mentioned previously, C++ is case sensitive. Consequently, because of the upper-case first letter, identifier *Sqrt* is not the same as the identifier *sqrt*, which refers to the standard C++ math function for computing the square root. *sqrt* was used in Chapter 1 in the program for computing square roots.

As an example of a function definition, consider the definition of function *swap*, which exchanges the values of two *int* variables (file *swap.cpp*):

```
void swap(int& a, int& b)
{
    int tmp = a;
    a = b;
    b = tmp;
}
```

Line 1 of the above definition specifies that *swap*

1. is a function,
2. has two *int* parameters *a* and *b*, and
3. does not return a result (specified by type *void*).

The & character after the type identifier *int* specifies that the parameter will become a synonym for the corresponding argument (in "technical" terms, it specifies that the corresponding argument will be passed "by reference"). This means that both the parameter and the argument will refer to the same object. Consequently, changing a parameter value changes the argument value if the argument is passed by reference. Suppose, for example, that *swap* is called as

```
swap(i, j)
```

Then, within the body of *swap*, parameters *a* and *b* become synonyms of the arguments *i* and *j*, respectively, The body of function *swap* starts with the left curly brace (line 2) and terminates with the right curly brace (line 6).

Function *swap* exchanges the values of its parameters *a* and *b* (and therefore the values of its arguments) by storing the

1. value of *a* in the local variable *tmp*,

2. value of *b* in *a*, and finally

3. the original value of *a*, which was saved in *tmp*, in *b*.

As mentioned previously, an object definition results in allocation of storage for the object. Storage for local variables is allocated when a function begins execution and this storage is deallocated just before the function terminates. Also, parameters behave like local variables in that they can be accessed only within the function body.

Now lets us take a look at the following code that contains a declaration of function *swap* and a pair of calls to *swap*:

```
void swap(int& a, int& b);
int i = 1, j = 2, m = 3, n = 4;
...
swap(i, j); //first call
swap(m, n); //second call
...
```

The prototype of function *swap* matches the first line of its definition. This prototype must be given if the definition of *swap* given after function *swap* is referenced (a function call is a reference) or if the definition of *swap* is in a different file.[2]

The effect of a function call is to jump to the corresponding function body. Upon completion of the function body, execution is resumed at a point just after the function call. In this example, function *swap* completes execution by completing the execution of its body, which consists of just three statements.

The first call to *swap* exchanges the value of the variables *i* and *j*, which are the arguments of the function call. The second *swap* function call exchanges the values of *m* and *n*.

Suppose that variables *i*, *j*, *m*, and *n* initially have the following values:

```
i = 1, j = 2, m = 3, n = 4
```

After the two calls to *swap*, these variables will have the following values

```
i = 2, j = 1, m = 4, n = 3
```

There are several advantages of using functions:

1. Using functions makes the program modular – a program, especially a large one, can be partitioned into several functions.

2. Each function call represents a "higher" level instruction than C++ statements because it typically encapsulates several C++ statements.

3. Functions encourage code sharing since a function can be called from several places in the program – the code in the function body does not have to be replicated. And if functions are stored in separate files, then they can also be "reused" in other programs.

---

2. If a C++ program is split into many source files, then it is the programmer's responsibility to compile and link together all the source files to produce an executable program.

1. FUNCTION DECLARATIONS OR PROTOTYPES

As in the case of variables and constants, a function must be declared or defined before it can be referenced. Function declarations are called "prototypes." A prototype can be thought of as an incomplete function definition. A prototype must "match" the corresponding function definition. A prototype contains information that a C++ compiler can use to ensure that the function is called correctly. For example, given a prototype, the compiler can ensure that

1. the number of arguments match the number of parameters;

2. each argument type matches the corresponding parameter type; and

3. the value returned by the function is used appropriately with respect to its type.

Prototypes do not really tell us what a function does although, if function names are selected properly, we may be able to guess their functionality.

Here are examples of prototypes:

```
int get(void);
void put(int);
double sin(double x);
int toupper(int c);
int max2(int a, int b);
```

These prototypes declare

1. *get* as a function that does not accept any arguments (that is why its argument type is declared as *void*) and returns a value of type *int*;

2. *put* as a function takes one argument of type *int* and does not return a result (indicated by the *void* result type);

3. *sin* as a function that takes one argument of type *double* and returns a result of type *double*;

4. *toupper* as a function that takes one argument of type *int* and returns a result of type *int*; and

5. *max2* as a function that accepts two *int* arguments and returns a result of type *int*.

The example programs in the previous chapter "called" (invoked) two standard C++ library functions *sin* and *toupper* whose prototypes were not given explicitly. Instead, appropriate standard header files, which contained the prototypes of these two functions, were included in the programs. C++ provides the prototypes of all the standard library functions in the standard header files.

2. FUNCTION DEFINITIONS (BODIES)

Function definitions (bodies) have the form

result-type function-name (parameter-declarations)
{
    statements
}

A function with a *void* result type (a function that does not return a result) completes execution by reaching the end of its body, or by executing a *return* statement of the form

```
return;
```

return statements are used in function bodies to allow a function to return from multiple points in the program, without forcing the programmer to write code that always jumps to the end of the function body.

As an example of a function that terminates by executing the *return* statement, consider the definitions function *order* (file *order.cpp*):

```
//reorder x, y so that x <= y
#include "swap.h"
void order(int& x, int& y)
{
    if (x <= y)
        return;
    else
        swap(x, y);
}
```

Function *order* reorders the values of its parameters x and y so that $x \leq y$. If $x \leq y$ when *order* is called, then it returns without doing anything (by executing the *return* statement). Otherwise, it exchanges the values of x and y by calling function *swap* (whose definition was shown earlier). Incidentally, the header file *swap.h* contains the prototype of function *swap*:

```
void swap(int& a, int& b);
```

The name of the header file in the *#include* statement, shown above in file *order.cpp*, is specified using double quotes instead of with angle brackets as in previous examples. The only difference between using double quotes and angle brackets is that in case of double quotes, C++ first looks for the file specified in the current directory and then in the "standard" places where the standard header files are kept. In case of angle brackets, C++ looks for the specified file only in the standard places. Typically, user-defined header files are included by specifying the file name in double quotes because such files are likely to be found in the current directory.

A function with a non-*void* result type (a function that returns a result) must terminate by returning a result of the appropriate type. Executing a *return* statement of the form

```
return expression;
```

causes a function to terminate and return the specified expression as its result.

To illustrate how a function returns a result, we will write a function *max2* that computes the maximum of its two parameters. Here is the prototype of *max2* (file *max2f.h*):

```
int max2(int a, int b);
```

Unlike in function *swap*, there is no & character after the parameter types (in "technical" terms, this means that the arguments will be passed "by value"). Because of this, parameters of function *max2* will not become synonyms of the arguments specified in a *max2* function call. Argument values will be simply copied to the parameters. Changing the parameter values will not the affect argument values.

Here is the definition of function *max2* (file *max2f.cpp*):

```
int max2(int a, int b)
{
    return a < b ? b : a;
}
```

Function *max2* compares the values of the parameters *a* and *b*

```
a < b ? b : a
```

The value of this expression is *b* if *a* is less than *b*; otherwise, it is *a*. Function *max2* returns the value of the above expression as its result.

2.1 DEFAULT PARAMETER VALUES

C++ allows default values to be specified for function parameters. Functions with default parameter values can be called with fewer arguments than specified in their prototypes and definitions. In such a case, parameters without corresponding arguments are assigned default values. Typically, default values are specified in prototypes and not in function definitions. Note that all arguments following an omitted argument must also be omitted (in other words, only trailing arguments can be omitted).

To illustrate the specification and the use of default parameter values, we will write a function, named *Sqrt*, to compute the square roots of *double* values We will use the following algorithm to compute the square root:

1. a. Let *x* be the value whose square root is to be computed. The square root computed must be accurate to within a precision of *accuracy*.
    b. Let zero be the first approximation of the square root of *x*; call this value *oldSqrt*.
    c. Let *x*/2.0 be the second approximation of the square root of *x*; call this value *newSqrt*.

    We need the two approximations (*oldSqrt* and *newSqrt*) to start our computation. The specific values selected do not matter provided the difference between them is more than the desired precision *accuracy*.

2. If the absolute value of the difference between *oldSqrt* and *newSqrt* is less than *accuracy*, then we are done. Both values will then represent the square root of *x* (within the desired precision).

3. To compute a better approximation for the square root, set *oldSqrt* to the value of *newSqrt* and set *newSqrt* to

    ```
    0.5 * (oldSqrt + 2.0/oldSqrt)
    ```

    Go to step 2.

Function *Sqrt*, which implements the above algorithm, has the prototype

```
double Sqrt(double x, double accuracy = 0.01);
```

Parameter *accuracy* has 0.01 as its default value. If the programmer does not specify an argument corresponding to *accuracy* as in the following assignment statement

```
a = Sqrt(b);
```

then *accuracy* will be assumed to be initialized to 0.01.

Of course, the programmer can always explicitly specify an argument corresponding to the parameter *accuracy*, for example,

```
a = Sqrt(b, 0.0005);
```

In C++, only the trailing set of parameters can be given default values. In other words, if a parameter has a default value, then all parameters that follow it must be given default values.

Now let us take a look at the definition of function *Sqrt* (file *sqrt.cpp*):

```
   #include <iostream.h>
   #include <math.h>
   #include <stdlib.h>
   #include "sqrt.h"
5  double Sqrt(double x, double accuracy)
   {
       double newSqrt = x/2, oldSqrt = 0;
       if (x < 0) {
           cout << "cannot compute square roots of";
10         cout << "negative numbers" << endl;
           exit(1);
       }
       while (fabs(newSqrt-oldSqrt) > accuracy) {
           oldSqrt = newSqrt;
15         newSqrt = 0.5 * (oldSqrt+x/oldSqrt);
       }
       return newSqrt;
   }
```

The first four instructions include header files:

1. *iostream.h* (line 1) contains the prototypes and other declarations for the stream input/output facilities.

2. *math.h* (line 2) contains the prototype of the function *fabs* (called in line 13), which computes the absolute value of its argument (of type *double*).

3. *stdlib.h* (line 3) contains the prototype of function *exit* (line 11), which is called to explicitly terminate a program. Function *Sqrt* terminates the program, if it is called with a negative argument, by calling *exit*.

4. *sqrt.h* (line 4) contains the prototype of *Sqrt*. It is not necessary to include this header file in *sqrt.cpp* because *sqrt.cpp* contains only the definition of *Sqrt*. Specifying the prototype is a must if the function is referenced before its definition is encountered. However, including the prototype in the file containing the function definition allows C++ to catch inconsistencies between the prototype and the function definition at compile time. Otherwise, such inconsistencies will be detected only when the object modules are "linked" together to form an executable program (discussed later).

The definition of *Sqrt* starts on line 5. Parameter *x* corresponds to the argument whose square root is to be computed. A prototype must match the first line of the corresponding function definition with respect to the number of arguments and their types, and the function result type. However, this matching does not extend to the default parameter values which are typically specified only in the prototype.

Within the body of *Sqrt*, identifiers *newSqrt* and *oldSqrt* are defined as local variables and given initial values in the same definition statement (line 7). If *x* is negative, then function *Sqrt* prints an error message and terminates the program by calling function *exit* (lines 8-12). *exit* is called, by convention, with its argument equal to one to indicate "failed" termination and zero to indicate "successful" termination.[3]

Then comes the *while* loop (lines 13-16). If the current approximation of the square root is not satisfactory (that is, it is not within the desired precision specified by *accuracy*), then a new approximation is computed. Eventually, the loop terminates and the computed square root is returned as the function result.

3. FUNCTION CALL

A function body is executed by "calling" the function. A function call, which is an expression, has the form[4]

function-name (*arguments*)

If the value returned by a function is to be ignored or if the function does not return a value, then a semicolon is appended after the function call to make it into a statement:

function-name (*arguments*) ;

4. ARGUMENTS PASSING

The relationship between the arguments in a function call and the corresponding parameters specified in the function definition depends upon the "argument passing mode." C++ supports two argument passing modes: "by value" and "by reference." The mode in which an argument is passed to a function is specified in the function definition (and in the prototype).

4.1 PASSING ARGUMENTS BY VALUE

Passing an argument "by value" means that the value of the argument specified in a function call will be copied to the corresponding parameter. Stated another way, this means that the argument value will become the initial value of the corresponding parameter. Changing the values of such parameters do not affect the values of the corresponding arguments.

---

3. The argument in an *exit* function call is passed on to the environment, such as the operating system, where it can be used to determine whether or not the program executed successfully.

4. The parentheses in a function call denotes the "function call" operator.

Storage is allocated and deallocated for "value" parameters just as it is done for local variables. Storage is allocated when a function begins execution and deallocated just before function termination.

Function *max2* defined above is one example of a function whose arguments are passed by value. As another example, we will write a function to compute the factorial. The factorial of a number *n*, denoted as *n*! is defined as

```
0! = 1
n! = n * (n-1)!
```

Another way of defining the factorial is

```
0! = 1
n! = n * (n-1) * (n-2) ... * 1
```

The first definition is "recursive" in that the factorial is defined in terms of itself. We will use the second definition, which is not recursive, to compute the factorial.

Here is the prototype of *fact*, which computes the factorial (file *fact.h*):

```
int fact(int n);
```

Function *fact* is defined as (file *fact.cpp*):

```
#include "fact.h"
int fact(int n)
{
    int result = 1;
    for (int i = n; i >= 1; i-- )
        result = result * i;
    return result;
}
```

Function *fact* computes the factorial of *n* by repeatedly multiplying the numbers from *n* down to 1. The intermediate products of the multiplication and the final product are stored in variable *result* (the old product is destroyed when a new one is stored). The final value of *result*, which is the factorial of *n*, is returned by *fact* as its result.

The *for* loop used in *fact* could also have been written to compute the product by multiplying the numbers from 1 up to *n* (instead of from *n* down to 1):

```
for (int i = 1; i <= n; i++ )
    result = result * i;
```

Also, the assignment statement

```
result = result * i;
```

could alternatively have been written using the compound assignment operator
`*=` as

```
result *= i;
```

Consider the following call to function *fact*:

```
fact(i)
```

The effect of this function call is to copy the value of argument *i* to the parameter *n*, jump to the body of function *fact*, compute the factorial, and return from the function body. The factorial of *n* is returned as the function result, which then becomes the value of this function call.

4.2 PASSING ARGUMENTS BY REFERENCE

Passing an argument "by reference" means that the corresponding parameter will become a synonym for the argument. Changing the value of such a parameter means changing the value of the corresponding argument. The value of a parameter upon function completion will be the value of the corresponding argument.

Function *swap*, defined above, is an example of a function whose arguments are passed by reference. To illustrate the necessity of passing arguments by reference, suppose that *swap* is erroneously defined (with a matching prototype) so that its arguments are passed by value. Here is its definition:

```
void swap(int a, int b)
{
    int tmp = a;
    a = b;
    b = tmp;
}
```

Calling this *swap* function will not affect the arguments specified – they will not be exchanged. Suppose, as an example, that *swap* is called to exchange the values of *x* and *y* as follows:

```
swap(x, y);
```

The values of *x* and *y* are copied to the parameters *a* and *b*, respectively. The values of *a* and *b* are then exchanged, but this does not have any impact on the values of *x* and *y* because *a* and *b* are not synonyms of *x* and *y*. After *swap* completes, *x* and *y* will have the same values as they had prior to the *swap* function call.

To further illustrate passing arguments by reference, we will write a function that computes the roots of a quadratic equation. We wrote a program to do this in Chapter 1. Now we will take the part of this program that computes the roots and make it into a function named *roots*. Here is the prototype of function *roots* (file *roots.h*):

```
int roots(float a,float b,float c,float& r1,float& r2);
```

The first three arguments of function *roots* are passed by value and the last two arguments are passed by reference. It is important to pass the last two arguments by reference because the roots computed by function *roots* will be stored in the parameters corresponding to these arguments. And because the parameters corresponding to arguments passed by reference are synonyms for the arguments, the roots will also be stored in the arguments.

Function *roots* is defined as (file *froots.cpp*):

```
   //compute real roots of a quadratic equation;
   //does not compute complex roots

   #include <math.h>
 5 #include "froots.h"
   int roots(float A,float B,float C,float& R1,float& R2)
   {
       float tmp = B*B - 4*A*C;
       if (A == 0 || tmp < 0)
10         return 0;
       tmp = sqrt(tmp);
       R1 = (-B+tmp)/(2*A);
       R2 = (-B-tmp)/(2*A);
       return 1;
15 }
```

Function *roots* returns zero (line 10) if it cannot compute the roots because the first coefficient of the quadratic equation is zero or because the equation has complex roots. If function *roots* is successful in computing the roots, then it returns one (line 14). It is the responsibility of the caller of function *roots* to determine whether or not the roots were computed successfully. When a value returned by a function is used to indicate success or failure, it is called a *status* value.

The task of reading input, printing error messages, and printing the roots is left to the *main* function which calls function *roots* (file *mroots.cpp*):

```
     #include <iostream.h>
     #include "froots.h"
     int main()
     {
 5       float a, b, c, r1, r2;
         while (cin >> a >> b >> c) {
             if (roots(a, b, c, r1, r2)) {
                 cerr << "Error! First coeff is 0 or ";
                 cerr << "equation has complex roots!";
10               cerr << endl;
                 continue;
             }
             cout <<"Coeff = " << a << ", " << b << ", " << c;
             cout <<"; Roots = " << r1 << ", " << r2 << endl;
15       }
     }
```

Consider the function call (line 7)

```
roots(a, b, c, r1, r2)
```

which is in effect the condition part of the *if* statement. Values of the arguments *a*, *b*, and *c*, which are passed by value, are copied to the parameters *A*, *B*, and *C* of the function *roots*. Parameters *R1* and *R2*, whose corresponding arguments *r1* and *r2* are passed by reference, become synonyms for the arguments. This relationship between *r1* and *r2*, and *R1* and *R2*, respectively, lasts until the completion (termination) of function *roots*. Note that it is not necessary for the argument names to be different from parameter names (as in this example).

The quadratic roots program is now contained in two files: *mroots.cpp* and *froots.cpp*. The complete program can be compiled as

```
bcc mroots froots
```

and can be executed by typing

```
mroots
```

4.2.1 ADVANTAGES OF PASSING ARGUMENTS BY REFERENCE
Arguments are passed by reference for two important reasons:

1. *Argument update*: The value of the argument passed by reference can be changed in the function body by changing the value of the corresponding parameter.

2. *Efficiency*: Passing an argument by reference does not require copying of the argument value to the parameter. Copying can be expensive when the size of the argument is large (as in the case of structure and class objects,

which are discussed later). When an argument is passed by reference, only its location (address) in memory needs to be copied. The cost of copying a memory address is typically less than or equal to the cost of copying an object whose size is equal to 4 bytes.

5. LOCAL AND GLOBAL VARIABLES

Local variables are variables which can be accessed from within only one function. Global variables are variables that are (typically) shared by several functions. Each variable has a "scope" and a "lifetime." The scope of a (variable) name is the region of the program text where the name can be referenced. The lifetime of an object (referenced by a variable) is the period for which the object exists. By default, the scope of and lifetime of an object are determined from the context. In this section, we will discuss the scope and lifetime of local and global variables.

5.1 SCOPE AND LIFETIME

Declarations and definitions are the mechanisms for introducing new names in a program. Each name (for example, a constant identifier or a variable name) in a C++ program has a scope. There are four kinds of scope in C++: local, function, file (global), and class:

1. *Local*: A name declared in a block (such as a function body) is local to the block – the name can be accessed from any where within the block following its declaration. As an example, consider the following program which computes the total of the first input values until it encounters a zero (from Chapter 4):

```
#include <iostream.h>
int main()
{
    int x, total = 0;
    cin >> x;
    while (x != 0) {
        total = total + x;
        cin >> x;
    }
    cout << "Total = " << total << endl;
}
```

The two variable names x and *total* are local to the block (body of function *main*) that starts with the left curly brace on line 3 and ends with the right curly brace on the last line. Their scope starts in line 4 just after their definitions.

Function parameters are also local to the function body. A nested block may hide a name if it contains the declaration of the same name.

2. *Function*: Only statement labels, which identify statements for the *goto* statement, have function scope.

3. *File*: Names declared outside blocks and classes have file (global) scope. Such names can be accessed from anywhere within a file following their declarations.

In the example shown above, the names x and *total* are local to the body of function *main*. These variables could have been defined outside the body of function *main* and they could have been shared by *main* and other functions, if any, in the file containing these declarations (they could also be shared by functions in other files). As an example, consider the following program skeleton:

```
...
int n = 0;
void f(int a, int b)
{
    ...
    n++;
    a = b+n;
    ...
}
int main()
{
    int x, y;
    ...
    n++;
    f(x, y);
    ...
}
```

Variable n has file scope and it can be referenced both in function *main* and in function *f*. Global variables are one mechanism in which functions can share information.

Function *f* has two parameters: *a* and *b*. Each call to function *f* must have two arguments. The values of these arguments become the values of *f*'s parameters. In our case, the values of x and y become the values of *a* and *b*, respectively. Parameters *a* and *b* have local scope – their scope is the body of function *f*.

4. *Class*: The class mechanism in C++, which is the most important facility in C++, is used for defining new types. Names of the members (components) of a class have class scope. These names can be referenced within the "member functions" of the class, used with proper qualification following the name of the object or a pointer to the object name, in

"derived" classes, and in "friend" functions. (Classes are discussed in detail in later chapters.)

As mentioned earlier, C++ objects are regions of storage that have properties such as names and types associated with them. The lifetime of an object starts when an object is created (say by a definition) and ends when it is destroyed (say at the end of the program).

The lifetime of objects defined within a block starts after their declarations and ends upon reaching the end of the block containing its declaration. The lifetime of a global object is the duration of the program. The lifetime of objects defined by "dynamically" allocating their storage extends from the point of storage allocation to the point when this storage is deallocated (see Chapter 7 for details).

5.2 STORAGE CLASS

The default scope and lifetime of a variable can be changed by explicitly specifying a "storage class" in a declaration/definition:

$$storage\text{-}class_{opt} \quad type\text{-}specification \quad declarator$$

There are two storage classes: *auto* and *static*. The first storage class is assigned, by default, to objects defined within a function. The second storage class is used to alter the lifetime of local variables.

Variables defined within a block, that is, local variables, are automatically allocated at the beginning of the block and deallocated at the end of the block. The default storage class of local objects is the *auto* storage class. Such local variables do not retain their values from previous "incarnations" of the block (function) containing them.

Global variables are allocated at the beginning of program execution and deallocated at the end of program execution. The storage class of global variables is *static*. The class of local variables can also be specified to be *static* by using the keyword *static*. Local *static* variables retain their values across different invocations of a function.

5.3 LINKAGE

A C++ program consists of one or more C++ source files that are compiled and linked together to form an executable program. A global variable is said to have "external" linkage, by default. Its scope can be extended to files other than the one containing it by giving a "matching" *extern* declaration in the other file. The scope of a global variable can be restricted to the file containing its declaration by prefixing the declaration with the keyword *static*. Such variables are said to have "internal" linkage.

Keywords *extern* and *static*, when used as discussed above, are called linkage specifiers. Declarations of global variables with the linkage explicitly specified have the form

linkage-specifier$_{opt}$ *type-specification declarator*

5.4 STORAGE CLASS AND LINKAGE EXAMPLE

Consider a program whose code is contained in two files *p.cpp* and *q.cpp*. Let us first look at the contents of file *p.cpp*:

```
    void f(int);
    extern const int max = 10;
    int n = 0;
    int main()
5   {
        int a;
        ...
        f(a);
        ...
10      f(a);
        ...
    }
```

The first three lines of file *p.cpp* are declarations and definitions:

1. The prototype of function *f* (line 1) declares *f* as a function with external linkage (default). Its definition must be given later in this file or in another file (in this example it is in the file *q.cpp*).

2. *max* is defined as an integer constant (line 2). The default linkage for constants is internal. So that *max* can be accessed in file *q.cpp*, its linkage is made external with the keyword *extern*.

3. *n* is defined as an integer variable (line 3). The default linkage for variables defined outside function bodies is external.

File *q.cpp* contains the following code:

```
   #include <iostream.h>
   extern const int max;
   extern int n;
   static float z = 0.0;
 5 void f(int k)
   {
       static int ncall = 0;
       int a;
       ...
10     ncall++;
       n++;
       a = max*z;
       ...
       cout << "f called " << ncall << " times " << endl;
15 }
```

The declarations on lines 2 and 3, and the definitions on lines 4 and 7 are the items of interest:

1. *max* is declared to have external linkage (line 2). A matching definition for *max* (with external linkage) must be appear in some file. In our example, the definition is in file *p.cpp*.

2. *n* is declared to have external linkage (line 3).

3. *z* is defined as a global variable with internal linkage (line 4).

4. The definition of *ncall* (line 7) specifies *ncall* to be a variable that retains its value across calls to function *f*. Unlike local variables with the default *auto* storage class, *ncall* will be initialized once, at the start of the program, and not once for each invocation of *f*. The storage class specifier *static* affects the lifetime of the local variable *ncall* and not its scope.

    The keyword *static* plays a double role. When used in the definitions of global variables, it specifies internal linkage. When used in the definitions of local variables, it specifies that the lifetime of the variable is to be the duration of the program (instead of being the duration of the function).

6. MAIN FUNCTION

Each program must have a *main* function, which is the first function that is executed by a C++ program. This function can be defined as

```
int main() { ... }
```

or in a form that accepts "command-line" arguments, which are supplied when invoking the program.

```
int main(int argc, char *argv[]) { ... }
```

argc is the number of command-line arguments plus 1 (*argc*−1 is the number of command-line arguments). Parameter *argv* defines an array of strings (discussed in the next chapter) which store the values of the command-line arguments. The array component *argv*[0] is the name of the executable program (full path name), and each array component *argv*[*i*] points to the *i*th argument. See Section 5.1.2 of Chapter 7 for an example of a program that accepts command-line arguments.

C++ programs terminate by completing execution of the body of *main*, executing a *return* statement in *main*, or by calling function *exit* from anywhere in the program.

7. RECURSION

C++ supports "recursion", that is, C++ allows functions to call themselves. To illustrate recursion, we will write a recursive version of the factorial program which uses the following recursive definition of factorial (as shown above):

```
0! = 1
n! = n * (n-1)!
```

Here is the recursive version of *fact* (file *factr.cpp*):

```
#include "fact.h"
int fact(int n)
{
    if (n == 0)
        return 1;
    else
        return n * fact(n-1);
}
```

5

When *fact* is called with *n* equal to 0, *fact* returns 1 and terminates. Otherwise, *fact* calls itself to compute *n*−1, multiplies this value with *n*, and returns the product as its result.

Recursion is more "expensive" than "equivalent" loop statements in terms of execution time and storage. Because we can easily compute the factorial using a loop, function *fact* is not a particularly good example of using recursion in practice. However, it is a simple example that can be used to explain recursion.

8. SEPARATE COMPILATION

A C++ program can be split across many source files. Suppose we write a *main* program that calls the square root function *Sqrt* to compute square roots. Function *Sqrt* is stored in the file *sqrt.cpp* (mentioned above). We can put the whole program, including function *Sqrt*, in one file. Alternatively, we leave *Sqrt* as it is and write the *main* program in another file, say *sqrtmain.cpp*. Then we can compile the files "separately" and then "link" them together to form an executable program. Before we see how to do this, here is the *main* function (file *sqrtmain.cpp*):

```
#include "sqrt.h"
#include <iostream.h>
#include <stdlib.h>
int main()
{
    double a;
    cout << "\tSQUARE ROOT COMPUTING PROGRAM" << endl;
    for (;;) {
        cout << ": ";
        cin >> a;
        if (!cin)
            exit(0);
        cout << "Square root of " << a << " is ";
        cout << Sqrt(a) << endl;
    }
}
```

We can compile the two files *sqrtmain.cpp* and *sqrt.cpp* and then link them together by invoking *bcc* (the Borland C++ compiler) as follows:

```
bcc sqrtmain sqrt
```

Based on the name of first file specified in the command *bcc*, the executable file produced is named *sqrtmain.exe* .

If we compile the above two files as

```
bcc sqrt sqrtmain
```

then the executable file produced will be named *sqrt.exe* .

Here is a sample user interaction with this program:

```
sqrtmain
     SQUARE ROOT COMPUTING PROGRAM
: 4
Square root of 4 is 2
: 3
Square root of 3 is 1.732051
: 2
Square root of 2 is 1.414216
: ^Z
```

Instead of compiling and linking the two files in one step as shown above, we can compile them and link them together in separate steps:

```
bcc -c sqrtmain
bcc -c sqrt
bcc sqrtmain.obj sqrt.obj
```

The –c flag tells the Borland C++ compiler to just compile the specified file(s) without performing the linking step. The result of the compilation is an object file (with the suffix .obj). The two object files are then linked together to produce an executable file (in the third line).

It may seem more convenient to compile all the source files in one line. However, when developing large systems, it is generally more convenient to compile C++ files individually or in groups. This way all files need not be compiled all the time. Of course, all files must be specified in the link step to produce an executable file.

9. EXERCISES

1. In the example that computes the square root, we used the math library function *fabs* to determine the absolute value of a double precision value. Write a function *myabs* that provides the same functionality as *fabs*.

2. What will happen if the factorial function *fact* is called with a negative argument? What can you do to prevent such a problem? Consider both the recursive and non recursive definitions of *fact* in your explanation.

3. Write a program to print the factorial of the numbers from 1 to 8. Use one of the factorial functions described in this chapter to perform the computation.

4. Function *roots* (contained in files *froots.h* and *froots.cpp*) as written returns one to indicate that the roots are computed successfully and zero if the roots are not computed. Rewrite function *roots* so that it returns zero to indicate success, one to indicate that the first coefficient was zero, and two to indicate that the roots were complex.

Function *roots* should now be called as follows:

```
...
switch (roots(a, b, c, x1, x2)) {
case 0:
    ...
    break;
case 1:
    ...
    break;
case 2:
    ...
    break;
default:
    ...
}
...
```

Chapter 7

ARRAYS, STRUCTURES, POINTERS

An "array" is an "aggregate" object whose components are variables of the same type. Pictorially, a simple variable can be thought of as a box

while an array can be thought of as a row of boxes:

A "structure" is an aggregate object whose components, unlike those of an array, are variables which can be of different types. A structure can be thought of as a row of boxes of different sizes (corresponding to the different types):

A "pointer" is an object that refers to an object in memory (it is not the name of the object itself):

The pointer is the left box; the arrow points to the object being referenced.

Arrays, structures, and pointers are types that are derived (constructed) from predefined types or from other previously defined types. C++ inherited facilities to define such types from C. Besides these derived types, C++ also provides facilities for defining classes (discussed in the next chapter).

1. ARRAYS

An array can be thought of as a mechanism for giving a single name to a collection of variables of the same type. Each array element is identified by its position in the array, called the "index" of the array element. The ability to reference an array element by specifying its index makes arrays a very valuable "data structure." For example, we can write a loop to print the value of each element of an array, regardless of the number of elements in the array. We do not have to explicitly write a statement for each array element to print its value.

An array definition has the form

$T\ a[n];$

where a is name of the array being declared. a will have n elements of type T (n is a constant integer expression). Elements of a will have index values ranging from 0 to $n-1$.

Here are examples of array definitions:

```
float sales[12];
int x[100];
char line[81];
```

These definitions specify

1. *sales* to be an array of twelve *float* elements, with indexes ranging from 0 to 11;

2. *x* to be an array of 100 *int* elements, with indexes ranging from 0 to 99; and

3. *line* to be an array of 81 *char* elements, with indexes ranging from 0 to 80.

Elements of an array a are referenced as

$a[i]$

where i specifies the index of the element. The value of i should be between 0 and the $n-1$ where n is the number of elements in a.

Suppose that a is defined as

```
int a[10];
```

Here is a pictorial representation of array a with element i initialized to i:

0	1	2	3	4	5	6	7	8	9

```
a[0] a[1] a[2] a[3] a[4] a[5] a[6] a[7] a[8] a[9]
```

Array *a* can be initialized, for example, as

```
for (int i = 0; i < 10; i++)
    a[i] = i;
}
```

The *for* loop makes it *unnecessary* to write ten assignment statements, one for each element to initialize *a*:

```
a[0] = 0;
a[1] = 1;
a[2] = 2;
a[3] = 3;
a[4] = 4;
a[5] = 5;
a[6] = 6;
a[7] = 7;
a[8] = 8;
a[9] = 9;
```

As an example illustrating the use of arrays, we will write a program that reads a list of integers (up to a maximum of 1000 integers) and prints them in the reverse order (file *rev.cpp*):

```
#include <iostream.h>
int main()
{
    const int max = 1000;
    int a[max], i;

    //read max numbers or up to end of file
    for (i = 0; i < max && cin >> a[i]; i++)
        ;

    //print numbers in reverse order
    while (--i >= 0)
        cout << a[i] << endl;
}
```

First, using the *for* loop (lines 8-9), the program reads the integers into the array *a*. This loop executes as long as the number of values read from input is not more than *max* (counting the number of values read is started from zero) and there are more values to be read. Operator >>, which performs the input, returns as its result the left operand, which is an input stream. An input stream evaluated as a condition yields true if the last operation on the stream was successful; otherwise, it returns false.

This *for* loop is another example of a loop with a null body (line 9). All the work, including reading the numbers, is done in the *for* loop header itself (line 8). The integers read are stored in the array elements in increasing index order. The ith number is read is stored in element *i* of array *a*.

After the numbers have been read, they are printed in reverse order by printing the array elements in the order (lines 12-13)

```
a[i-1], a[i-2], ..., a[0]
```

In the *while* loop expression (line 12)

```
--i >= 0
```

variable *i* is decremented (reduced by one) before performing the comparison. Note that upon the termination of the *for* loop (lines 8-9), the last integer read (provided *i* is greater than zero) is in the array element

```
a[i-1]
```

and not in

```
a[i]
```

because *i* is incremented (increased by one) prior to reading the next input value.

1.1 MULTI-DIMENSIONAL ARRAYS

Multi-dimensional arrays are arrays whose elements are themselves arrays. For example, a two-dimensional array (also called a "matrix") is a one-dimensional array whose elements are one-dimensional arrays. A two-dimensional array can be pictorially thought of boxes arranged in rows and columns:

As an example of a multi-dimensional array, here is the definition of a two-dimensional *int* array which is a one-dimensional array of 2 elements, each of which is an array of 3 *int* elements:

```
int m[2][3];
```

The size of *m* is 2×3, that is, it has two rows and three columns. This array can be pictorially described as

m[0]	m[0][0]	m[0][1]	m[0][2]
m[1]	m[1][0]	m[1][1]	m[1][2]

The elements of this array are $m[0][0]$, $m[0][1]$, $m[0][2]$, $m[1][0]$, $m[1][1]$, and $m[1][2]$.

The two rows of this two-dimensional array can be referenced as the one-dimensional arrays $m[0]$ and $m[1]$.

Multi-dimensional arrays, especially two-dimensional arrays, are quite useful for a variety of applications. A two-dimensional array can, for example, be used to store the distances between pairs of points. To illustrate such an array, we will write a program that reads distances between pairs of points (representing cities), which are stored in a "data" file, and responds to user queries, from the keyboard, about distances between specific pairs of points.

The distance data is stored in file *dist.dat*. The first line in this file specifies the number of points *n*, which will be numbered from 0 to *n*−1. The remaining lines in *dist.dat* specify distances between pairs of points. The reverse distances are not specified; for example, if the distance from point *a* to point *b* is specified, then the distance from *b* to *a* is not specified in the data file because the two distances are the same.

Here are the contents of file *dist.dat*:[1]

---

1. I have used a small data file for ease of presentation.

```
4
1 0 25.0
2 0 30.0
2 1 35.0
3 0 29.0
3 1 45.0
3 2 50.0
```

To hold the distance information, we will define a two-dimensional array d of size $max \times max$ (this is a programmer-defined constant). However, we will use only the first n rows and n columns of d, where n ($n < max$) is the number of points. Before reading the data, all the diagonal elements of this array will be initialized to 0.0 (the distance from point i to point i is zero). Assuming that the number of points is 4, here is array d with its diagonal elements initialized (only 5 rows and 5 columns of d are shown):

	0	1	2	3	4
0	0.0				
1		0.0			
2			0.0		
3				0.0	
4					0.0

After reading the distance data, d will have the following values:

	0	1	2	3	4
0	0.0	25.0	30.0	29.0	
1	25.0	0.0	35.0	45.0	
2	30.0	35.0	0.0	50.0	
3	29.0	45.0	50.0	0.0	
4					0.0

Here is the distance query program (file *dist.cpp*):

```
  // distance lookup program
  #include <iostream.h>
  #include <fstream.h>
  #include <stdlib.h>
5 const int max = 16;
  int main()
  {
      float d[max][max], distance;
      int i, j, n = 0;
10    ifstream data("dist.dat");

      for (i = 0; i < max; i++)
          d[i][i] = 0.0;

15    data >> n;
      if (n <= 0 || n > max) {
          cerr << "Error, number of points must be ";
          cerr << "between 1 and " << max << endl;
          exit(1);
20    }
      while (data >> i >> j >> distance) {
          if (i < 0 || i >= n || j < 0 || j >= n) {
              cerr << "Error, point number must be ";
              cerr << "between 0 & " << n-1 << endl;
25            exit(1);
          }
          d[i][j] = d[j][i] = distance;
      }
      cout << "\t\tDistance Lookup Program" << endl;
30    cout << "Use spaces to separate points." << endl;
      for (;;) {
          cout << "Points:";
          if (!(cin >> i >> j))
              break;
35        if (i < 0 || i >= n || j < 0 || j >= n) {
              cerr << "Invalid points!" << " Points must";
              cerr << " be between 0 & " << n-1 << endl;
              continue;
          }
40        cout << "  Distance between points " << i;
          cout << " & " << j << " is " << d[i][j] << endl;
      }
      exit(0);
  }
```

Much of the code in this program deals with detecting and handling error conditions. In fact, in many large systems, a significant portion of the code does just this: detect and handle error conditions.

Let us examine the distance program code in detail. d is declared as a two-dimensional array of *float* elements (line 8); each of its two dimensions is of size *max* (defined on line 5).

The distance program must read input from two sources: the distance data from the file *dist.dat* and user requests from the standard stream *cin* (which is associated with the keyboard). Assume that file *dist.exe* contains the executable version of the distance program. Redirecting the standard input stream *cin* to read the data from file *dist.dat*

```
dist <dist.dat
```

will not be appropriate in this example, because the program will now not be able to read user requests from the keyboard.

Instead, to read the distance data from file *dist.data*, we will define a new stream *data* and associate it with the file *dist.dat* (line 10). Input operations performed on stream *data* will read data from the file *dist.dat*. Type *ifstream*, which is a predefined type defined in the header file *fstream.h* (included in line 3), is used for defining new input streams and associating them with data files.

The diagonal elements of matrix d, which have the same first and second subscripts (the row number is equal to the column number), are initialized to zero by the following loop (lines 12-13):

```
for (i = 0; i < max; i++)
    d[i][i] = 0.0;
```

The distance program then reads the number of points from stream *data* (line 15).

```
data >> n;
```

If file *dist.dat* is empty, then the value of n, which is initialized to zero (line 9), will not be affected by the input operation. if n is less than zero, or larger than the maximum number of points array m can hold (*max*), then the distance program will print an error message and terminate by calling *exit* (lines 16-20).

After reading the number of points, the program will read the distances between pairs of points. While doing this, the program checks to make sure that the points are numbered between zero and $n-1$ (lines 21-28):

```
while (data >> i >> j >> distance) {
    if (i < 0 || i >= n || j <0 || j >= n) {
        cerr << "Error, point number must be ";
        cerr << "between 0 & " << n-1 << endl;
        exit(0);
    }
    d[i][j] = d[j][i] = distance;
}
```

The distance from point *i* to point *j* and the reverse distance are both set to the same distance.

This loop terminates when the stream (*data*) returned by the expression

```
data >> i >> j >> distance
```

evaluates to false. As mentioned earlier, the input stream operator returns its left operand, which must be a stream, as its result. When an input stream is evaluated as a condition, it evaluates to true if the last operation on the stream (input performed by >> in our case) did not encounter the end of input (or any other error); otherwise, the stream will evaluate to false.

The distance program then prints a message on the monitor (lines 29-30) and enters a loop where it interacts with the user (lines 31-42):

```
for (;;) {
    cout << "Points";
    if (!(cin >> i >> j))
        break;
    if (i < 0 || i >= n || j < 0 || j >= n) {
        cerr << "Invalid points!" << " Points must";
        cerr << " be between 0 & " << n-1 << endl;
        continue;
    }
    cout << "  Distance between points " << i;
    cout << " & " << j << " is " << d[i][j] << endl;
}
```

The program first prints (line 32) the message

```
Points:
```

and then waits for user input. The input operations are embedded within the *if* statement expression (line 33):

```
!(cin >> i >> j)
```

The program continues only when the user types a request or when the user signals the end of input by typing control-Z (^Z) followed by carriage return (or simply by typing ^D on UNIX systems). The loop (lines 31-42) will then terminate by executing the *break* statement (line 34). After exiting the loop, the program terminates by calling function *exit* (line 43).

If the user types an invalid point (outside the range zero to $n-1$), the distance program prints an appropriate message (lines 36-37) and continues with the next iteration of the loop (line 38). The program then waits for the user to type another request.

If the user types valid input, the program looks up the distance between the specified points and prints the distance between them (lines 40-41). The program then continues with the next iteration of the *for* loop (lines 31-42).

Here is an example of user interaction with the distance program:

```
dist
                Distance Lookup Program
Use spaces to separate points.
Points: 2 1
  Distance between points 2 & 1 is 35
Points: 3 1
  Distance between points 3 & 1 is 45
Points: ^Z
```

1.2 INITIALIZING ARRAYS

Like variables of the simple types, array variables can be initialized in their definitions. For example, the following definition of *a*

```
int a[10] = {0, 1, 2, 3, 4, 5, 6, 7, 8, 9};
```

initializes element i ($1 \leq i \leq 9$) of *a* to i (a[0] is initialized to 0, a[1] is initialized to 1, and so on).

When a one-dimensional array is initialized in its definition, it is not necessary to give its dimension explicitly. For example, *a* could also have been defined and initialized as

```
int a[] = {0, 1, 2, 3, 4, 5, 6, 7, 8, 9};
```

Let us now look at an example illustrating the initialization of a multi-dimensional array:

```
int b[2][2] = {{1, 1}, {1, 1}};
```

b is defined as a two-dimensional array and each of its elements is initialized to 1 (b[0][0] is initialized to 1, b[0][1] is initialized to 1, and so on).

When initializing a multi-dimensional array such as *b*, a set of values must be given for each sub-array. For example, in the above definition, one set of values

```
{1, 1}
```

is given for the elements of each of the one-dimensional sub-arrays *b*[0] and *b*[1] of *b*.

In case of multi-dimensional arrays, only the first dimension can be omitted when initial values are specified in the array definition. For example, the above definition could also have been written as

```
int b[][2] = {{1, 1}, {1, 1}};
```

Initializing an array in its definition has advantages: it can be more efficient and it makes the initialization explicit to the reader. Unfortunately, such initialization can be conveniently used only for small arrays and when the initial values do not involve extensive computation.

1.3 ARRAY ARGUMENTS

C++ interprets an array name as the address of the array (discussed later). For an array argument, it is this address that is actually passed as the argument. The parameter corresponding to an array argument can therefore be specified either as an array or as a "pointer" of the right type (pointers are discussed later). If the parameter is specified as an array, then the array argument is effectively passed by reference (without using the reference designator &). In C++, array arguments are not passed by value!

When declaring array parameters, the bound for the first subscript can be omitted, for example,

```
int a[]
float s[][12]
```

Only the first bound of a multi-dimensional can be omitted. For example, declaring the two-dimensional array parameter *s* as

```
float s[][]
```

is illegal.

1.4 EXAMPLES

In this section we will write two functions: one to find the index of an element in a sorted array that has a specific value and the other to sort an array.

1.4.1 SEARCHING A SORTED ARRAY Function *find*, which has the prototype (file *find.h*),

```
int find(int a[], int l, int u, int key);
```

takes as an argument an integer array *a*, which is sorted in increasing order, and looks in the "sub-array" specified by the lower and upper bounds *l* and *u* for the value *key*. If *find* is successful, then it returns the index of the array element with the value *key*; otherwise, it returns −1.

Function *find* is based on the following search algorithm:

1. If the *l* is greater than *u*, then the sub-array $a[l]$ ... $a[k]$ does not have elements. Return −1 indicating failure.

2. Determine the index, say *k*, of the middle element of the above sub-array.

3. If $a[k]$ is equal to *key*, then return *k*.

4. If $a[k]$ is greater than *key*, then narrow the search to the sub-array $a[l]$ ... $a[k-1]$ Do this by setting *u* to *k*−1 and then going to step 1.

   Otherwise, $a[k]$ must be less than *key*; narrow the search to the sub-array $a[l]$ ... $a[k-1]$ Do this by setting *l* to *k* and then going to step 1.

I will now explain this algorithm pictorially. Suppose that the array to be sorted is the ten-element array *a* shown earlier. Elements of array *a* are initialized as shown:

−22	−2	3	5	6	6	7	7	8	11
a[0]	a[1]	a[2]	a[3]	a[4]	a[5]	a[6]	a[7]	a[8]	a[9]

We want to find the index of an element with the value −22 in the above array (the sub-array is the array itself, i.e., *l* is 0 and *u* is 9). We first look at the value of middle element $a[4]$ (*l*+*u* divided by 2 yields 4.5 which is truncated to 4 because of integer division). This element has the value 6, which is greater than −22. As a result, the search is narrowed to the sub-array starting with element $a[0]$ up to element $a[3]$.

We again look at the middle element of this sub-array, that is, $a[1]$ (*l*+*u* divided by 2 yields 1). This element has the value −2 which is greater than −22. We now narrow the search to the sub-array starting with element $a[0]$ up to element $a[0]$ (sub-array of just one element). The middle element is now $a[0]$ (*l*+*u* divided by 2 yields 0). This element has the value we are searching for −22.

Function *find*, which implements the above algorithm, is defined as (file *find.cpp*):

```
   // find index of key value in elements
   // a[l] .. a[u] of sorted array a

   #include "find.h"
 5 int find(int a[], int l, int u, int key)
   {
       int k;

       while (l <= u) {
10         k = (l+u)/2;
           if (a[k] == key)
               return k;
           else if (a[k] < key)
               l = k+1;
15         else
               u = k-1;
       }
       return -1;
   }
```

find keeps searching for the element until it runs out of elements to examine (as specified by the *while* loop condition on line 9). The index of the middle element is computed on line 10 and stored in variable k. If a[k] is equal to *key*, then *find* returns k. Otherwise, if a[k] is less than *key*, then *find* narrows the search to the elements a[k+1] to a[u] (line 14); otherwise, the search is narrowed a[l] to a[k-1] (line 16). If *find* does not find the element in the sub-array specified for searching (line 5), which happens when the *while* loop condition becomes false (line 9), then *find* returns −1 and terminates.

The argument corresponding to a is passed by reference (by default),[2] while the other three parameters are passed by value. The values of the parameters l and u are changed in the program, but this has no effect on the values of the corresponding arguments. Had we passed arguments corresponding to the parameters l and u by reference, then these arguments would have been updated in *find*, which is not what we want.

I will now show you a recursive version of *find*. The recursive *find*, like the *while* loop version, looks for the element with the desired value by repeatedly narrowing the sub-array to be searched until it finds the element. The smaller sub-arrays are examined by recursively calling *find* with these sub-arrays. The recursive version of *find* has the same prototype as the *while* loop version. Here

---

2. As explained earlier, an array argument is effectively passed by reference.

is its definition (file *findr.cpp*):

```
     // find index of key value in elements
     // a[l] .. a[u] of sorted array a
     #include "find.h"
     int find(int a[], int l, int u, int key)
 5   {
         int k;

         if (l > u)
             return -1;
10       else {
             k = (l+u)/2;
             if (a[k] == key)
                 return k;
             else if (a[k] < key)
15               return find(a, k+1, u, key);
             else
                 return find(a, l, k-1, key);
         }
     }
```

If the sub-array to be searched has no elements (the lower bound of the sub-array is greater than its upper bound), then *find* returns −1 and terminates (lines 8-9). Otherwise, it computes the index *k* of the middle element (line 11). If the value of the middle element is equal to the value *key* that is being searched, then *find* returns *k*. Otherwise, if $a[k]$ is less than *key* (line 14) then *find* calls itself recursively with the smaller sub-array that has the elements $a[k+1]$ through $a[u]$ and then returns the value returned by the recursive call (line 15); otherwise, *find* calls itself recursively with the smaller sub-array that has the elements $a[l]$ through $a[k-1]$ and then returns the value returned by the recursive call (line 17).

1.4.2 SORTING ARRAYS We will write a function *sort* that takes an integer array *a* of size *n* as an argument and sorts the array (rearranges the elements of the array so that they are stored in the array in increasing order). The sorting technique we will use is called "insertion" sort. Before writing function *sort*, I will illustrate the insertion sort technique pictorially.

Suppose the array to be sorted is array *a*:

7	3	5	8	−2	7	6	−22	6	11
a[0]	a[1]	a[2]	a[3]	a[4]	a[5]	a[6]	a[7]	a[8]	a[9]

The insertion sort technique divides the array into two parts: the left one is sorted and the right one is unsorted. It takes elements, one by one from the unsorted part, and inserts them in the right place in the sorted part. If necessary, elements greater than the one to be inserted are shifted one place to the right.

Initially, the sorted part of the array (the left part) consists only of one element:

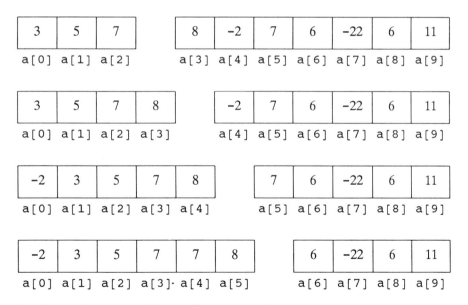

The idea is to take the first element of the unsorted part, which is 3 ($a[1]$), and incorporate it into the sorted part. We store its value in a temporary variable and this frees up element $a[1]$. Then we push values greater than 3 in the sorted part one place to the right and then insert 3 in the element thus freed:

This process is repeated until we reach the end of the array. I will show you a few more steps:

Here is how the array will look after it is sorted:

| -22 | -2 | 3 | 5 | 6 | 6 | 7 | 7 | 8 | 11 |

a[0] a[1] a[2] a[3] a[4] a[5] a[6] a[7] a[8] a[9]

It is now time to look at function *sort*. First, here is its prototype (file *sort.h*):

```
void sort(int a[], int n);
```

Here is the body of function *sort* (file *sort.cpp*):

```
   //sort array a which has n int elements
   #include "sort.h"
   void sort(int a[], int n)
   {
5      int j, tmp;

       for (int i = 0; i < n-1; i++) {
           tmp = a[j = i+1];
           while (j != 0 && a[j-1] > tmp) {
10             a[j] = a[j-1];
               --j;
           }
           a[j] = tmp;
       }
15 }
```

sort starts off by taking the second element of *a* (*i*+1 is 1 at this point) and storing it in *tmp* (line 8). The assignment statement within the subscript operator [] sets *j* to 1 and yields 1 as its result. Storing the value of a[1] in *tmp* frees up element a[1]. a[0] is shifted right if it is greater than *tmp*, which is the original value of a[1] (lines 9-12). The value stored in *tmp* is then inserted in the free slot which will be either a[0] or a[1] (line 13). After this step, a[0] will be less than or equal to a[1].

The above process is then repeated starting with a[2] and for each element up to a[n-1]. At the end of this, elements in array *a* will be in sorted order.

Note that the *while* loop expression

```
j != 0 && a[j-1] < tmp
```

evaluates to true only if *j* is not equal to 0 and a[j-1] is less than *tmp*. The comparison against zero ensures that *j* is greater than 0 (*j* was at least 1 initially and we only decrement it). Remember that arrays in C++ do not have negative subscripts.

2. STRUCTURES

A structure can be thought of as a mechanism for giving a single name to a collection of variables which need not be of the same type. Structures are used to group together logically related variables. For example, each point on a plane, specified using Cartesian coordinates, has an x coordinate and a y coordinate. Each point must thus be represented by two variables. These variables can be grouped together into a structure type, say *point*, defined as follows:

```
struct point {
    float x, y;
};
```

Variables, say *p1* and *p2*, representing points can now be defined to be of type *point* as follows:

```
point p1, p2;
```

Each *point* variable has two component variables with the names x and y. Components of *p1*, for example, can be referenced using the selection operator . as *p1*.x and *p1*.y. Similarly, the components of *p2* can be referenced as *p2*.x and *p2*.y. Except for the fact that these components are prefixed by the name of the structure variable to which they belong and the selection operator, they can be used just like ordinary *float* variables.

Structure variables are assigned values by assigning values to their components. For example, *p1* can be assigned the coordinates (0.0, 0.0) as follows:

```
p1.x = 0.0;
p1.y = 0.0;
```

Structure variables, like array variables, can also be initialized in their definitions. For example, the *point* variable *a* can be initialized to the coordinates (1.0, -3.0) in its definition as

```
point a = {1.0, -3.0};
```

The first component is assigned the first value within the curly braces, the second component is assigned the second value, and so on.

C++ supports structure assignment. In other words, a structure variable can be assigned to another structure variable provided they are both of the same type. For example, the *point* variable *p1* can be assigned to *p2* as follows:

```
p2 = p1;
```

This structure assignment is equivalent to the component-wise assignments

```
p2.x = p1.x;
p2.y = p1.y;
```

Structure types are a special case of the more general "class" types, which are discussed in subsequent chapters.

As another example of illustrating structures, consider the structure type *person* defined as (file *person.h*):

```
     const int MAX_NAME = 32
     const int MAX_CHILD = 16

     struct date {
 5       int m, d, y;
     };

     enum marital {
         SINGLE, MARRIED, DIVORCED
10   };

     struct person {
         char first[MAX_NAME+1], mi, last[MAX_NAME+1];
         char sex;
15       date birth;
         marital status;
         char spouse[MAX_NAME+1];
         date marriage;
         date divorce;
20       char nchild;
         char child[MAX_CHILD][MAX_NAME+1];
     };
```

The definition of the structure type *person* (lines 12-22) uses two other user-defined types: the structure type *date* (defined on lines 4-6) and the enumeration type *marital* (defined on lines 8-10). *MAX_NAME* and *MAX_CHILD* are constants (lines 1-2) that specify the maximum length of a name and the maximum number of children that can be handled by a variable of type *person*. There are several character arrays in the structure type *person*: *first*, *last*, *spouse*, and *child* (to be precise, *child* is a two-dimensional array each of whose elements is a character array). These arrays are used for holding names which are strings, that is, character arrays (strings are discussed in Section 5).

By defining type *person*, we can give a collective name to the different variables that may otherwise be required to store all the information about a person.

Here are example definitions of variables of type *person* and examples illustrating their use:

```
person p, q;
...
if (p.age < 18) {
    ...
}
p = q;
```

2.1 UNIONS

Unions are special types of structures that are used to save space. Unlike components of a structure, all components of a union share the same storage space. In other words, they are "overlayed" on top of each other in memory.

Here is an example of a *union* type:

```
union simpleType {
    int i;
    float f;
    double d;
    char c;
};
```

Components *i, f, d*, and *c* will occupy the same storage in memory. The storage allocated for an object of a *union* type is equal to (or more than) the storage required for the largest component, which in this case is *d* (of type *double*).

An object of type *simpleType* can, at any given time, be used to store a value of one of the following types:

- *int*: using component *i*;
- *float*: using component *f*;
- *double*: using component *d*; and
- *char*: using component *c*.

When accessing the value of a *simpleType* object, it is the programmer's responsibility to ensure that the right component is used. For example, consider the following code fragment:

```
simpleType s;
s.f = 1.0;
... // s contains a float
s.i = 1;
... // s contains an int
s.c = 'a';
... // s contains a char
```

After assigning a *float* value to *s*, via component *s.f*, a programmer should access *s* only using component *f* (that is, as *s.f*) until a value of another type is stored in *s*. If the programmer does not obey this discipline, and instead accesses object *s* using a component of another type, say by using component *c*, then this will become the programmer's problem: C++ will not flag this as an error. Instead, C++ will take whatever is stored in *s* and interpret the bit pattern as a value of type *char*. Some "system" programmers, who manipulate bit patterns of objects stored in memory, like to do such things. In the final analysis, it is the programmer's responsibility to ensure that a union object is accessed correctly.

The type of the value stored in a *union* object should be recorded in another variable, say of an enumeration type. The component of the *union* object used to access the value stored in the *union* object should be based on the value of this enumeration variable as illustrated below:

```
      enum componentType { intT, floatT, doubleT, charT };
      ...
      simpleType s;
      componentType c;
   5  s.i = 1; c = intT;
      ...
      switch (c) {
      case intT:
           ... s.i ...
  10       break;
      case floatT:
           ... s.f ...
           break;
      case doubleT:
  15       ... s.d ...
           break;
      case charT:
           ... s.c ...
           break;
  20  }
```

Initially, using component *s.i*, an integer is stored in the *union* object *s* (line 5). The type of value stored in *s* is noted by storing the enumeration identifier *intT* in the enumeration variable *c* (line 5)

Use of the value stored in the *union* object *s* is based on an examination of the value's type. This examination is performed in the expression of *switch* statement (line 7) which ensures that the appropriate component of *s* is used for accessing the value stored in *s*.

2.2 STRUCTURE AND UNION ARGUMENTS

Structure and union arguments are, by default, passed by value. They can also be passed by reference; this mode, as mentioned earlier, is specified with the &

operator.

As an example illustrating arguments of a structure type, consider function *length* that computes the length of a line specified by two points. The prototype of function *length* is contained in the header file *length.h*:

```
#include "point.h"
float length(point a, point b);
```

File *points.h* contains the structure type *point*:

```
struct point {
    float x, y;
};
```

Here is the definition of function *length* (file *length.cpp*)

```
    #include <math.h>
    #include "point.h"
    float length(point a, point b)
    {
5       float dx = a.x - b.x;
        float dy = a.y - b.y;
        return sqrt(dx*dx + dy*dy);
    }
```

Function *length* uses the differences between the *x* and *y* coordinates of the two points to compute the line length.

These arguments could also have been passed by reference. Here is the revised prototype:

```
#include "point.h"
float length(point& a, point& b);
```

The matching function body is

```
     #include <math.h>
     #include "point.h"
     float length(point& a, point& b)
     {
5        float dx = a.x - b.x;
         float dy = a.y - b.y;
         return sqrt(dx*dx + dy*dy);
     }
```

However, there is no advantage in passing arguments by reference to *length* since the arguments are not being changed and the arguments are not big objects (to avoid the overhead of copying in passing arguments by value).

3. POINTERS

A pointer is a variable that refers (points) to another object. The value of a pointer is the address of the object to which it points. Pointers are typically used for referencing "dynamically created" objects (created by calling operator *new*, which is discussed below). Pointers can, however, also be used to reference objects created "statically" using definition statements whose addresses are extracted using the "address of" operator (&).

As an example, suppose that *p* is a pointer that refers to an object of type *T* that has the value *t*:

$$p$$

The dereferencing operator * can be used to access the value of the object referenced by a pointer. For example, the value of

`*p`

will be *t*.

The specific value of a pointer does not matter much – the item of interest is the object referenced by the pointer. Pointer values can be dereferenced, assigned, passed as arguments, and C++ allows a limited form of pointer arithmetic.

The dereferencing operator should be applied only to valid pointer values (addresses). Dereferencing invalid or prohibited addresses can cause program termination.

The null pointer, denoted by zero, is often used to indicate that a pointer does not refer to any object. The null pointer is also denoted by the constant identifier *NULL*, which is defined in several header files, e.g., *stdlib.h* and *stdio.h*. Dereferencing the null pointer can also cause program termination.

3.1 DYNAMIC OBJECTS

Pointers are typically used to reference "dynamically created" objects. The number of objects created with a definition statement is fixed. On the other hand, an arbitrary number of objects can be created dynamically at run time by calling operator *new*. The only limitation on the number of objects that can be created dynamically is the size of the "heap", which is the area of memory from which storage is allocated for dynamic objects.

Objects created dynamically can be deleted by calling operator *delete*. The storage thus freed is returned to the heap from where it can be reallocated for new objects.

3.1.1 OPERATOR NEW Objects of type *T* are dynamically created by calling operator *new* as

```
new T
```

new returns a pointer of type *T* * that refers to the newly allocated object. If for some reason *new* cannot allocate storage, then it returns the null pointer.

Here are three examples illustrating dynamic creation of objects:

```
new int
new point
new person
```

Operator *new* always returns a pointer of the appropriate type. For example, in the above three calls *new* returns pointers to objects of type *int*, *point*, and *person*, respectively.

To allocate an array of objects of type *T*, the bounds of the array must be specified:

```
new T [size_1] ... [size_n]
```

Here are two examples illustrating dynamic array allocation:

```
new node[10];
new float[n][5];
```

In the first case a ten-element array of elements of type *node* is allocated and in the second case an $n \times 5$ two-dimensional array of *float* elements is allocated.

3.1.2 OPERATOR DELETE Objects allocated with the *new* operator can be deleted by calling the *delete* operator as follows:

```
delete p;
```

p must be a pointer returned by *new*. The effect of applying the *delete* operator to a pointer not obtained by calling *new* is unspecified. Calling *delete* with the null pointer as its argument is harmless.

Unlike *new*, *delete* does not return any value. The effect of accessing a deleted object is undefined.

Dynamically created arrays are deleted using the *delete* operator as

```
delete [] p;
```

where *p* is a pointer that refers to a dynamically created array.

3.2 VOID POINTERS

"*void*" pointers are pointers of type

```
void *
```

void pointers are "generic" pointers that can be used to store a pointer regardless of the actual pointer type.

C++ automatically converts a pointer of any type to a *void* pointer when appropriate. But the reverse is not true. The reverse type conversion must be explicitly specified. Suppose, for example, that *p* is a *void* pointer. It can be converted to a pointer of type *T* * using a "type cast" as follows:

```
(T *) p
```

void pointers are often used to

    a.   define variables that will hold values of different pointer types,
    b.   declare parameters that will be passed different types of pointers as arguments, and
    c.   specify the result type of a function; the pointer returned by the function will be explicitly cast to an appropriate pointer type, if necessary, by the caller.

3.3 POINTER CONVERSIONS

C++ allows programmers to convert pointers of one type to another. Some conversions are performed automatically while others must be performed explicitly. The following conversions are performed automatically:

1.   A pointer of any type will be automatically converted to a *void* pointer if needed. Thus a pointer of any type can be assigned to a *void* pointer, but *not* vice versa.

2.   Zero is the null pointer. C++ will automatically convert it to an appropriate pointer type as determined from the context. Thus a zero can be assigned to a pointer variable of any type and compared with a pointer of any type.

3. A pointer to any derived type will be automatically converted to a pointer to the base class of this derived type (classes are discussed in later chapters).

All other conversions must be specified explicitly using the cast operator:

(*pointer-type*)

Thus a *char* pointer defined as

```
char *s;
```

can be converted to an *int* pointer as

```
(int *) s
```

The above expression is of type "pointer to *nt*." Conversions between pointer types do not change the pointer value (the address stored in the pointer) except in cases involving base classes and derived classes (discussed in later chapters).

3.4 POINTER ARGUMENTS

Pointer arguments are, by default, passed by value much like structure arguments or arguments of predefined types.

3.5 SELECTION USING POINTERS

Consider the structure type *point* (shown earlier) and a pointer that refers to an object of type *point*:

```
struct point {
    float x, y;
};
point *p;
```

Components *x* and *y* of the *point* object referenced by *p* can be referenced as

```
(*p).x
(*p).y
```

Using the selection operator ->, these components can be referenced as

```
p->x
p->y
```

which is more convenient than using the **.** selection operator.

3.6 POINTER ARITHMETIC

C++ allows you to add an integer to and subtract an integer from a pointer, and subtract one pointer from another. However, other arithmetic operations on pointers, such as adding or multiplying two pointers, are not allowed. The effect of adding an integer i to a pointer p that points to objects of type T is to add the value $i*sizeof(T)$ to p; that is, the value added is the number of bytes occupied by i objects of type T. To add the integer value i, and not the space occupied by i objects of type T, type casts must be used, for example,

```
p = (T *) ((int) p + i);
```

Similarly, the effect of subtracting an integer i from a pointer p, which points to objects of type T, is to subtract the value $i*sizeof(T)$ from p.

When subtracting one pointer from another, say p from q, both pointers being of the same type T, then the result is the number of items of type T that can be fitted in memory between p and q. The result can be converted to bytes by multiplying it by $sizeof(T)$.

3.7 LISTS: AN EXAMPLE OF POINTER USE

After arrays, lists are probably the most important data structure used in programming. A list consists of one or more items that are linked together. Besides containing data, each list item indicates where the next item will be found, that is, it specifies the address or the location of the next item.

We will implement lists by defining an element type *list* which contains data members for storing information, and a pointer that points to the next element in the list. A null pointer value signals the end of the list.

Lists such as those described above are called *singly-linked* lists because there is only one pointer (link) from one list element to the next. Using this pointer, the list can be traversed in one direction: you can go from one list element to the next element but not to the previous element. Other types of lists, such as *doubly-linked* lists, allow list traversal in both directions: forward to the next element and back to the previous element. In doubly-linked lists two pointers must be kept: one for the next element and one for the previous element.

Building lists is straightforward. We start with the list head and insert a new element at an appropriate place in the list, e.g., the element can be inserted at the beginning of the list, in the middle of the list, or at the end of the list. In our list, we will insert elements at the beginning of the list (it is simpler to do this).

Here is the definition of type *list* and the prototypes of functions for manipulating the lists (file *list1.h*):

```
   struct list {
       int x;
       list *next;
   };
5  void add(list& l, int a);
   void print(list& l);
```

The list argument must be passed to *add* by reference because its component *next*, which points to the first element of the list, is changed when a new element is added to the list. The newly added element becomes the first element of the list. We pass the list argument to *print* by reference simply for (minor) efficiency. If it is passed by value, then the *list* argument (which consists of two components) will have to be copied.

Here are the definitions of the list manipulation functions (file *list1.cpp*):

```
   #include <stdlib.h> //get NULL
   #include <iostream.h>
   #include "list1.h"

5  void add(list& l, int a)
   {
       list *p = new list;
       p->x = a;
       p->next = l.next;
10     l.next = p;
   }
   void print(list& l)
   {
       for (list *p = l.next; p != NULL; p = p->next)
15         cout << p->x << endl;
   }
```

Here is some sample code illustrating the use of lists:

```
     #include "list1.h"
     int main()
     {
         list q;
5        q.next = 0;
         add(q, 3);
         add(q, -5);
         add(q, 7);
         add(q, 2);
10       print(q);
     }
```

Variable *q* will point to the list (line 4). The end of the list is signaled by the null pointer. Initially, there are no elements in the list. It is therefore the programmer's responsibility to ensure that the list variable *q* points to an empty list by setting *q.next* to the null pointer (line 5). Note that no data item will be stored in *q* itself. Its sole use is to act as a pointer to the first element.

The following figures depict the state of list *q* just after its definition (line 4), just after setting *next* to zero (line 5), and after the insertion of each of four items:

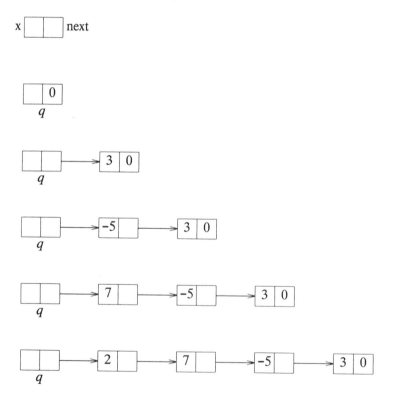

The arrows indicate pointers.

Here is the output produced by the above program:

```
2
7
-5
3
```

Unlike in an array, items can be inserted between any two list elements without having to shift the adjacent elements (the *add* operation shown inserts elements at the beginning of the list). We simply adjust the pointers. For example, we can insert the integer 8 between 7 and –5 as follows:

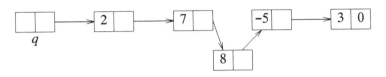

The above picture is equivalent to the picture

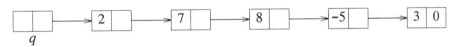

Any item can be deleted without creating a gap in the list. As in the case of insertion, we just have to adjust the pointers. Both inserting an item into a list and deleting an item from a list requires only a few operations.

If a list is initially sorted, then this ordering can be preserved if new elements are added at appropriate places in the list. For example, when inserting a new element in a list that is sorted in increasing order, the new element should be added after an element less than or equal to the new element, but before an element greater than it.

4. ARRAYS AND POINTERS

In C++, there is a very strong relationship between pointers and arrays. Arrays can be treated as pointers and vice versa. C++ array names are really *const* pointers.[3]

---

3. There is one exception: array parameters, corresponding to array arguments passed by value, can be treated as non-*const* pointers.

In many ways, arrays are just a convenient mechanism for manipulating objects referenced by pointers. Suppose, for example, that a is declared as a character array. Then the ith element of array a is accessed using the array element notation $a[i]$. An array name is also a pointer to the first element of the array. For example, the array name a can be thought of as a pointer that points to the first element of a, that is, it points to the beginning of the storage allocated for a. Hence, the ith element of a can also be accessed as $*(a+i)$.

Similarly, any pointer value can be thought of as the name of an array that begins at the address specified by the pointer value. As an example, suppose that p is a *char* pointer that has been initialized properly. Then the ith byte of storage, relative to the address pointed to by i, can be referenced as $p[i]$. In general, if p is a pointer of type T, then $p[i]$ refers to the ith block of storage of size *sizeof*(T) beginning from p.

Because array elements can be accessed using pointers and the storage referenced by a pointer can be accessed as array elements, C++ has no way of knowing whether or not a user is referring to a valid array element. Consequently, the C++ run-time system will not give a "subscript-out-of-range" error when an invalid array element is referenced, i.e., when an array subscript is negative or when it is greater than the upper bound of the array.

Strictly speaking, C++ can flag a subscript error for array elements accessed using the array subscript notation. One reason why C++ compilers do not check for invalid array subscripts is that array subscript checking is expensive. In general, it must be done at run time and this slows program execution. Recognizing the importance of subscript checking, at least in the program debugging phase, some C++ debugging tools check for invalid subscripts.

4.1 ARRAY ARGUMENTS

Parameters corresponding to array arguments can be declared as pointers. For example, suppose that two arrays a and s, declared as follows

```
int a[100];
float s[6][12];
```

are to be passed as arguments:

1. C++ will pass a as a pointer to *int*. Therefore, the parameter corresponding to a can be declared as an *int* pointer, for example, as

   ```
   int *p
   ```

   Of course, the parameter corresponding to a could also have been declared as

   ```
   int p[]
   ```

2. C++ will pass array *s* as a pointer to an one-dimensional array of twelve *float* elements. Therefore, the parameter corresponding to *s* can be declared as a "pointer to an one-dimensional array of twelve *float* elements", for example,

```
float (*q)[12]
```

The parentheses, which bind the * to *q*, are necessary because the array subscript operator [] has a higher precedence than the pointer (dereference) operator *. Declaring *q* as

```
float *q[12]
```

means that *q* is an array of twelve pointers to *float* elements, which is not what we want.

Of course, the parameter corresponding to *s* could also have been declared as

```
float q[][12]
```

which is our preferred declaration. As mentioned earlier, only the first array dimension may be omitted.

To illustrate the treatment of an array argument as a pointer, we will rewrite function *find* to treat its array argument as a parameter. The original version of *find* treats its array argument as an array; it has the prototype

```
int find(int a[], int l, int u, int key);
```

The revised version of *find*, which treats its array argument as a pointer parameter, has the prototype (file *findp.h*)

```
int find(int *a, int l, int u, int key);
```

The two prototypes are "equivalent" because using an array parameter is equivalent to using a pointer parameter. Both versions of *find* can be called in the same way, i.e., with an *int* array or with a pointer to an *int* as the first argument. In the latter case, the pointer should refer to the first element of an *int* array.

Here is the revised version of *find* (file *findp.cpp*):

```
     #include "findp.h"
     int find(int *a, int l, int u, int key)
     {
         int k;
5
         while (l <= u) {
             k = (l+u)/2;
             if (*(a+k) == key)
                 return k;
10           else if (*(a+k) < key)
                 l = k+1;
             else
                 u = k-1;
         }
15       return -1;
     }
```

a is now declared as a pointer to an *int* (line 2). Element *k* of the array pointed to by *a* is now referenced using pointer arithmetic. The pointer expression $a+k$ yields the address of element $a[k]$. And the expression $*(a+k)$ yields the value of element *k* (lines 8 and 10).

Arrays and pointers are so strongly related that we can declare the parameter corresponding to an array argument as a pointer, but within the body we can treat it as an array (the reverse is also allowed):

```
     #include "findp.h"
     int find(int *a, int l, int u, int key)
     {
         int k;
5
         while (l <= u) {
             k = (l+u)/2;
             if (a[k] == key)
                 return k;
10           else if (a[k] < key)
                 l = k+1;
             else
                 u = k-1;
         }
15       return -1;
     }
```

4.2 DYNAMIC ARRAYS

Bounds of C++ arrays specified using definitions must be constant expressions. However, this restriction does not apply to arrays created dynamically. Creating an array dynamically is a two-step process: first a pointer variable is defined and then it is set to point to an array allocated using operator *new*. Here is example code illustrating the dynamic allocation of an *int* array with n elements, where n is an arbitrary expression:

```
int *a;
    ...
if ((a = new int[n]) == NULL) {
    cerr << "Error, not enough heap storage" << endl;
    exit(1);
}
```

The above *if* statement can also be written as

```
if (a = new int[n])) {
    ...
}
```

Instead of comparing the value of the pointer returned by *new* with the null pointer *NULL*, the above code relies on the fact that in C++ the null pointer is zero. If *new* returns the null pointer, then this will be interpreted as false; any other value returned by it will be interpreted as true.

5. STRINGS

C++ implements strings as character arrays. For example, C++ stores the string literal

```
"C++ Programming"
```

in a character array, appends the null character '\0', and returns a pointer to the array. Here is the C++ representation of the above string:

C	+	+		P	r	o	g	r	a	m	m	i	n	g	'\0'
1	2	3	4	5	6	7	8	9	10	11	12	13	14	15	16

Every string in C++ must be terminated by the null character \0. C++ automatically terminates every string literal with the null character. But in case of strings constructed by the programmer, say by storing characters in a *char* array, it is the programmer's responsibility to terminate the string with the null character. Using the null character to signal the end of a string is a very important C++ convention. Almost all manipulation of strings in C++, including that performed by string library functions, relies on this convention to detect the end of string.

Header file *string.h* contains the prototypes of the functions for manipulating strings. For example, it contains prototypes of the functions to determine the length of a string (*strlen*), copy a string (*strcpy*), append a string (*strcat*), and so on. For complete details, see Section 2.7 in Chapter 16.

To illustrate the relationship between pointers and arrays in the context of strings and string output, consider the following program that prints strings (file *str.cpp*):

```
     #include <iostream.h>
     #include <string.h>
     int main()
     {
5        char a[] = "C++ Programming", b[100];

         for(int i = 0; i < strlen(a); i++)
             cout << a[i];
         cout << endl;
10
         for(char *p = a; *p != '\0'; p++)
             cout << *p;
         cout << endl;

15       cout << a << endl;

         strcpy(b, a);
         cout << b << endl;

20       strcat(b, ", the new technolgy!");
         cout << b << endl;
     }
```

Variable *a* is defined as a character array and initialized to the string

```
"C++ Programming"
```

(on line 5). C++ computes the size of the array based on the number of characters in the initial value (plus one more for the terminating null character). *b* is defined as an array of 100 character elements (also on line 5).

The string stored in array *a* is first printed by printing each element of *a* up to the length of the string (lines 7-8). The same string is now printed by using a character pointer *p* to point to each element of *a* and then dereferencing the pointer (lines 11-12). This time characters are printed until the null character is encountered. Instead of printing the string *a* one character at a time, the whole string can also be printed in one statement (line 15).

The program next illustrates string copying and appending. String *a* is copied to array *b* with the library function *strcpy*, which also copies the terminating null character.

Then the string

```
", the new technology!"
```

is appended to string *b* using the library function *strcat*, which overwrites the terminating character in *b* with the first character from the above string (the comma character).

The output of the above program is

```
C++ Programming
C++ Programming
C++ Programming
C++ Programming
C++ Programming, the new technology!
```

To illustrate string manipulation, we will write a function that reverses its string argument. Here is the prototype of this function (file *reverse.h*):

```
void reverse(char a[]);
```

The body of function *reverse* is (file *reverse.cpp*):

```
    #include <string.h>
    #include "reverse.h"
    void reverse(char a[])
    {
5       const int n = strlen(a);
        char *p = new char[n+1];

        for (int i = 0; i < n; i++)
            p[i] = a[n-1-i];
10      p[n] = '\0';
        strcpy(a, p);
    }
```

Function *reverse* dynamically allocates a temporary array and sets pointer *p* to point to this array (line 6). The size of this array is equal to one more than the size of the string supplied in the argument matching parameter *a* (line 3). The array allocated has an extra element to accommodate the null character used for terminating a string. The string is reversed by copying the characters in *a* starting from the end of *a* to the beginning of the array pointed to by *p* (lines 8-9). The

terminating character is added after all the characters have been copied (line 10)
Then the reversed string is copied to the parameter (line 11). Remember that
array arguments are passed by reference which means that the array parameter
becomes a synonym for the argument.

The following figures illustrate how *reverse* works. Suppose, for example, that the
array parameter *a* is initially the following string:

Characters are copied in the reverse order to the temporary array pointed to by
p. Here is how this array looks after two characters have been copied:

And here is the temporary array after all the characters have been copied:

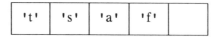

Finally, the terminating null character is appended to the end of this array:

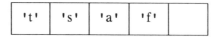

The temporary array is then copied to parameter *a* and this completes execution
of the function.

Function *reverse*, as defined above, requires the allocation of an array equal in
size to the array being reversed to temporarily hold the reverse version of the
string as it is being constructed. We do not need this array. Instead, we can
reverse the string by using a simple character variable (file *reverse2.cpp*):

```
#include <string.h>
#include "reverse.h"
void reverse(char a[])
{
    const int n = strlen(a);
    char c;

    for (int i = 0; i < n/2; i++) {
        c = a[i];
        a[i] = a[n-1-i];
        a[n-i-1] = c;
    }
}
```

This version of *reverse* exchanges the first character of *a* with the last character, the second character with the second last character, and so on.

Assuming parameter *a* is initially

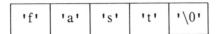

then it will look as follows after the first and last characters have been exchanged:

't'	'a'	's'	'f'	'\0'

Note that the terminating null character is not touched by the exchanges performed.

The second version of function *reverse* performs $3n/2$ character copies (assignments). The first version performed $2n$ character copies. Thus the second version of *reverse* not only uses less storage, but is also faster.

5.1 EXAMPLES

5.1.1 COMPUTING THE LENGTH OF A STRING Suppose that C++ does not provide function *strlen* for determining the length of a string. Our task is to write function, say *slen*, for computing the length of a string.

Here is the prototype of function *slen* (file *slen.h*):

```
int slen(char *s);
```

Here is the definition of function *slen* (file *slen.cpp*):

```
#include "slen.h"
int slen(char *s)
{
    for(int n = 0; s[n] != '\0'; n++)
        ;
    return n;
}
```

5.1.2 COMMAND-LINE ARGUMENTS C++ programs, as discussed in the previous chapter, can accept command-line arguments, which are specified when invoking the program. The following simple program shows how to write a program that accepts command-line arguments. This program simply prints the name of the program and each of the command-line arguments on a new line (file *cmd.cpp*):

```
    #include "slen.cpp"
    #include <iostream.h>
    int main(int argc, char *argv[])
    {
5       cout << "Program Name is ";
        cout << argv[0] << endl;
        for(int i=1; i <= argc; i++)
            cout << argv[i] << endl;
    }
```

Suppose we compile this program, using the Borland C++ compiler, as follows:

```
bcc cmd
```

The executable version of the program produced is named *cmd.exe*. Now suppose that *cmd.exe* is stored in the directory

```
D:PROGS
```

and we execute it from this directory as

```
cmd one two three
```

where *one*, *two*, and *three* are the command-line arguments.

Program *cmd* produces the following output:

```
Program Name is D:\PROGS\CMD.EXE
one
two
three
```

The program name is automatically stored by C++ in the array element *argv* [0].

6. EXERCISES

1. Write a function *sum* that computes the sum of the elements of an array with elements of type *lfloat*. Function *sum* has the prototype

   ```
   double sum(float a[], int n);
   ```

   Explain:

   > Why has the result type been declared to be *double* instead of *float*?

   a. Will it be advantageous to pass the argument corresponding to *a* by reference (instead of by value)?

2. Write a function *len* that takes a string as its argument and returns the length of the string as its result. Function *len* has the prototype

   ```
   int len(char *s);
   ```

3. When should objects be created dynamically (instead of simply creating them using definitions)?

4. Explain what can as a result of dereferencing a pointer variable whose value is null or one that refers to an object deleted using the *delete* operator.

Chapter 8

CLASSES

The C++ "class" facility allows programmers to define full-fledged types that can be used just like the predefined types. Unlike types defined with the *typedef* statement, class types are new types and not synonyms for existing types. A new type is defined by grouping together items that implement the new type. Components of a class type or of an object of a class type are called "members." Class members can be data items, functions, operators, and type definitions. A class "semantically" specifies the

1. range of values associated with a new type and

2. operations that can be legally performed on objects of these types.

Class members can be

1. "public" members, which can be referenced by all class users,

2. "private" members, which are for "internal" use only, or

3. "protected" members, which are for use by classes derived from the class containing them (see Chapter 9).

A C++ structure is really a class whose members are all public members. C++ structure members can therefore be data declarations, functions, operators, and type definitions.

Before discussing C++ classes in detail, we will look at an example class definition.

1. COMPLEX DATA TYPE

A large scientific application uses and manipulates complex numbers. We need to define a *complex* type so that users can define *complex* variables and perform standard arithmetic and comparison operations on *complex* numbers.

Here is the definition of the *complex* type (file *complex.h*):

```
    class complex {
        float r, i;
    public:
        complex(float a = 0, float b = 0);
5       float real();
        float imag();
        complex operator +(complex a);
        complex operator -(complex a);
        complex operator *(complex a);
10      complex operator /(complex a);
        int operator ==(complex a);
    };
```

The above class specification defines a new type *complex* (line 1) which can be used much like the predefined types in C++. To store complex values, *complex* defines *r* and *i* as *private* data members (line 2) which cannot be accessed directly. By default, class members are *private* members.

public class members are specified following the keyword *public* (lines 4-11). The first *public* member (line 4) is a function with the name *complex* (*complex::complex* to be precise). A function with the same name as the class is called a "constructor."

A constructor is always called automatically to initialize a newly created object. A constructor function call does not return a value. Although not shown in this example, the counterpart of a constructor is a "destructor", which is automatically called when an object is destroyed or deleted. Destructors are used for performing cleanup, such as closing files and deleting objects referenced by the members of the object being deleted.

Continuing with our example, let us examine the prototype of the *complex* constructor

```
complex(float a = 0, float b = 0);
```

in more detail. This constructor takes two arguments which are used to initialize *complex* objects. The default initial values for these arguments, specified in the parameter declarations, make the corresponding arguments optional (if an argument is omitted, then all arguments following it must also be omitted).

The *complex* constructor is called when a *complex* object is defined or dynamically created. Consider, for example, the objects created by the following variable definitions and the call to operator *new*:

```
complex a, b(2.0, 2.0), c(5.0), *d;
...
d = new complex(3.0);
```

The newly created *complex* objects are initialized by calling the *complex* constructor (the calls are automatically generated by C++) as follows:

1. *a* is initialized by calling the constructor with both arguments equal to 0.0 (default parameter values),

2. *b* is initialized by calling the constructor with both arguments equal to 2.0,

3. *c* is initialized by calling the constructor with the first argument equal to 5.0 and the second argument equal to 0.0 (default parameter value), and

4. the dynamically created object referenced by *d* is initialized by calling the constructor with the first argument equal to 3.0 and the second argument equal to 0.0 (default parameter value).

The *complex* constructor is also called to perform type conversions. For example, this constructor is automatically called to create a *complex* value from a *float* value as illustrated by the following assignment of a *float* value to the *complex* variable *a*:

```
a = 2.5;
```

The assignment that will actually take place is

```
a = complex(2.5);
```

which assigns to *a* the *complex* value constructed by invoking the *complex* constructor with the first argument equal 2.5 and the second argument equal to 0.0.

Following the definition of the *complex* constructor are the prototypes of the member functions *real* and *imag* for extracting the real and imaginary parts of a *complex* object (lines 5-6). These functions are called using the "selected component" notation as follows:

```
complex a;
float r, i;
...
r = a.real();
i = a.imag();
```

The *complex* object specified (*a* in this case), when calling a member function or operator, is passed as an implicit argument to the member function or operator.

There is one important difference between ordinary functions and member functions: in the case of member functions, the object associated with the member function call is passed as an implicit argument to the function. Within the member function, components of the implicit argument can be referenced simply by using their names.

Following the definitions of the member functions *real* and *imag* are the prototypes of several operators for manipulating *complex* objects (lines 7-11). By defining these predefined operators to work on *complex* values, we have "overloaded" these operator symbols with additional semantics. Overloading an operator symbol (a function identifier) simply means that there is more than one operator (function) definition denoted by the operator symbol (function identifier). The actual definition invoked by a call to an overloaded operator (function) depends upon the argument types.

Member operators are like member functions except that are declared or defined slightly differently, they can have only one or two arguments, and they can be invoked using the "infix" notation commonly used in mathematics, for example,

```
a + b
```

where the operator + is specified between its two operands. Only existing C++ operators can be overloaded (new operators cannot be defined) and their predefined precedences and association rules cannot be changed.

Each *complex* operator takes two operands. In the prototypes and in the definitions of the operators, the parameter corresponding to the right operand is specified explicitly but the parameter corresponding to the left operand is not specified. The left operand is passed implicitly and its components can be referenced, within the operator body, directly without using the selected component notation.

Here is code illustrating the use of the *complex* operators:

```
#include "complex.h"
...
complex x(6.0, 6.0), y(5.0), z;
...
z = x*y+x;
```

The expression in the above assignment, written in infix notation, could also have been written in functional form using the selected component notation as follows:

```
z = (x.operator*(y)).operator+(x);
```

For obvious reasons, the infix notation is to be preferred. Except for the difference in how operator names are specified, member operator bodies are specified just like member function bodies. Because the left-hand operand of an operator becomes the implicit argument and the right-hand operand, if any, becomes the explicit argument, binary operators are specified with one explicit parameter and the unary operators are specified without an explicit parameter.

Now, it is time to look at the bodies of the *complex* member functions (file *complex.cpp*):

```
    #include "complex.h"
    complex::complex(float a, float b)
    {
        r = a; i = b;
5   }
    float complex::real()
    {
        return r;
    }
10  float complex::imag()
    {
        return i;
    }
    complex complex::operator +(complex a)
15  {
        complex b(r+a.r, i+a.i);
        return b;
    }
    complex complex::operator -(complex a)
20  {
        complex b(r-a.r, i-a.i);
        return b;
    }
    complex complex::operator *(complex a)
25  {
        complex b(r*a.r-i*a.i, r*a.i+i*a.r);
        return b;
    }
    complex complex::operator /(complex a)
30  {
        complex b;
        float denom = a.r*a.r+a.i+a.i;
        b.r = (r*a.r+i*a.i)/denom;
        b.i = (i*a.r-r*a.i)/denom;
35      return b;
    }
    int complex::operator ==(complex a)
    {
        return r == a.r && i == a.i;
40  }
```

Variables *r* and *i*, which are referenced within the *complex* member functions (for example, line 4), are data members of the *complex* class and are associated with the *complex* object passed as the implicit argument. The operators shown simply implement complex arithmetic. For example, the *complex* addition operator (lines 14-17) adds two *complex* numbers by adding their real and imaginary components. The *complex* + operator does this by initializing the real and imaginary components of a new *complex* variable *b* to the sum of the real and imaginary components of its two *complex* operands (line 16). The value of *b* is returned as the result of the addition (line 17). The addition operator used on line 16 is the predefined addition operator that adds *float* operands. Components of the left operand of the *complex* + are referenced directly as *r* and *i* (line 16). Components of the right operand, which is denoted by the parameter *a*, are referenced using the selected component notation as *a*.*r* and *a*.*i* (line 16).

Having defined class *complex*, we will now write a program, a desk calculator, to do *complex* arithmetic (file *ccalc.cpp*):

```
     #include <iostream.h>
     #include "complex.h"
     int main()
     {
 5       float ar, ai, br, bi;
         complex r; char opr;
         for(;;) {
             cout << "Enter first complex number: ";
             cin >> ar; cin >> ai;
10           cout << "Enter operator: "; cin >> opr;
             cout << "Enter second complex number: ";
             cin >> br; cin >> bi;
             switch (opr) {
             case '+':
15               r = complex(ai, ar) + complex(bi, br);
                 break;
             case '-':
                 r = complex(ai, ar) - complex(bi, br);
                 break;
20           case '*':
                 r = complex(ai, ar) * complex(bi, br);
                 break;
             case '/':
                 r = complex(ai, ar) / complex(bi, br);
25               break;
             default:
                 cerr << "Bad operator!" << endl;
             }
             cout << "Result is: ";
30           cout << r.imag() << " " << r.real() << endl;
         }
     }
```

The program is straightforward. It repeatedly requests input from the user, performs the desired operation, and prints the result. It converts the input into *complex* numbers by calling the *complex* constructor so that the *complex* operators can be used to perform *complex* arithmetic (lines 15, 18, 21, 24).

The program is terminated by typing the interrupt character control-C. The above program can be compiled as follows

```
bcc ccalc complex
```

to produce the executable program *ccalc.exe* .

As we shall see in Section 6 of Chapter 11, the calculator program will become smaller and more elegant when we use extended definitions of the operators >> and << for *complex* input/output.

2. CLASS DEFINITIONS

A class definition consists of two parts: the specification and the bodies of its member and "friend" functions (friends will be discussed later in detail). The bodies of these functions can be given "inline" within the class specification or they can be given separately. For example, the following version of the specification of class *complex* contains the definitions of the *complex* constructor, and those of the member functions *real* and *imag*:

```
     class complex {
         float r, i;
     public:
         complex(float a = 0, float b = 0) {r=a; i=b;}
 5       float real() {return r;}
         float imag() {return i;}
         complex operator +(complex a);
         complex operator -(complex a);
         complex operator *(complex a);
10       complex operator /(complex a);
         int operator ==(complex a);
     };
```

Visibility of a class member determines who can access the member. A member's visibility is determined by whether the member has been specified as a *private*, a *public*, or a *protected* member. A class specification therefore consists of three parts or sections:

1. *private*: Members specified here can be accessed only from within bodies of member functions or friends of the class. Private members follow the class header or they follow the keyword *private* (terminated by a colon).

2. *public*: Members specified here can be accessed from within any function including member functions and friends of the class. Such members represent the class user interface. Public members follow the keyword *public* (terminated by a colon).

3. *protected*: Members specified here can be accessed from within classes that have been "derived" from (based on) this class and from within member and friend functions specified in the class specification itself. *protected* members behave like *private* members except when referenced from within derived classes in which case they behave like *public* members. Protected members follow the keyword *protected* (terminated by a colon).

Class specifications have the form[1]

```
class class-name {
    private-member-declarations
public:
    public-member-declarations
protected:
    protected-member-declarations
};
```

Typically, the *private* components are specified following the class header which makes them *private* by default. It is therefore not necessary to explicitly use the keyword *private* to indicate the beginning of the *private* section of a class specification.

A class name can be used just like a predefined type name to specify variable types, function result types, parameter types, and so on.

Within member functions, class members are referenced simply by using their names. In other instances, they must be qualified with a reference to the associated object (using the selected component notation).

The keyword *struct* can be used instead of the keyword *class* to declare a class. Members of such a class are, by default, *public* members. Members of a class declared using the keyword *class* are, by default, *private* members.

Functions declared in a class specification can be of several types. We have already seen constructors, and member functions and operators. I will later discuss the various types of functions in detail. But to give you an idea what these functions are used for, here is a brief summary:

1. *Constructors* are special functions, which are automatically called when objects are created to initialize newly created objects. A newly created object is passed as an implicit argument to the constructor called to initialize it. Constructors do not return values (no result type is specified in their declarations or definitions).

2. *Destructors* are special member functions, which are automatically called to cleanup when class objects are deleted (deallocated). The object being deleted is passed as an implicit argument to the destructor. Destructors do not return values (no result type is specified in their declarations or definitions).

---

1. Specifications of classes that are derived from (based upon) existing classes are like those of ordinary (non-derived) classes except that these classes list the (immediate) base classes in the class header. Derived classes will be discussed in the next chapter.

3. *Member functions* are like ordinary functions except that they are intended for operating on objects of the class containing them. A member function is called in association with a class object using the selected component notion; this object is passed as an implicit argument to the member function. The object associated with the member function invocation is specified explicitly by using the selected component notation or implicitly when a member function is invoked from within another member function.

4. *Member operator functions* (member operators or simply operators) are similar to member functions except that their definitions are syntactically slightly different from those of member functions.

    Like member functions, member operators can be called using the selected component notation and the object specified in the call is passed as an implicit argument. C++ also allows member operators to be invoked in infix notation. Unary operators are defined without any explicit parameters and binary operators are defined with one explicit parameter.

5. *Virtual functions* are like member functions except that classes ("derived" classes) based on the class containing these functions can replace the virtual functions with alternative functions. A pointer to a base class object can store a pointer to a derived class object. Invocation of a member function via a base class pointer will automatically call the "right" virtual function – the base class function is invoked if the base class pointer refers to a base class object and the derived class function is invoked if the base class pointer refers to a derived class object.

6. *Friends* are ordinary functions or operators which have been given permission to access the *private* and *protected* members of a class. Unlike member functions and member operators, friends are not passed an implicit argument and they are called using the ordinary function call or infix operator notation (i.e., the selected component notation is not used).

    All components of a class, including *private* and *protected* components, can be accessed from within the above functions.

    We will now discuss in detail the different kinds of members: data items and functions including constructors, destructors, member functions, operators friend and *static* functions. *virtual* functions will be discussed in the next chapter.

3. CLASS OBJECTS

A class can be used much like the predefined types to declare objects, arrays of objects, pointers and so on. A constructor is invoked to perform initialization for each new class object (including each element of an array). Class objects may be created statically using variable definitions or dynamically by calling the object allocator *new*. A destructor is automatically called to perform cleanup when a class object is destroyed – implicitly by leaving the scope of the object or explicitly by calling the *delete* operator.

4. CLASS MEMBERS

The members of a class can be data members or functions (operators are treated like functions). Data members specified in the class specification are like the components of a structure. Initial values for the data components can be specified using constructors.

In case of member and *friend* functions, the prototype must be given within the class specification but the body can be given separately. The function body can be given, within the class specification itself, in lieu of the prototype. Each invocation of a member function is associated with an object of the class to which the member function belongs.

The general notation for accessing members of a class object is (provided there are no "access" restrictions)

class-object . member

or

pointer-to-class-object–>member

Within member functions, components of the associated object can be referenced simply by using their names.

Suppose we have defined *c* as a *complex* object and *pc* as a pointer to a *complex* object. Then we can refer to the member function *real* as

```
c.real()
```

and

```
pc->real()
```

To call function *real* from within a member function of class *complex* to determine the value of the real component, we can simply write

```
real()
```

but this is not necessary because within a member function we can get the real value of a *complex* object by just examining the value of member *r*.

4.1 THE SPECIAL VARIABLE this

Within a member function, the special variable *this* points to the object associated with the invocation of the member function. The type of *this* in a member function of class *T* is

```
T *const
```

i.e., a constant pointer to an object of type *T*.

Within a member function, references to the members of the object associated with the invocation of the member function can be prefixed with *this* and the selection operator `->`. However, this is generally unnecessary since C++ automatically does this. As an example, consider the following *complex* class constructor that was shown previously:

```
complex::complex(float a, float b)
{
    r = a;
    i = b;
}
```

This constructor can alternatively be written with the members *r* and *i* explicitly qualified by the special variable *this*:

```
complex::complex(float a, float b)
{
    this->r = a;
    this->i = b;
}
```

This use of the special variable *this* is redundant and unnecessary. Examples of situations (within member functions) where it is necessary to use the special variable *this* explicitly are listed below:

1. As an argument in a function call to pass a pointer to the object associated with the member function invocation, for example,

   ```
   f(this);
   ```

2. To make a copy of the object associated with the invocation or to assign a whole new value to the object, for example,

   ```
   void T::g(T& a, T& b)
   {
       ...
       a = *this;
       ...
       *this = b;
   }
   ```

   As discussed earlier, notation

```
T&
```

is used to specify that parameters *a* and *b* will be passed by reference.

3. To explicitly reference a member hidden as a result of another declaration as illustrated by the following code in which parameter *size* of the *U* constructor "hides" the *private* member *size* of class *U* within the body of the constructor:

```
class U {
    int size;
    ...
public:
    U(int size) { this->size = size; ... }
    ...
};
```

4. To store a pointer to the object associated with the invocation of the member function (or constructor).

5. To return a reference to the object associated with the invocation of a member function, for example,

```
T& T::f(int a)
{
    ...
    return *this;
}
```

A reference, of type *T*, to the object associated with the invocation of the member function is specified as *this*.

The result type

```
T&
```

specifies that function *f* will return a reference to an object. In our example, *f* returns a reference (synonym) to the object associated with the invocation of *f*.

4.2 CONSTRUCTORS

A *constructor* is a member function whose name is the same as that of the class in which it is declared. Its purpose is to "construct" a value of its class type, say by properly initializing a newly created object. A constructor is automatically called when a (class) object is created.

A constructor prototype, say for class *T*, has the form

T (*parameter-declarations*) ;

and the corresponding constructor body has the form

T : : T (*parameter-declarations*)
{
    ...
}

If the constructor definition is given within the class definition in lieu of its declaration, then the constructor definition has the form

T (*parameter-declarations*)
{
    ...
}

A class can have several constructors, but each constructor must have a unique *signature*, i.e., each constructor must differ in the number of parameters or at least one of the corresponding parameter types should not match. In other words, constructors can be overloaded provided each constructor has a unique signature. In deciding which constructor to call, C++ uses contextual information to select the appropriate constructor.

Here are examples of constructor declarations:

```
class set {
    ...
public:
    set(int lo, int hi);
    set(int hi);
    ...
};
```

The specification of class *set* specifies two constructors: one with two parameters and one with a single parameter. Consequently, when declaring or creating *set* objects, one or two initial values must be supplied for use as constructor arguments. Here are examples of *set* variable definitions and the dynamic creation of a *set* object:

```
set s(16), t(10, 100);
extern set w;
set *ps;
...
ps = new set(256);
```

The definition of *s* invokes the *set* constructor with one parameter and the definition of *t* invokes the *set* constructor with two parameters. The declaration specifying *w* as an external variable does not invoke the constructor because no object is created. The definition of *ps* as a pointer to a *set* object also does not invoke any constructor, but when a new *set* object is dynamically allocated by calling the object allocator *new*, then a *set* constructor (the one with one parameter) is invoked.

One or more constructors are automatically generated under the following conditions:

1. If no constructor has been explicitly specified for a class, say *T*, then a default (argumentless) constructor is automatically generated for class *T*. This constructor is invoked when objects of type *T* are created.

2. "Copy" constructors are used to copy class objects, that is, the copy constructor of class *T* is used for copying objects of class *T*. A copy constructor is automatically generated for a class if no copy constructor has been specified explicitly. Copy constructors are discussed later in Section 6.2.

4.3 INITIALIZATION

Class objects are initialized by means of constructors. One exception to this rule is a class which has only *public* members, no virtual functions, and is not derived from any other class. Such a class is essentially like a structure. Objects of such classes can be initialized just like structure variables are initialized by specifying their initial values (aggregate values are specified using curly braces) in their definitions.

Constructors initialize class objects regardless of whether they are created statically using variable definitions or dynamically by calling the object allocator *new*. In both cases, appropriate constructors are invoked at run time.

Let us take another look at the constructor of class *complex*:

```
    class complex {
        float r, i;
    public:
        complex(float a = 0, float b = 0);
5       float real();
        float imag();
        complex operator +(complex a);
        complex operator -(complex a);
        complex operator *(complex a);
10      complex operator /(complex a);
        int operator ==(complex a);
    };
```

The *complex* constructor (line 4) has two *float* parameters with each having zero as a default value. Because of the default values, this constructor does triple duty and is equivalent to specifying three constructors with the following prototypes and essentially the same body:

```
complex();  //a and b replaced by 0 in constructor body
complex(float b); //a replaced by 0 in constructor body
complex(float a, float b); //constructor body as before
```

We will now examine class object initialization in more detail by discussing how the objects in the following examples are initialized:

```
complex e(1.0, 1.0);
complex f = complex(1.0, 1.0);
complex g = e;
complex h = 1.0; //parentheses not required
```

The initialization process used for each of the variables *e, f, g,* and *h* is different:

1. *e* is initialized by simply invoking the *complex* constructor.

2. *f* is initialized to a *complex* value constructed by invoking the *complex* constructor (with the arguments as specified on the right of the =) and then copying this value to *f* using a "copy" constructor. A *copy* constructor, say for type *complex*, is a constructor that takes one argument: a reference to a *complex* object. Since a copy constructor has not been specified explicitly for class *complex*, C++ will automatically generate one.

    When used in a variable definition, the = symbol denotes initialization and not assignment. Such initialization is performed using a "copy" constructor.

3. *g* is initialized by the copy constructor for class *complex*, which copies the value of *e* to *g*.

4. *h* is initialized to the *complex* value constructed by calling the constructor with 1.0 as its only argument. When a single simple value is specified using the initialization symbol =, as in the initialization of *h*, then there is no need to explicitly specify the conversion as in

    ```
    complex h = complex(1.0);
    ```

4.4 INITIALIZATION: INITIALIZERS VS. MEMBER ASSIGNMENT

Class objects can be initialized in two ways using constructors: by using *initializers* specified in the constructor definition or by giving assignment statements in the constructor body. Execution of a constructor consists of two parts: execution of the initializers followed by execution of the constructor body.

Initializers are specified in the constructor of class T as follows:

$T::T$ (*parameter-declarations*) : *initializer-list*
{
    ...
}

In case of an inline constructor (one whose body is given within the class specification), initializers are specified as follows:

T (*parameter-declarations*) : *initializer-list*
{
    ...
}

The initializer list is a comma-separated list of initializers for initializing the members of class T (in this example).[2] Class member initializers have the form

x (*arguments*)

where x is the name of the member and the arguments are the values to which x is to be initialized (by calling a constructor, if necessary). The arguments are expressions composed of operands that include the constructor parameters.

Here is an example illustrating member initialization (file *queue1.h*):

```
     class queue {
         int size;
         ...
     public:
5        queue(int n): size(n) { ... }
         ...
     };
```

In the above code member *size* will be initialized to n, which is *queue* constructor parameter. The body of the constructor is given within the specification itself. Had the body been given separately, then the initializer would not be specified in the constructor prototype, but instead in the constructor definition, as shown below:

---

2. Initializers are also used for initializing base classes (see Chapter 9).

```
class queue {
    int size;
    ...
public:
    queue(int n);
    ...
};
    ...
queue::queue(int n): size(n)
{
    ...
}
```

This initialization could also have been accomplished by using assignments (file *queue2.h*):

```
class queue {
    int size;
    ...
public:
    queue(int n) { size = n; ... }
    ...
};
```

Both methods for initializing members (using initializers or using assignments) have their pros and cons. Initializers must be used to initialize

1. *const* members, for example, if *size* is declared as a *const* identifier, then it must be initialized as shown below (file *queue3.h*):

```
class queue {
    const int size;
    ...
public:
    queue(int n): size(n) { ... }
    ...
};
```

2. members that can only be initialized by calling constructors with arguments (their classes do not have argumentless constructors).

Assignments are used to initialize members (except for the above cases) when the initialization is complicated. For example, assignments are used when initialization requires the use of statements such as *while* loops, etc., or when it is necessary to allocate some storage (say for a dynamic array) within the constructor itself.

4.5 ARRAY INITIALIZATION

Initializing an array with elements of a class type is similar to initializing an array with elements of a predefined type. Here are some examples:

```
#include "complex.h"
...
complex ca[5];
complex cb[] = {1.0, 2.0, 3.0, 4.0, 5.0};
complex cc[10] = {complex(1.0, 1.0), complex(2.0, 2.0),
                  complex(3.0, 3.0), complex(4.0, 4.0),
                  complex(5.0, 5.0)};
...
```

For array *ca*, the argumentless *complex* constructor is called for each element. For array *cb*, the constructor that takes one *float* argument is called for each element. And in the case of array *cc*, the constructor that takes two *float* arguments is called for each element. Note that when there are multiple constructor arguments, initial values of the right type (*complex* in our example) must be explicitly constructed (as in case of *cc*).

If initial values are not supplied for all the array elements, as in case of *cc*, then the argumentless constructor is invoked for the elements that are not explicitly initialized.

Arrays of class objects cannot be initialized using the notation that can be used for single objects, for example,

```
complex a(1.0, 2.0);
```

Array initialization using this notation is not allowed because this notation cannot be used to specify different initial values for the various array elements.

4.6 ORDER OF CONSTRUCTOR INVOCATION

Suppose a class, say *T*, contains members that are class objects. When an object of type *T* is created, constructors for members that are class objects are called first and then the body of the constructor for the class *T* is executed. Constructors for the members are called in the order in which the members are declared in the class. If constructors with arguments are to be called for the members, then these calls must be specified in the member initialization list.

4.7 DESTRUCTORS

A *destructor* is a special member function whose name is identical to the name of the class containing it, but it is prefixed with the ˜ (tilde) character. Destructors are used for "cleaning up" prior to the deallocation (deletion) of objects. For example, a constructor may initialize objects by opening files while a destructor may cleanup by closing the files.

Unlike constructors, a class can have only one destructor. If a destructor has not been explicitly specified, then C++ will automatically generate one. Destructors do not return values and they do not have any parameters. Destructors are automatically invoked when an object is deleted – implicitly by leaving the scope containing the object or explicitly by calling the *delete* operator.

Destructors can be used to implement "garbage" collection (freeing space allocated for objects that are no longer referenced), close files, and other actions that need to be performed when an object is no longer needed.

A destructor for class, say *T*, is declared (within the class specification) as

```
~T();
```

The destructor body has the form

```
T::~T()
{
    ...
}
```

Of course, as in case of all member functions, the destructor body can be given inline within the class specification itself in lieu of the prototype. In such a case, the destructor body has the form

```
~T()
{
    ...
}
```

As an example illustrating the use of a destructor, suppose that each object of type *T* contains a pointer, say *p*, that refers to an object of type *E* allocated by calling the storage allocator *new*. These *E* type objects are to be deallocated (by calling *delete*) when objects of type *T* are deleted. The straightforward way of freeing these objects is to place the statement

```
delete p;
```

in the destructor of class *T*.

In the examples shown so far, for example, *complex*, destructors have not been defined explicitly because there was no need to perform any special cleanup at object deletion time. All that needs to be done is to deallocate the storage used by the *complex* objects, which is done automatically.

As an example of an explicitly specified destructor, consider class *stack* (discussed later in detail):

```
     class stack {
         int max;
         int sp;
         float *stk;
  5  public:
         stack(int size); //constructor
         ~stack(); //destructor
         ...
     };
 10  stack::stack(int size) //constructor body
     {
         stk = new float[max = size];
         sp = 0;
     }
 15  stack::~stack() //destructor body
     {
         delete [] stk;
     }
     ...
```

The *stack* constructor sets pointer *stk* to point to an array of *float* elements (line 12) and the destructor deallocates this array (line 17). The destructor is called automatically when a *stack* object is deleted. In the absence of the *stack* destructor, deleting a *stack* object will free the storage occupied by the pointer *stk*, but will not deallocate the object referenced by *stk*.

4.8 ORDER OF DESTRUCTOR INVOCATION

The destructor invocation order is the reverse of the constructor invocation order. Suppose, for example, that class *T* contains members that are class objects. When an object of type *T* is deallocated, first the body of the destructor for type *T* is executed and then the destructors for the members that are class objects are called.

The destructors for the members that are class objects are called in the reverse of the order in which they are declared in the class specification.

4.9 MEMBER FUNCTIONS

A member function (one that is not a constructor or a destructor) for a class, say *T*, is declared as

result-type function-name (*parameter-declarations*) ;

This prototype must be declared within the class specification.

The corresponding member function body has the form

result-type `T::`*function-name* (*parameter-declarations*)
{
   ...
}

The member function body can be given inline within the class specification itself in place of the prototype, using the following form:

result-type *function-name* (*parameter-declarations*)
{
   ...
}

4.10 OPERATORS

Member operator definitions are similar to member functions definitions. An operator prototype given in a class specification has the form[3]

result-type `operator` *symbol* (*parameter$_{opt}$*) ;

Only existing C++ operator symbols can be used to define new operators.

The corresponding operator body has the form

result-type `T::operator` *symbol* (*parameter$_{opt}$*)
{
   ...
}

where *T* is the class to which the above operator belongs.

The operator body can be given inline within the class specification itself in place of the prototype. In such a case, the operator body has the form

result-type `operator` *symbol* (*parameter$_{opt}$*)
{
   ...
}

Here is an example of an operator prototype:

---

3. Subscript *opt* denotes an optional item.

```
class complex {
    ...
public:
    ...
    complex operator +(complex a);
    ...
};
```

The body of operator + looks like

```
#include "complex.h"
    ...
complex complex::operator +(complex a)
{
    complex b(r+a.r, i+a.i);
    return b;
}
    ...
```

This operator could alternatively have been specified inline within the class specification as

```
class complex {
    ...
public:
    ...
    complex operator +(complex a)
      { complex b(r+a.r, i+a.i); return b; }
    ...
};
```

As mentioned earlier, unary and binary member operators are specified with zero or one parameters, respectively. This is because member operators, like member functions, are invoked in association with an object which corresponds to the left operand of the operator. In case of a binary operator, the explicitly specified parameter corresponds to right operand.

5. STACKS: AN EXAMPLE

A stack is a data structure which implements the last-in-first-out (LIFO) discipline for providing service. Stacks are used in a variety of applications. For example, they are used for implementing compilers, implementing recursive functions, accounting, simulation, and a host of other applications. We will implement stacks by defining a class *stack*. An application using stacks can simply include the specification of class *stack* and define *stack* objects. The application must be "linked" with the file containing the object code version of the *stack* member functions.

Class *stack* will provide functions (including a constructor and a destructor) to

1. initialize the *stack*,

2. free the dynamically allocated storage pointed to by components of *stack* objects when *stack* objects are deleted,

3. add an item to the stack,

4. retrieve the top item from the stack (without deleting it),

5. delete the top stack item, and

6. determine whether the stack is empty or full.

The items stored in class *stack* will be *float* values.

5.1 STACK SPECIFICATION

Here is the specification of class *stack* (file *stack.h*):

```
     class stack {
         int max;
         int sp;
         float *stk;
  5  public:
         stack(int size);
         ~stack();
         int push(float a);
         int pop();
 10      float top();
         int empty();
         int full();
     };
```

Members *max*, *sp*, and *stk* (lines 2-4) represent the implementation details of a *stack* object. Because these members are specified as *private* members, they cannot be accessed directly by users of *stack* objects. *private* members can be referenced only from within member functions. Member *max* stores the maximum stack size, The dynamically allocated array pointed to by *stk* will be used to hold the items inserted in the stack. *sp* points to the first free slot for storing a new stack element in this dynamically allocated array.

Class *stack* has one constructor (line 6) which requires one argument: the stack size. This argument must be supplied when a *stack* object is created, either as a result of a variable definition or dynamic allocation. The stack implementation uses a dynamically allocated array which is allocated by the *stack* constructor. This dynamically allocated array will be freed when the *stack* object containing it is deallocated (implicitly by exiting the scope of the object definition or explicitly by calling operator *delete*). Otherwise, the storage used by this array will not be available for reuse. This deallocation is performed within the class *stack* destructor, that is, ˜*stack*.

Besides the constructor and destructor, class *stack* has five member functions (lines 8-12)

1. *push*: put an element on the top of the stack,

2. *pop*: remove the top stack element,

3. *top*: return the value of the top stack element,

4. *empty*: check if the stack is empty, and

5. *full*: check if the stack is full.

Functions *push* and *pop* return 1 if they are successful; otherwise, they return 0.

Here are examples illustrating the use of *stack* objects:

```
     #include "stack.h"
     #include "error.h"
     int main()
     {
5        const int max = 100;
         stack s(max), *ps;
         stack t = stack(max);
         float a = 5.0, b = 3.0, c, x;
         ...
10       s.push(a); s.push(b); t.push(c); //add to stack
         if (!s.empty())
             x = s.top();
         ps = new stack(max);
         if (!ps->pop())
15           error("empty stack popped");
         delete ps;
         ...
     }
```

The above program code declares two *stack* variables *s* and *t*, and one *stack* pointer *ps* (lines 6-7). One *stack* is dynamically created by calling the storage allocator *new* and it is assigned to the stack pointer *ps* (line 13). The *stack* objects are manipulated by calling the member functions using the selected component notation.

To give you an idea of how class *stack* will be implemented, here is how the *stack* object *s* will look after it is created but before it is initialized with the constructor:

max	100
sp	0
stk	

$$s$$

The components of s will not be accessible to the user of the *stack* object s. After the constructor call, s will look like

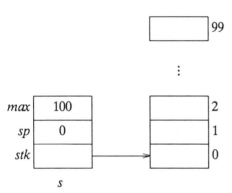

Then after *a* and *b* have been put on the stack s, it will look as follows:

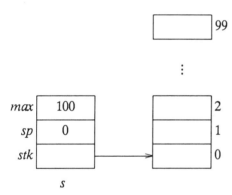

5.2 STACK IMPLEMENTATION

C++ does not have a syntactic facility for encapsulating the bodies of the member functions specified in the class specification. Member functions are defined individually, separate from the class specification (assuming they are not given inline within the class specification), and they can be in separate files. The member function name is prefixed with the name of its class. Here are the bodies of the *stack* member functions (file *stack.cpp*):

```
#include <stdio.h>
#include "stack.h"
#include "error.h"
stack::stack(int size)
{
    stk = new float[max = size]; sp = 0;
}
stack::~stack()
{
    delete [] stk;
}
int stack::push(float a)
{
    if (sp < max) {
        stk[sp++] = a; return 1;
    }
    else
        return 0;
}
int stack::pop()
{
    if (sp > 0) {
        sp--; return 1;
    }
    else
        return 0;
}
float stack::top()
{
    if (sp > 0)
        return stk[sp-1];
    else
        error("stack::top: under flow error");
}
int stack::empty()
{
    return sp == 0;
}
int stack::full()
{
    return sp == max;
}
```

Implementing the stack member functions is fairly straightforward. Of particular interest is the allocation of the array for implementing the stack data structure in the constructor *stack* and its deallocation in the destructor ˜*stack*. The *stack* constructor allocates a *float* array of the size specified for the stack (line 6). The destructor deletes this array (line 10). *error* (line 33) is a previously defined function that simply prints its argument on the standard error stream *stderr* and then terminates the program by calling function *exit*.

6. COPYING CLASS OBJECTS

Class objects can be copied in two ways: by assignment and by initialization. Assignment is performed with the assignment operator; initialization is performed with the copy constructor.

6.1 ASSIGNMENT

A programmer can explicitly define an assignment operator that is to be used for objects of a class. In the absence of an explicitly defined assignment operator, C++ automatically generates a default assignment operator which performs "member-wise" assignment. Members of the source (right-hand) class object are assigned to the corresponding members of the destination (left-hand) class object. The default assignment operator generated by C++ for a class, say *T*, has the prototype

```
T& operator=(T& right);
```

Suppose *a* and *b* are objects of type *T* and that we have the following assignment statement:

```
a = b;
```

The left operand *a* of the assignment operator is accessed as the implicit argument within the body of the assignment operator. The right operand *b* is the argument that corresponds to parameter *right*. This argument is passed by reference.

Member-wise assignment performed by the default assignment operator may not be appropriate in some cases. For example, member-wise copy of pointers will result in two pointer members pointing to the same object instead of pointing to two different copies of the object. Member-wise copy also does not perform cleanup such as deallocating the object referenced by a pointer member that is being assigned a new value. In such cases it is appropriate to explicitly define an assignment operator with semantics that are appropriate for the application.

We will now examine two situations involving assignment – in one the default assignment operator does just fine and in the other the semantics of the default assignment operator are inappropriate, making it necessary to explicitly define an assignment operator. As an example, consider the following code:

```
#include "complex.h"
...
complex a, b;
...
a = b;
```

The effect of this assignment is equivalent to the following pair of assignments (which must take place in a member function since components *i* and *r* are *private*):

```
a.r = b.r;
a.i = b.i;
```

The default assignment operator does the job for *complex* objects and its member-wise copy semantics are appropriate. But its semantics are not appropriate, for example, when pointers are involved as in the following *stack* object assignments:

```
     #include "stack.h"
     #define MAX 256
     ...
     stack s1(MAX), s2(MAX), s3(MAX);
5    ...
     s2 = s1;
     s3 = s2;
```

Here again is the definition of class *stack* (which was defined earlier):

```
     class stack {
         int max;
         int sp;
         float *stk;
5    public:
         stack(int size);
         ~stack();
         int push(float a);
         int pop();
10       float top();
         int empty();
         int full();
     };
```

The effect of the above assignments is equivalent to the following assignments (which must take place in a member function since the members involved are *private*):

```
s2.max = s1.max; s2.sp = s1.sp; s2.stk = s1.stk;
s3.max = s2.max; s3.sp = s2.sp; s3.stk = s2.stk;
```

Remember that stacks are implemented using dynamically allocated arrays (member *stk* points to such an array). As a result, after the *stack* assignments we encounter the following problems:

1. The arrays implementing stacks *s2* and *s3* become "dangling" or unreferenced arrays. They are lost for all practical purposes to the program since they can no longer be referenced.

2. Stacks *s1*, *s2*, and *s3* now all refer to the same array.

3. But the problem resulting from (2) is worse than it seems. It is not that *s1*, *s2*, and *s3* are now different ways of manipulating the same stack. Although each of these *stack* variables refers to the same *stack* array, each *stack* variable has its own idea about the state of the stack. Specifically, each *stack* variable has its own data member *sp* that tracks the number of objects in the stack. This causes strange behavior. Consider the effect of adding elements to the stack using the objects *s1*, *s2*, and *s3* as follows:

```
s1.push(1.0);
s2.push(2.0);
s3.push(3.0);
```

Assume that the stack is initially empty, that is, the shared stack array referenced by *s1*, *s2*, and *s3* contains no elements as indicated by the value of member *sp* of *s1*, *s2*, and *s3*. Then after these three *push* calls, the stack will contain one element, not three elements. First, the value 1.0 is stored as the top stack element. This value is then replaced by 2.0 which is inserted next into the stack. Finally, 3.0 replaces 2.0.

These problems can be avoided by explicitly defining an appropriate *stack* assignment operator. Instead of copying the array pointer, the customized assignment operator copies the contents of the array.

Here is the *stack* specification modified to include the prototype of the assignment operator (file *stack3.h*):

```
    class stack {
         int max;
         int sp;
         float *stk;
 5  public:
         stack(int size);
         ~stack();
         stack& operator =(stack& s);
         int push(float a);
10       int pop();
         float top();
         int empty();
         int full();
    };
```

The body of the assignment operator is (file *stack3.cpp*):

```
    #include "stack3.h"
         ...
    stack& stack::operator =(stack& s)
    {
 5       int i;
         sp = s.sp;
         for(i=0; i<sp; i++)
             stk[i] = s.stk[i];
         return *this;
10  }
```

This solution relies on the fact that the stacks involved in the assignment are of the same size. It is unreasonable to put this restriction on the programmer. The assignment operator can be modified as follows to allow assignment of different sizes of stack to each other:

1. Delete the storage pointed to by the destination (left-hand) stack.

2. Allocate the correct amount of storage using information from the source (right-hand) stack.

3. Perform the stack copy.

This solution has one problem: it cannot handle the assignment of a stack to itself (item 1 would destroy the stack). Consequently, the above operations must be performed only if a stack is not being assigned to itself. Here is the modified version of the assignment operator that does not suffer from the above problem (file *stack4.cpp*):

```
    #include "stack3.h"
        ...
    stack& stack::operator =(stack& s)
    {
5       int i;
        if (this != &s) {
            sp = s.sp;
            delete stk;
            stk = new float[max = s.max];
10          for(i=0; i<sp; i++)
                stk[i] = s.stk[i];
            return *this;
        }
    }
```

This assignment operator does not perform the assignment if the left operand of the assignment is also the right operand. The special variable *this* points to the left operand, which is the implicit operand associated with the invocation of the assignment operator. Expression &*s* is a pointer to the object *s*, which is the right operand (&, as used here, is the address-of operator). Note that parameter *s* is a synonym for the right operand since it is passed by reference (indicated by the second & on line 3).

6.2 INITIALIZATION – COPY CONSTRUCTORS

Copy constructors are used for making copies of class objects. Here is a list of situations when the copy constructor is used to copy class objects:

1. Initialization of class variables as illustrated by the following code:

    ```
    complex f = complex(1.0, 1.0);
    ```

2. copying arguments to parameters, and

3. returning function values.

We have previously discussed the role of copy constructors for initializing objects (item 1). Let us now examine items 2 and 3. When a class object is passed by value, the argument value must be copied to the parameter. (The parameter is actually a temporary variable automatically created by C++ in the function caller.) The argument value is copied using the copy constructor, and then the "function jump" takes place.

Similarly, to hold the function result, a temporary variable created by the caller (this creation is done automatically by C++) is initialized using the copy constructor, to the value returned by the function.

C++ automatically generates a default copy constructor for a class provided a copy constructor has not been explicitly specified. The default copy constructor generated for class *T* has the prototype

```
T(T&)
```

The sole parameter of a copy constructor must be a reference parameter and not a "value" parameter (the argument must be passed by reference and not by value). Otherwise, the result will be infinite recursion: initializing the copy constructor's parameter to the argument value will recursively invoke the copy constructor [Ellis & Stroustrup 1990].

Here are examples of declarations with initializations that invoke the copy constructor:

```
complex f = complex(1.0, 1.0);
complex g = e;
```

The copy constructor is also invoked (three times) in the following code:

```
complex a, b, c, d;
complex f(complex c, complex d);
...
c = f(a, b) + d;
```

The copy constructor is invoked once each for the two parameters of *f* and once to copy the result value returned by *f* to a temporary variable. Note the assignment operator is used for assigning a value to the variable *c*.

Except for the possible invocation of the copy constructor, the following declarations are equivalent:

```
complex p(1.0, 1.0);
complex q = complex(1.0, 1.0);
complex r = q;
```

The default copy constructors generated by C++ perform member-wise copy. In other words, members of the destination (receiving) class are initialized by copying values of the corresponding members of the source class. As in the case of the default assignment operator, depending upon the application, member-wise copy semantics of the default copy constructor semantics may or may not be satisfactory. In such cases, the programmer can explicitly define a copy constructor with the desired semantics. C++ does not generate the default copy constructor for a class for which a copy constructor has been explicitly specified.

6.3 INITIALIZATION VS. ASSIGNMENT

Initialization semantics are quite different from assignment semantics. The two operations may superficially look the same, since the same operator symbol = is used to denote both initialization and assignment. Initialization occurs whenever a new object is created, that is,

- in a definition,

- as a result of a call to the object allocator *new*,

- when an argument is passed to a function (initialization of the parameter), and

- when returning a value from a function (initialization of the result).

On the other hand, assignment occurs only when the assignment operator is executed during expression evaluation.

To illustrate the difference between initialization and assignment, consider class *date* which is defined as follows (file *date.h*):

```
     #include <iostream.h>
     class date {
         int m, d, y;
     public:
5        date() {}
         date(int month, int day, int year);
         date(const date& d1);
         friend int operator <(date& d1, date& d2);
         friend ostream& operator <<(ostream& os, date& d);
10   };
```

Class *date* has three *private* members of type *int* (line 2): *m*, *d*, and *y* which are used to store the month, day, and year respectively. There are three constructors (lines 5-7):

1. line 5: this constructor does not accept any arguments; its body, which is null, is give inline within the class specification itself. C++ will not automatically generate an argumentless constructor if the class explicitly defines one or more constructors. An argumentless constructor must be specified if variables are to be defined without explicitly specified initial values. Note that C++ will not automatically generate such a constructor if any constructor has been explicitly specified.

2. line 6: this constructor takes three arguments corresponding to the components of a date; and

3. line 7: this is a copy constructor that takes one argument, an object of type *date*, which is passed by reference.

Finally, class *date* has two *friend* operators (lines 8-10): one operator comparing dates, and one for printing dates.

Now here are the bodies of the *date* member functions (file *date.cpp*):

```
    #include "date.h"
    date::date(int month, int day, int year)
    {
        m = month; d = day; y = year;
5   }
    date::date(const date& d1)
    {
        *this = d1;
    }
10  int operator <(date& d1, date& d2)
    {
        if (d1.y < d2.y)
            return 1;
        if (d1.y == d2.y && d1.m < d2.m)
15          return 1;
        if (d1.y == d2.y && d1.m == d2.m && d1.d < d2.d)
            return 1;
        return 0;
    }
20  ostream& operator <<(ostream& os, date& d)
    {
        cout << d.m << "-" << d.d << "-" << d.y;
        return os;
    }
```

The *date* constructor (lines 2-5) assigns the values of its parameters to the corresponding components of the associated *date* object (line 4). The *date* copy constructor (lines 6-9) assigns the value of its *date* parameter to the associated *date* object (line 8). Remember that the special variable *this* points to the object associated with a member function call, and **this* refers to the object itself. The *date* assignment on line 8

```
    *this = d1;
```

could also have been written as the following set of component assignments:

```
    d = d1.d;
    m = d1.m;
    y = d1.y;
```

Next comes the definition of the *friend* operator < (lines 10-19), which compares two dates to determine whether or not the first date is "less than" the second date. If the year in the first date is less than the year in the second date, then < returns 1. Otherwise, if the years are equal, but the month in the first date is less than the month in the second date, then < returns 1. Otherwise, if the years and months are equal, but the day in the first date is less than the day in the second date, then < returns 1. Otherwise, the first date is not less than the second date and < returns 0.

Finally, the output operator << is defined to print *date* values (lines 20-24). The output operator returns a reference its first argument, the output stream, as its result. This allows operator << to be used multiple times within an expression to print multiple complex values, for example,

```
...
complex c, d;
...
cout << c << d;
```

Now let us look at the following code that defines *date* variables:

```
  #include "date.h"
      ...
  date d0, d1;
  date d2(5, 23, 91);
5 date d3 = date(5, 23, 91);
      ...
  d0 = date(0, 0, 0);
  d1 = d2;
```

The first definition defines *d0* and *d1* as variables of type *date* without specifying any initialization parameters. As a result, the argumentless constructor is invoked to initialize these two *date* objects. The second constructor, which takes three integer arguments, is invoked to initialize the *date* object defined by variable *d2*. The third declaration which declares *d3* as a variable of type *date* causes the following steps to be taken:

i.   First, the second constructor is invoked to construct a value of type *date* as specified on the right-hand side of the = symbol.

ii. Next, the copy constructor (the third constructor) is invoked to copy this value to *d3*. Note that the = symbol denotes initialization and not assignment, because it appears in a variable definition.

Now we come to the first assignment statement. First, a *date* value is constructed using the second *date* constructor. Then this *date* value is assigned to *d0* using the assignment operator. Finally, the assignment operator is used to assign the value of *d2* to *d1*.

7. DYNAMIC OBJECT CREATION AND DELETION

Class objects, like objects of other types, can also be dynamically created and deleted using the operators *new* and *delete*. Earlier we saw simple forms of these operators, which are used for allocating and deleting objects of non-class types.

7.1 OPERATOR NEW

Objects of any type T can be dynamically allocated by calling the *new* operator using one of the following forms of invocation:

```
new  T
new  T(constructor-arguments_opt)
```

As mentioned before, *new* returns a pointer of type T that refers to the newly allocated object. If for some reason *new* cannot allocate storage, then it returns the null pointer. If T is of a class type, then *new* invokes a constructor to initialize the object. The first form can only be used if T has an argumentless constructor, a constructor that can be invoked without arguments, or no constructors (in which case an argumentless constructor is generated by C++). If the second form is used, then a constructor with matching parameters is invoked for object initialization.

Here are examples illustrating dynamic object allocation:

```
     #include "complex.h"
     #include "stack.h"
     ...
     complex *c, *d;
5    stack *s;
     ...
     s = new stack(100);
     c = new complex(1.0, 2.0);
     d = new complex;
```

In the first two calls (lines 7-8), *new* invokes the appropriate constructors with the specified arguments. In the third call (line 9), *new* invokes the *complex* constructor without arguments; default parameter values are used.

Operator *new* always returns a pointer of the appropriate type. For example, in the above calls *new* returns pointers to objects of type *stack* (line 7) and *complex* (lines 8-9), respectively.

7.1.1 DYNAMIC ARRAY ALLOCATION When allocating an array of objects of a class type, say T, C++ requires that

1. the array bounds are specified and

2. T have an argumentless constructor or no constructors. C++ syntax does not permit the allocation of arrays of objects with class types that only have constructors that must be called with arguments.

To allocate an n-dimensional array of type T, *new* is used as

$$\text{new } T[size_1] \; ... \; [size_n]$$

Here is an example of dynamic array allocation:

```
ac = new complex[10];
```

7.2 OPERATOR DELETE

Dynamically created objects are deleted as

```
delete p;
```

where p is a pointer returned previously by *new*. Before the storage used for the object is deallocated, the *delete* operator calls the destructor, if any, for the object pointed to by p.

Dynamically allocated arrays are deleted using the *delete* operator as

```
delete [] p;
```

where p points to an array of objects, say of type T. *delete* calls the destructor $T::\tilde{\;}T$, if specified, once for each of the array elements being deallocated. If the array pointed to by p is deleted using the *delete* operator without the square brackets as

```
delete p;
```

then from a programmer's perspective the difference will be noticed only if a destructor has been specified for type T. The destructor will be called only for the first element of the array.

8. FRIENDS

A class can specify as its "friends" ordinary functions, member functions of other classes, and other classes. Friends of a class are trusted with access to the *private* (and *protected*) members of the class. Specifying a class as a friend is shorthand for specifying all member functions of the class as friends. A function or a class can be the friend of more than one class.

A *friend* prototype is similar to an ordinary (non-member) prototype except that it is preceded by the keyword *friend*. Friend function definitions and calls are like ordinary function definitions and calls. Unlike for a member function, the class object whose components are to be accessed in a *friend* function must be explicitly passed as an argument to the *friend* function. A *friend* class declaration consists simply of the keyword *friend* followed by the class name.

8.1 SYMMETRIC INTERFACE EXAMPLE

The operators defined for class *complex* all require the left operand to be a *complex* value; however, the right operand can be a *complex*, an integer, or a floating-point value. Consider the following expression where *a* is a *complex* variable and *i* is an integer variable:

```
a+i
```

This expression is interpreted as the expression

```
a.operator+(i)
```

The C++ compiler knows that + expects a *complex* value. It therefore applies the *complex* constructor to construct a *complex* value from *i* (that is, C++ converts *i* to a *complex* value):

```
a.operator+(complex(i))
```

Unfortunately, this scheme does not work when the operands of + are reversed. When translating the expression,

```
i+a
```

the C++ compiler, based on the type of the left operand (the integer variable *i*), assumes that the + operator is the integer addition operator and thus expects the second argument to be an integer expression. On finding the second argument to be a *complex* variable, the C++ compiler flags an error.

Friend operators can be used to provide a symmetric interface to users of a class. Either operand will be converted to the right type, if appropriate and if possible. As an example, consider the following definition of class *complex* that declares its operators as friends:

```
     class complex {
         float r, i;
     public:
         complex(float a = 0, float b = 0);
5        float real();
         float imag();
         friend complex operator +(complex a, complex b);
         friend complex operator -(complex a, complex b);
         friend complex operator *(complex a, complex b);
10       friend complex operator /(complex a, complex b);
         friend int operator ==(complex a, complex b);
     };
```

Now consider the following expression where *a* is a *complex* variable and *i* is an integer variable:

```
a+i
```

C++ interprets this expression as

```
a+complex(i)
```

Operator + is interpreted as the *complex* addition operator. Similarly, C++ interprets the expression

```
i+a
```

as

```
complex(i)+a
```

As in the previous case, C++ interprets + as the *complex* addition operator, which is exactly what we want. However, it does this only because + is specified as a *friend*.

Of course, if both arguments are integers, then C++ will interpret + as the integer addition operator.

Here are the bodies of the member functions and operators of this version of class *complex*:

```
    #include "complex2.h"
    complex::complex(float a, float b)
    {
        r = a; i = b;
5   }
    float complex::real()
    {
        return r;
    }
10  float complex::imag()
    {
        return i;
    }
    complex operator +(complex a, complex b)
15  {
        complex c;
        c.r = a.r+b.r; c.i = a.i+b.i;
        return c;
    }
20  complex operator -(complex a, complex b)
    {
        complex c;
        c.r = a.r-b.r; c.i = a.i-b.i;
        return c;
25  }
    complex operator *(complex a, complex b)
    {
        complex c;
        c.r = a.r*b.r-a.i*b.i;
30      c.i = a.r*b.i+a.i*b.r;
        return c;
    }
    complex operator /(complex a, complex b)
    {
35      complex c;
        float denom = b.r*b.r+b.i+b.i;
        c.r = (a.r*b.r+a.i*b.i)/denom;
        c.i = (a.i*b.r-a.r*b.i)/denom;
        return c;
40  }
    int operator ==(complex a, complex b)
    {
        return a.r == b.r && a.i == b.i;
    }
```

Note that the definitions of *friend* function bodies are similar to those of ordinary functions.

8.2 ADVANTAGES OF FRIENDS

The following is a list of the advantages of using *friend* functions:

1. An ordinary (non-friend) member function can access the *private* and *protected* components of only one class, but a *friend* function can access the *private* and *protected* components of multiple classes.

2. A *friend* function can bypass member functions and access *private* and *protected* class members directly thus avoiding the overhead associated with calling member functions.

3. Arguments of *friend* functions and operators are treated symmetrically. Automatic conversions are performed, as necessary, for all the arguments and operands, respectively.

4. *friend* function calls use the standard function call notation whereas member function calls use the "selected component" notation.

5. Without the friend facility, the only way of making the *private* members of a class accessible to a non-member function would be to make the components *public*. This would make the internal details of a class accessible to users who should not be aware of such details.

9. CONSTANT MEMBERS AND MEMBER FUNCTIONS

Objects that must not be updated after they have been initialized are specified as *const* (constant) objects. C++ guarantees that *const* objects will not be modified. Only *const* member functions can be applied to *const* objects. *const* member functions are specified by using the keyword *const* in their declarations. Within a *const* member function, the class object associated with its invocation cannot be modified. *const* member functions can, of course, be applied to non-*const* objects.

As an example of a *const* member function, consider the following class *point* (file *point.h*):

```
class point {
    float a, b;
public:
    ...
    void y() {...}
    void z() const {...}
};
```

5

Member function z is declared as a *const* member function; it can be applied to *const* objects of type *point*. Within a *const* member function, members of the associated object cannot be modified. This is ensured by making the type of the special variable *this* be "*const* pointer to a *const* object" instead of "*const* pointer to object."

Consider the following code:

```
point j;
const point k;
...
j.y(); j.z();
k.z();
```

Member functions y and z can both be called in conjunction with object j but only member function z can be called in conjunction with object k. The member function call

```
k.y();
```

will be flagged as an error by the C++ compiler because k is a *const* object and only *const* member functions can be applied to such objects.

10. PERFORMING TYPE CONVERSIONS (CASTS)

Explicit conversion of one type to another can be performed using either the functional notation or the cast notation. Suppose a value of type E can be converted to a value of type T because C++ predefines the conversion or because the conversion has been explicitly specified by the programmer. Then an expression e of type E can be converted to a value of type T using the functional notation

```
T(e)
```

or using the cast notation

```
(T) e
```

Here is code illustrating the above forms of type conversions:

```
float f, g;
int i, j;
...
i = (int) f;
j = int(g);
```

Casts are typically used for converting between the fundamental types, pointers and integers, between different pointer types, between different reference types, and as explicitly defined by the user within a class.

Explicit conversions to types that do not have a simple name must be performed using the cast operator. For example, a cast must be used to convert a pointer to class *T* to a pointer to class *E*.

Constructors that take one argument, in essence, convert the argument to the associated class type. Type conversions using constructors are specified in functional notation:

type (*expression*)

As illustrated earlier, the *complex* constructor could be used to convert *float* values to *complex* values. For example, the expression

```
complex(3.0)
```

converts 3.0 to the *complex* value (3.0, 0.0).

11. SPECIFYING TYPE CONVERSIONS (CASTS)

Constructors and conversion functions are used to specify how one type is converted to another. Facilities for specifying type conversions are important because they allow the programmer

1. to perform conversions between logically related types using the notation used for specifying conversions between the predefined types, and

2. tell C++ how to convert a value of one type to another, just as C++ can convert between the predefined types.

The latter allows the programmer to define fewer routines. Suppose, for example, that function *max* takes three arguments of type *T*, i.e., it has the prototype

```
T max(T, T, T);
```

and that it should be possible to call *max* with either *float* arguments or with arguments of type *T*. Without a type conversion from *float* to *T*, eight *max* functions with the following prototypes will have to be defined:

```
T max(T, T, T);
T max(T, T, float);
T max(T, float, T);
T max(T, float, float);
T max(float, T, T);
T max(float, T, float);
T max(float, float, T);
T max(float, float, float);
```

Both constructors and type conversion functions are associated with a class. Constructors are used for converting values to values of the class with which they are associated. Conversion functions are used for converting values of the class with which they are associated to values of other types. Unlike constructors, conversion functions can be used

1. to define conversions from a class to the predefined types,

2. to define conversions from one class (source) to another class (destination) without modifying the source class, and

3. in both functional and cast notation to perform conversions.

11.1 CONSTRUCTORS

Here are two examples of constructors that can be used for type conversion:

```
     class complex {
         ...
     public:
         complex(float a);
 5       ...
     };
     class vector {
         ...
     public:
10       vector(int i);
         ...
     };
```

Constructor *complex* is invoked to construct a *float* value to a *complex* value and constructor *vector* is invoked to convert an *int* value to a *vector* value.

11.2 CONVERSION FUNCTIONS (OPERATORS)

A conversion function of class *ST* is a parameterless member function declared using the keyword *operator*, as illustrated below:

```
class ST {
    ...
public:
    ...
    operator DT();
    ...
};
```

DT is a type name. This conversion function converts values of the source type *ST* to the destination type *DT*. The destination type can be the name of any type, but it must be a single identifier. This identifier can denote one of the predefined types or it can be an identifier that is associated with a "complex" type such as an array type defined by using the *typedef* statement.

Here is code showing the conversion of *ST* values to *DT* values:

```
ST s;
DT d;
...
d = DT(s);
d = (DT) s;
d = s;  //conversion function is implicitly invoked
```

Conversion functions cannot have parameters. Consequently, conversion functions cannot be overloaded.

Class *polar* illustrates the use of both constructors and conversion functions for type conversion. The *complex* type can be used to store *x* and *y* coordinate pairs representing points on the Cartesian plane. An alternative representation, implemented by class *polar*, is to store the radius of a point from the origin and the angle formed by the radial line through the point with the x-axis.

To facilitate the free use of both *polar* and *complex* representations of points, class *polar* contains a constructor to convert *complex* values to *polar* values and a conversion function to perform the reverse conversion:

```
     #include "math.h"
     #include "complex.h"
     class polar {
         float rad, theta;
 5   public:
         polar(float r, float t) { rad=r; theta=t; }
         polar(complex c);
         float radius() { return rad; }
         float angle() { return theta; }
10       ...
         operator complex();
     };
     ...
     polar::polar(complex c)
15   {
         float x = c.real();
         float y = c.imag();
         rad = sqrt(x*x + y*y);
         theta = atan(x/y);
20   }
     polar::operator complex()
     {
         float x, y;
         x = rad * cos(theta);
25       y = rad * sin(theta);
         return complex(x, y);
     }
```

We are particularly interested in

1. the constructor that can take a *complex* value and convert it to a *polar* value (lines 7, 14-20) and

2. the conversion function that can convert a *polar* value to a *complex* value (lines 11, 21-27).

A *complex* value is converted to a *polar* value by computing the radius from the origin (line 18) and the angle made by the radial line through this point with respect to the x-axis (line 19). What is important is not the mathematics, but the mechanism for specifying the conversion (that is the constructor). The "mathematical reverse" is performed to convert a *polar* value to a *complex* value (lines 24-25).

The *polar* constructor (as is the case with all constructors) does not return any value: it simply initializes the components of the associated object to the right values. The conversion function on the other hand must return the converted value (line 26).

Here is code illustrating the implicit and the explicit use of user-defined conversions:

```
polar p(1.0, 1.0);
complex c;
...
//implicit conversions
    p = c;
    ...
    c = p;
    ...
//explicit conversions
    c = (complex) p;
    ...
    p =  polar(c);
    ...
    c = complex(p);
```

12. INLINE FUNCTIONS

Inline functions are functions whose calls are replaced by the corresponding function bodies but only after the parameters have been replaced by the corresponding arguments. Inline functions can speed up program execution because the code for jumping to and back from the function body, and the code for saving and restoring registers, is not needed. Execution speedup is minimal except in cases of

1. very small functions, such as those with minimal bodies consisting of one or two simple expressions; execution time of such functions should be of the same order of magnitude as the time it takes to execute the function call and the return, and

2. functions that are called frequently, for example, from within a "tight" loop.

However, because function calls are replaced by the corresponding function bodies, inline functions can result in a significant increase in object code size.

Consider, as an example, the following modified definition of function *swap* (discussed in Chapter 6), which specifies *swap* as an *inline* function (file *swapiri.h*):

```
inline void swapir(int& a, int& b)
{
    int tmp = a;
    a = b;
    b = tmp;
}
```

It is important to note that *inline* expansion will be performed only if the body of the *inline* function is available in the file containing the call to be expanded. The *inline* definition of *swapir* has therefore been placed in a header file so that source files can include it. If the body of an *inline* function will be in the file containing the call, but will appear after the call, then a prototype of the *inline* function must be given, for example,

```
inline void swapir(int& a, int& b);
```

If a function has been specified as an *inline* function in its prototype, then it is not necessary to use the *inline* qualifier again in the function definition; however, using the *inline* qualifier will do no harm.

Finally, replacement of an *inline* function call by the corresponding function body is performed only the body of the *inline* is encountered before the call.

13. FORWARD (INCOMPLETE) CLASS DECLARATIONS

C++ requires that all entities be declared or defined before they are referenced. Defining a class before it is referenced is not possible when two classes reference each other or a set of classes form a "reference cycle." Consider, as an example, two classes *doctor* and *patient* that reference each other. Here is a skeleton of the specification of *doctor*:

```
class doctor {
    patient *p;
    ...
public:
    ...
};
```

p points to a dynamically allocated array of *patient*s. However, using class *patient* before it is declared is an error. This problem can be solved by declaring class *patient* before class *doctor*. However, the solution will not work if class *patient* also contains a reference to the class *doctor*.

```
class patient {
    doctor *d;
    ...
public:
    ...
};
class doctor {
    patient *p;
    ...
public:
    ...
};
```

This "recursive reference cycle" resulting from classes that refer to each other can only be "broken" by using "forward" ("incomplete") class declarations which have the form

```
class name;
```

The above two classes can now be declared as

```
class doctor;
class patient { doctor *d; ... public: ... };
class doctor { patient *p; ... public: ... };
```

Classes for which only a forward declaration is given can be used only for defining pointers and references. Complete class definitions are not required for declaring pointers and references because C++ allocates a fixed amount of storage for such variables regardless of their type.

Incomplete types can also be used to specify arbitrary parameter and result types in function prototypes and in external variable declarations, but these functions and variables cannot be used until after the complete type definition has been given.

14. LISTS: A FINAL EXAMPLE

In Chapter 7, Section 3.7, we implemented lists using C++ structures. Now we will implement lists by using objects of the class type *list* (file *list.h*):

```
   class list {
       int x;
       list *next;
   public:
5      list();
       ~list();
       void add(int a);
       void print();
   };
```

Class *list* has two *private* members, *x* and *next*. Note that *next* is a pointer to an object of type *list*, the type being declared. There are four public members: a constructor (line 5), a destructor (line 6), and two member functions (lines 7 and 8).

The member functions in the above list are implemented as (file *list.cpp*):

```
   #include <stdlib.h> //get NULL
   #include <iostream.h>
   #include "list.h"
   list::list()
5  {
       next = NULL;
   }
   list::~list()
   {
10     if (next)
           delete next;
   }
   void list::add(int a)
   {
15     list *p = new list;
       p->x = a;
       p->next = next;
       next = p;
   }
20 void list::print()
   {
       for (list *p = next; p != NULL; p = p->next)
           cout << p->x << endl;
   }
```

The constructor *list* (lines 4-7) just initializes the *next* pointer to the null pointer. The destructor determines whether or not the object being deleted points to another *list* object. If the answer is yes, then that object is deleted first, before the current object is deleted (lines 10-11). Thus a list is deleted recursively.

Here is code illustrating the use of class *list*:

```
   #include "list.h"
   int main()
   {
       list q;
5      q.add(3);
       q.add(-5);
       q.add(7);
       q.add(2);
       q.print();
10 }
```

The constructor is called automatically to initialize the list variable *q*. And the destructor is called to delete the list objects (and thus free the storage used by them) at the end of function *main*. In this example, deleting the objects is not important because the objects are deleted at the end of the program. However, in cases where the list is freed in the middle of the program, say at the end of a function other than *main*, then the freed storage can be reused in the rest of the program.

Incidentally, executing the above program produces the following output:

```
2
7
-5
3
```

15. EXERCISES

1. List the different kinds of members a C++ class can have and explain their use.

2. What is the advantage of specifying *private* members? Would it not be simpler to specify all members as *public* members?

3. What constructors and operators are generated automatically for each class? When are they not generated?

4. Explain the difference between specifying parameters for a member function and for an ordinary function?

5. What symbols can used as the names of operators?

6. Explain the differences between constructors and destructors?

7. List the possible situations in which a constructor is invoked?

8. Can a class have more than one constructor? If yes, then when are the constructors called and how does C++ determine which constructor to

call?

9. State the restriction C++ imposes on the definition of arrays of class types.

10. Extend the list program as follows:

   a. Modify class *list* to add the member function *in* with the prototype

   ```
   void in(int a);
   ```

   in checks to see whether or not *a* is the list. If *a* is in the list, then it returns one; otherwise, it returns zero.

   b. Modify the *main* program to read a list of numbers from a data file and put them in a list. Accept numbers interactively from the user and inform the user whether or not the number is in the list. See the distance example in Chapter 7, Section 1.1 on how to read input simultaneously from a file and the terminal.

Chapter 9
INHERITANCE

"Inheritance" is used in C++ to "derive" new types from existing classes. The derived class inherits the members of the "base" classes, that is, the classes it is derived from (based upon). The most important advantage of deriving a class from existing classes instead of defining the class from "scratch" is that it lets C++ know that the classes are related.

The derived class inherits the members of the base class; it can also define more members. Unless a base class member is redefined, a base class member can be referenced just like a member of in the derived class. In case of ambiguity, a base class member can be referenced by using the "scope resolution" operator :: to explicitly qualify the member name with the name of the base class.

A derived class may be viewed as a specialization of its base class. Inheritance allows users to develop customized classes by allowing new attributes to be added to existing classes without requiring changes to the original classes. Inheritance thus supports both code reuse and tracks the relationship between derived and base classes.

As an example of inheritance, suppose we have defined a class *vehicle* which contains data members to store information common to all vehicles. The common members store information such as the name and address of the owner, the manufacturer, and the year and date of manufacture. To represent the different types of vehicles, new classes such as *car* and *van* are derived using class *vehicle* as the base class. Cars and vans can be treated as vehicles when appropriate. The same code can be used to manipulate cars and vans provided the members specific to the *car* and *van* classes are not referenced.

Before discussing inheritance in detail, I will show you a specific example of inheritance. Consider an application that needs a type to store both the time (hour and minute) and the date a particular transaction took place. In Chapter 8 we defined class *date* as follows:

```
     #include <iostream.h>
     class date {
         int m, d, y;
     public:
 5       date() {}
         date(int month, int day, int year);
         date(const date& d1);
         friend int operator <(date& d1, date& d2);
         friend ostream& operator <<(ostream& os, date& d);
10   };
```

Class *date* stores the date but not the time. We can define a class that stores both the time and the date in one of several ways:

1. Modify class *date* to include time; this has the bad side effect of affecting programs that are already using class *date*. Class *date* will now store more information than required by some programs and use more storage for each object. Class *date* must be written to allow the time values to be unspecified (say by using default parameter values). Also, executable programs will become inconsistent with respect to the modified definition of *date* and must be recompiled.

2. Define a new class *time* that can be used along with class *date* to store both the time and date. This is inelegant, because now the programmer must manipulate two objects instead of one.

3. Use inheritance to "refine" or "specialize" class *date* to define a new class *timedate*, which provides facilities for storing both date and time. This technique allows reuse of existing code, class *date*, without modifying class *date*.

Class *timedate* is specified as (file *timedate.h*)

```
     #include "date.h"
     class timedate: public date {
         int hr, min, sec;
     public:
 5       timedate() {};
         timedate(int month, int day, int year,
                  int hour, int minute, int second);
         friend int operator <(timedate& t1, timedate& t2);
         friend ostream& operator <<(ostream& os,timedate& t);
10   };
```

Line 2 of class *timedate* specifies that it is derived from or based upon class *date*. Specifying the base class *date* as *public* means that all the *public* members of class *date* will in effect become *public* members of class *timedate*.

Class *timedate* defines two constructors (line 5 and 6). The body of the first constructor, which does not take any arguments, has a null body specified in the class specification itself. As in the case of class *date*, an argumentless constructor must be explicitly specified; C++ does not generate an argumentless constructor if any constructor is explicitly specified. An argumentless constructor must be defined to allow definition of class objects without requiring the specification of initial values.

Because class *timedate*, unlike class *date*, does not explicitly define a copy constructor, C++ will automatically generate one. A copy constructor was explicitly defined for class *date* for pedagogical reasons. Finally, *timedate* defines the less than and output operators (lines 8-9).

Here are the bodies of the member functions of class *timedate* (file *timedate.cpp*):

```
      #include "timedate.h"
      timedate::timedate(int month, int day, int year,
                         int hour, int minute, int second):
                         date(month, day, year)
 5    {
          hr = hour; min = minute; sec = second;
      }
      int operator <(timedate& t1, timedate& t2)
      {
10        if (date(t1) < date(t2))
              return 1;
          else if (date(t2) < date(t1))
              return 0;
          if (t1.hr < t2.hr)
15            return 1;
          if (t1.hr == t2.hr && t1.min < t2.min)
              return 1;
          if (t1.hr==t2.hr && t1.min==t2.min && t1.sec<t2.sec)
              return 1;
20        return 0;
      }
      ostream& operator <<(ostream& os, timedate& t)
      {
          cout << date(t) << " ";
25        cout << t.hr << ":" << t.min << ":" << t.sec << endl;
          return os;
      }
```

The body of the first constructor was specified within the specification of *timedate* itself. The body of the second constructor, shown above (lines 2-7), contains a call to the constructor of the base class *date* (line 4), which initializes the base class part of a *timedate* object. Such a constructor call, called an "initializer", is used to initialize the base class component of a derived class. If the derived class constructor does not contain an initializer calling a base class constructor, then C++ will automatically generate a call to the argumentless constructor of the base class. The base class must, in such a case, have an argumentless constructor, either generated by C++ or explicitly specified by the programmer. Otherwise, C++ will flag an error.

The "less than" operator < of class *timedate* (lines 8-21) compares two *timedate* objects by first comparing their *date* base class components (lines 10-11) and then comparing the data members added by class *timedate* (lines 12-20). Converting the two *timedate* objects to *date* objects and then comparing them with than operator < invokes the less than operator for class *date*. Note that any derived class object can be converted to a base class object as

base-class (*derived-class-object*)

The output operator << for class *timedate* (lines 22-27), prints a *timedate* object by first printing its *date* object (line 24), and then printing the time components.

1. DERIVED CLASS SPECIFICATION

The specification of a derived class has the form

`class` *derived*: *private-or-public*$_{opt}$ *base* {
    ...
`};`

Class *derived* is derived from class *base*. *base* is called the "direct" base class of *derived*. If a class, say *B*, is the direct or the indirect base class of class *base*, then *B* becomes the "indirect" base class of *derived*.

A derived class object consists of the components of the base class plus its members. The derived class inherits from the base class all data members and all function members except constructors, destructors, and the assignment operator. Base class member functions specified as *virtual* functions can be overridden in the derived class.

Access to the *public* and the "protected" members of the base class by users of the derived class is determined by whether the base class is specified as a *public* base class or as a *private* base class. See Section 1.1 for more details.

C++ allocates storage for a derived class object by first allocating storage for its base class parts and then allocating storage for the data members explicitly specified in the derived class itself.

A derived class object is initialized by

1. initializing its base class component, which is done by calling the base class constructor;
2. calling constructors to initialize members of class types;
3. executing the body of the derived class constructor body.

(These actions are performed by C++; the last two items also apply to the initialization of non-derived class objects).

The body of a derived class constructor must therefore contain, in its "initializer" list, calls to the base class constructor and to the constructors of the derived class members. Argumentless base class and member constructor calls can be omitted.

1.1 ACCESS TO THE BASE CLASS MEMBERS

Besides *public* and *private* members, class members can be specified to be *protected* using the keyword *protected* (much like *public* members are declared using the keyword *public*). *protected* members behave as *private* members for ordinary class users, but they can behave as *public* members in the member functions of the classes derived from the class containing them.

public and *protected* members of a *public* base class become the *public* and *protected* members of the derived class. And the *public* and *protected* members of a *private* base class become the *private* members of the derived class.

A derived class cannot directly access the *private* components of a base class.

1.2 CONVERSIONS BETWEEN DERIVED AND BASE CLASSES

C++ automatically performs conversions between pointers (references) to base class objects and pointers (references) to derived class objects under the following conditions:

1. A derived class pointer is implicitly converted to a *public* base class pointer. Except for *virtual* functions, only base class members can be accessed using a base class pointer that refers to a derived class object. If the base class has *virtual* member function, say *f*, then the member function *f* invoked via a base class pointer is the derived class function *f* with an identical signature, provided there is such a function. Otherwise, if the derived class does not have such a function, then the base class function is invoked.

2. A reference to a derived class is implicitly converted to a reference to its *public* base class. Using a base class reference that refers to a derived class object, the members of the base and derived classes accessed are as described for pointers in (1).

1.3 ASSIGNMENT BETWEEN DERIVED AND BASE CLASS OBJECTS

An object of a derived class, say class *D*, can be assigned to an object of its base class, say *B*. Unless the assignment operator is explicitly defined in the derived class *D*, the expected thing happens: data members of class *D* that correspond to those of the base class *B* are copied from the *D* object to the *B* object. However, the reverse assignment is not allowed, that is, a base class object cannot be assigned to a derived class object, because the derived class object will in general have data members that are not in the base class and it will not be possible to assign values to these members.

2. MULTIPLE INHERITANCE

C++ supports "multiple inheritance" by allowing a class to be derived from multiple base classes, as shown below:

class *derived*: *private-or-public*$_{opt}$ *base*$_1$, ..., *private-or-public*$_{opt}$ *base*$_n${
    ...
};

Here is an example of multiple inheritance:

```
#include "employee.h"
#include "children.h"
class divorced_employee:public employee,public children{
public:
    date divorce;
    virtual void print(ostream& os);
    virtual void print_status(ostream& os);
};
```

Class *divorced_employee* is derived from classes *employee* and *children*. All members explicitly specified in class *divorced_employee* are *public* members.

3. ORDER OF CONSTRUCTOR / DESTRUCTOR CALLS

Suppose a class, say *T*,

1. contains members that are class objects, and

2. is derived from one or more base classes.

When an object of class *T* is created,

1. constructors for the base classes are called first,

2. constructors for the members that are class objects are called next, and

3. finally the body of the constructor for the class *T* is executed.

Constructors for *virtual* base classes, if any, are invoked before those for the non-*virtual* base classes. Subject to this rule, base class constructors are invoked in the order the base classes are listed in the derived class definition. Member initialization, which occurs next, follows the order in which the members are listed in the class definition.

Destructors are invoked in reverse of the order in which the constructors are invoked. When an object of a class, say T, is deleted or deallocated,

1. the body of the destructor for class T is first executed, then

2. the destructors for the members that are class objects are called, and finally

3. the destructors of the base classes are called.

The destructors for class objects and the base classes are called in the reverse of the order in which they are declared and listed, respectively, in the class specification.

4. ASSIGNMENT & CONSTRUCTORS FOR DERIVED CLASSES

For each class, C++ automatically generates an assignment operator and an argumentless constructor, provided no assignment operator and constructor, respectively, have been explicitly specified. A copy constructor is also automatically generated if one has not been explicitly specified.

4.1 ASSIGNMENT OPERATOR

C++ generates a default assignment operator for every class, provided an assignment operator has not been explicitly specified. The default assignment operator performs member-wise assignment. The default assignment operator class first calls the base class assignment operators to perform the assignment of the base class parts of the derived class, and then performs the assignment for the data members added by the derived class.

If an assignment operator has been explicitly specified for a derived class, then the semantics of assignment become the responsibility of the programmer. Simply taking care of the assignment for the additional members specified in the derived class is not enough. In particular, it is the programmer's responsibility to ensure that the base class parts of the derived class are assigned appropriately.

The prototype of assignment operator for a class, say T, looks like

```
T& operator=(const T& t);
```

As an example of an explicitly specified assignment operator, suppose that an assignment operator has been explicitly defined for class *timedate*, which has class *date* as its *public* base class. First, class *timedate* will have to be modified to include the prototype of the assignment operator:

```
timedate& operator=(const timedate& t);
```

This assignment operator must ensure that the *date* components of *timedate* objects are assigned properly, as shown below:

```
timedate& timedate::operator=(const timedate& t)
{
    (date&)(*this) = t;
    hr = t.hr; min = t.min; sec = t.sec;
    return *this;
}
```

Expression

```
*this
```

specifies the left operand of the assignment operator (special variable *this* points to the object).

Expression

```
(date&)(*this)
```

refers to the *date* part of the left operand.

The assignment statement

```
(date&)(*this) = t;
```

assigns the base class part of parameter *t* (right operand) to the base class part of the left operand.

Finally, the statement

```
return *this;
```

returns the left operand of the assignment operator as the result of the assignment operator.

4.2 DEFAULT (ARGUMENTLESS) CONSTRUCTOR

If no constructor is explicitly specified for a class, say *T*, then C++ automatically generates a default argumentless constructor with the prototype

```
T();
```

If *T* is a derived class, then the default constructor will call the argumentless constructors of the base classes. The base classes must have such constructors; otherwise, C++ will flag an error.

4.3 COPY CONSTRUCTOR

C++ automatically generates a copy constructor for a class if one has not been explicitly specified. The copy constructor for a derived class calls the base class copy constructors to copy the base class portions of a derived class object, and then copies the members specified in the derived class itself. If a copy constructor has been explicitly specified for a derived class, then it is the programmer's responsibility to ensure that the base class components of the derived class are also copied by invoking the base class copy constructors.

5. VIRTUAL FUNCTIONS

Pointers to derived class objects can be stored in base class pointer variables. Consider, as an example, an array whose elements are of type "pointer to class *shape*." Such a pointer can refer to objects of class *shape* or of classes derived from class *shape*. Each class derived from *shape* defines its own version of the function *area* to compute the surface area of an object. For each array element, it should be possible to invoke the appropriate *area* function even though the element type is a *shape* pointer. C++ will call the right *area* function provided *area* is declared as a "virtual" function in class *shape*. The actual *area* function invoked will depend upon the type of the object referenced by the array element; it will not be the *area* function associated with class *shape*.

"Virtual" member functions are similar to ordinary member functions with one important difference: *virtual* function calls are bound "dynamically" at run time (instead of being bound at compile time) to the function that will be called. When a *virtual* function is invoked through a pointer (reference) to an object, the function invoked depends upon the type of the object referenced by the pointer (reference). It is *not* automatically the function associated with the class of the object referenced by the pointer (reference).

The "dynamic" binding of *virtual* function calls and the ability of pointers (references) to a specific class to refer to objects of classes derived from this class, facilitates the construction of heterogeneous data structures. Examples of heterogeneous data structures are arrays and lists whose elements point to objects of different classes.

Typically, *virtual* functions are redefined in the derived classes, but this is not necessary. In such a case, the base class *virtual* function will be invoked even if the call is made in association with a derived class object.

6. EXAMPLES

In this section, we will discuss two examples: the first illustrates the need for a *virtual* destructor and the second illustrates multiple inheritance and virtual functions.

6.1 VIRTUAL DESTRUCTOR

Member functions that may be replaced in derived classes should be declared as *virtual* functions in the base class. In fact, even destructors should be declared as *virtual* member functions [Apple 1990]. As an example, consider the classes *vehicle* and *truck* defined as follows:

```
class vehicle {
    ...
public:
    ...
    ~vehicle();
};

class truck : public {
    ...
public:
    ...
    ~truck();
};
```

Now consider the following code:

```
vehicle *pv;
...
pv = new truck;
...
delete pv;
```

The destructor called by *delete* will be

```
vehicle::~vehicle
```

and not the destructor

```
truck::~truck
```

which is the one that should be called. Declaring the destructors (at least *~vehicle*) as *virtual* solves the problem.

6.2 PERSONNEL DATA

Consider a program for storing and manipulating the personnel data belonging to a company. The following data is to be stored for each employee:

1. first name,
2. middle initial,
3. last name,
4. sex,
5. date of birth,
6. marital status,
7. spouse name and date of marriage for married employees,
8. date of divorce for divorced employees,
9. number of children, and
10. first names of the children.

Names will be at most 31 characters long and the maximum number of children planned for is 16.

We will use inheritance to derive classes corresponding to the marital and family status of the employees. Specifically, using two base classes *employee* and *children*, and multiple inheritance, the following three new classes will be derived: *married_employee*, *divorced_employee*, and *single_parent_employee*. Definitions of these classes are given below. To focus on inheritance and *virtual* functions, all members of these classes have been made *public* by using the keyword *struct* to specify the classes. Otherwise, additional member functions would have to be defined to access and manipulate the employee data.

First, here is the definition of class *employee* (file *employee.h*):

```
     #include <iostream.h>
     #include "lmts.h"
     #include "date.h"
     struct employee {
 5       char first[MAX_NAME], mi, last[MAX_NAME];
         date birth;
         char sex;
         virtual void print(ostream& os);
         virtual void print_status(ostream& os);
10   };
```

File *employee.h* includes file *lmts.h* (line 2), which contains the following constant definitions:

```
#define MAX_NAME 32
#define MAX_CHILD 16
```

#define statements are used to give symbolic names to strings of characters. In this case, they define the identifiers *MAX_NAME MAX_CHILD* as the strings 32 and 16, respectively.

File *employee.h* also includes file *date.h*, which contains the specification of class *date* (see the beginning of this chapter). Class *employee* is defined (lines 4-10) using the keyword *struct* (line 4) which means that all its members will be *public* members by default. *employee* has five data members (lines 5-7) and two *virtual* member functions, *print* and *print_status* (lines 8-9). Function *print* prints all employee information except the marital status, which is printed by *print_status*. Functions *print* and *print_status* are defined as *virtual* functions to allow classes derived from *employee* to supply their own alternative versions of these functions.

Here are the bodies of the member functions *print* and *print_status* of class *employee* (file *employee.cpp*):

```
#include "employee.h"
void employee::print(ostream& os)
{
    os << "Employee: " << first << " ";
    if (mi)
        os << mi << ". ";
    os << last << endl;
    os << "Birthdate: " << birth;

    if (sex == 'f' || sex == 'F')
        os << "Sex: " << "Female" << endl;
    else
        os << "Sex: " << "Male" << endl;
    print_status(os);
}
void employee::print_status(ostream& os)
{
    os << "Status: Single" << endl;
}
```

Class *children* is used for storing information about children (file *children.h*):

```
#include <iostream.h>
#include "lmts.h"
class children {
public:
    char nchild;
    char child[MAX_CHILD][MAX_NAME];
    void print(ostream& os);
};
```

Here is the body of the *print* function of class *children* that prints information about the children (file *children.cpp*):

```
    #include "children.h"
    void children::print(ostream& os)
    {
        for (int j = 0; j < nchild; j++)
5           os << "Child " << j+1 << ": " << child[j] << endl;
    }
```

Class *married* is derived from two base classes: *employee* and *children*. Here is its specification (file *married.h*):

```
    #include "employee.h"
    #include "children.h"
    class married_employee:public employee,public children {
    public:
5       char spouse[MAX_NAME];
        date marriage;
        virtual void print(ostream& os);
        virtual void print_status(ostream& os);
    };
```

Besides specifying additional data members, *married_employee* defines its own versions of the *print* and *print_status* functions (file *married.cpp*):

```
    #include "married.h"
    void married_employee::print(ostream& os)
    {
        employee::print(os);
5       children::print(os);
    }
    void married_employee::print_status(ostream& os)
    {
        os << "Status: Married, " << marriage << ". ";
10      if (sex == 'f' || sex == 'F')
            os << "Husband's name " << spouse << endl;
        else
            os << "Wife's name " << spouse << endl;
    }
```

Class *married_employee* inherits all the members of its base classes. It prints information about the employee and the employee's children by calling the *print* functions belonging to its base classes. These function are called by explicitly specifying the base classes (lines 4-5). Had references to *print* not been qualified by the base class names, then referencing *print* will (recursively) invoke member function *print* of class *married_employee*.

Class *divorced_employee*, like class *married_employee*, is derived from the classes *employee* and *children*. Here is its specification (file *divorced.h*):

```
#include "employee.h"
#include "children.h"
class divorced_employee:public employee,public children{
public:
    date divorce;
    virtual void print(ostream& os);
    virtual void print_status(ostream& os);
};
```

Here are the bodies of the *print* member functions of class *divorced_employee* (file *divorced.cpp*):

```
#include "divorced.h"
void divorced_employee::print(ostream& os)
{
    employee::print(os);
    children::print(os);
}
void divorced_employee::print_status(ostream& os)
{
    os << "Status: Divorced, " << divorce << endl;
}
```

Class *single_parent_employee* is specified as (file *single.h*):

```
#include "employee.h"
#include "children.h"
class single_parent_employee:
        public employee, public children {
public:
    virtual void print(ostream& os);
};
```

Finally, here is the definition of the member function *print* of class *single_parent_employee* (file *single.cpp*):

```
#include "single.h"
void single_parent_employee::print(ostream& os)
{
    employee::print(os);
    children::print(os);
}
```

Because class *single_parent_employee* does not explicitly redefine the member function *print_status* of the base class *employee*, the base class function is used to print the marital status of a *single_parent_employee*.

Consider the following code:

```
employee *e;
divorced_employee *d;
int kind;
...
if (kind)
    e = d;
...
e->print(cout);
...
```

Since *print* is a *virtual* function, the function actually invoked by the call

```
e->print(cout);
```

will be either *employee*::*print* or *divorced_employee*::*print* depending upon whether *e* refers to an *employee* object or to a *divorced_employee* object. Note that for this example to work, member function *divorced_employee*::*print* does not have to be declared *virtual*. Declaring it as *virtual* would be of value to classes derived from *divorced_employee*.

In C++, all work is done in class definitions; each class is associated with the appropriate functions. This simplifies the task of the application writer. For example, writing a function to print information about each of the *employee* objects referenced by the elements of an array of *employee* pointers is now a trivial exercise:

```
     #include "employee.h"
     #include <iostream.h>
     void printemp(employee *e[], int n, ostream& os)
     {
 5       int i;
         for (i=0; i<n; i++)
              e[i]->print(os);
     }
```

The *print* function invoked by C++ depends upon whether an element of *e* points to an object of the base class *employee* or to an object of one of the derived classes *married_employee*, *divorced_employee*, or *single_parent_employee*.

Array *e* (or the argument corresponding to it) is a heterogeneous array since its elements may point to an object of class *employee* or to one of the classes derived from *employee*, such as *part_time_employee* and *single_parent_employee*.

7. EXERCISES

1. Give three examples illustrating multiple inheritance.

2. a. Can a derived class object be assigned to a base class object and vice versa? Explain your answer.

    b. Can a pointer to a derived class be assigned to a pointer to its base class and vice versa? Explain your answer.

Chapter 10
OVERLOADING

Functions (and operators) can be "overloaded" in C++; that is, the same identifier (or operator symbol) can be used to denote multiple functions (or operators). The overloading capability of C++ makes C++ more attractive as an extensible programming language because it allows the use of identifiers and operator symbols that are natural to the application. For example, the standard operator symbols can be used as *complex* arithmetic operators.

Overloaded functions (operators) must have different "signatures." A *signature* consists of the function name (operator symbol) and an ordered list of the parameter types. Two signatures are different if the function names (operator symbols) are different or if the corresponding parameter types do not match.

When comparing signatures, note the following type equivalences:

1. a *typedef* type name matches its definition,
2. an array type with a bound matches one without a bound, and
3. an array type matches a pointer type provided the array elements and the object referenced by the pointer are of the same type.

As a consequence of the above type equivalences, the following function pairs have identical signatures as determined by examining their definitions or prototypes:

```
void f(int a[]) { ... }
void f(int *a) { ... }

void g(int a[]) { ... }
void g(int a[10]) { ... }

void h(int a[10]);
void h(int a[110]);
```

C++ does not consider the function (operator) result type to be part of the signature. Consequently, two functions with identical signatures, but with different result types are not allowed.

Some C++ types are considered to be equivalent because the same set of values can be used to initialize them:

type	equivalent type

`const T`
`T&`
`const T&`
	`T`

`T *const`	`T *`
`T`	`const T`

As an example illustrating the above type equivalences, suppose that function *f* is been overloaded as follows:

```
int f(const T);
int f(T);
```

Then the following call to *f*

```
T t;
...
f(t);
```

is flagged as ambiguous because C++ cannot decide which of the two *f* functions is being called. According to the above table, an object of type *T* can be used in place of an object of type *const T* and vice versa.

Consider, as another example, the following overloaded prototypes associated with identifier *sort*:

```
void sort(int a[], int n);
```

Each of the *sort* function prototypes has a unique signature. Based on the types of arguments supplied in a *sort* function call, C++ automatically determines which definition of *sort* is to be called. Here is some code that contains calls to function *sort*:

```
#include "sort.h"
        ...
int x[MAX];
float y[MAX];
char *z[MAX];
int nx, ny, nz;
...
sort(x, nx);
sort(y, ny);
sort(z, nz);
```

1. OPERATOR OVERLOADING

Overloading operators is similar to overloading functions. As an example of operator overloading, consider type *complex* (defined earlier) in which the operators +, −, *, /, and == are overloaded:

```
     class complex {
          float r, i;
     public:
          complex(float a = 0, float b = 0);
 5        float real();
          float imag();
          complex operator +(complex a);
          complex operator -(complex a);
          complex operator *(complex a);
10        complex operator /(complex a);
          int operator ==(complex a);
     };
```

These operators are overloaded to operate on *complex* objects. Note that in an operator prototype or an operator definition, the operator symbol is preceded by keyword *operator*.

Some comments about operator overloading:

1. Only the predefined operators can be overloaded.

2. Operators can be overloaded as ordinary functions, *friend* functions, and member functions. Operators not overloaded as member functions *must* have an operand of a class type.

3. All operators except the following operators can be overloaded:

    . .* :: ?:

4. The symbols # and ## cannot be overloaded.

5. Associativity, precedence, and the number of operands associated with the predefined operators cannot be changed by overloading them.

6. An operator defined as a member has one less parameter than if it were defined as a *friend* (as in case of member functions) or as an ordinary function. This is because the first parameter of the member operator is the object associated with its invocation and is passed as an implicit argument to the operator.

7. An operator defined as a member function can be invoked using the member function notation or using the ordinary prefix, infix, or suffix notations as appropriate. As an example, consider class *T* which overloads the binary plus operator:

```
class T {
    ...
public:
    ...
    T operator+(T);
    ...
};
```

Assuming *a* and *b* are variables of type *T*, then operator $T::operator+$, can be invoked as

```
a.operator+(b)
```

or as

```
a+b
```

The latter invocation is exactly the way the operator + would be invoked had it been defined as a *friend* function

```
class T {
    ...
public:
    ...
    friend T operator+(T, T);
    ...
};
```

or as the ordinary function

```
T operator+(T, T);
```

To avoid ambiguity, an operator can be defined to operate on specific operand types only in one of the three ways shown above. Otherwise, C++ will not be able to determine which operator definition is to be invoked.

8. Both the prefix and suffix forms of the increment and decrement operators, i.e., ++ and --, can be overloaded. The prefix version of the increment operator is overloaded by defining a one parameter version of ++. The postfix version is overloaded by defining a two parameter version of ++. The second argument must be of type *int*. Note that when operators ++ and -- are overloaded as members of a class, the prefix versions do not have any explicit parameters, while the postfix versions have one explicit parameter (of type *int*). When these operators are used in infix notation, the left operand becomes the implicit argument and when these operators are invoked using the selected component notation, the

object to the left of the selection operator becomes the implicit argument.

When the postfix version of ++ is invoked in infix notation, C++ automatically calls the definition of ++ with two parameters, with the second argument equal to 0.

The following code contains two prototypes specifying the overloaded versions of the prefix and suffix ++:

```
class complex {
    float r, i;
public:
    complex(float a = 0, float b = 0);
    ...
    complex operator ++();
    complex operator ++(int);
};
```

Assuming that *c* is a *complex* variable, the ++ operator can be invoked in the standard unary operator notation as

```
++c
```

or as

```
c++
```

or in the member function notation as

```
c.operator++()
```

or as

```
c.operator++(0)
```

The first member function form is the prefix version of ++ and the second form represents the postfix version.

The prefix and postfix versions of the decrement operator -- are overloaded in a similar fashion.

9. Only the assignment and the "address-of" operators are predefined for a class. All other operators must be defined explicitly.

10. Overloaded versions of the following operators must be specified as member functions:

symbol	operator
=	assignment
( )	function call
[ ]	subscripting
->	dereferencing

11. Although the dereferencing operator -> is predefined as a binary operator, its overloaded version can be defined only as a unary operator that returns

   a. a value of type "pointer to a class" or
   b. a class object that has -> defined as a member function.

   In either case, C++ takes the resulting value and reapplies the -> operator to it. If the result returned by -> is a pointer, then C++ applies the default (i.e., predefined) -> to the result. Otherwise, C++ applies the class specific -> to the class object returned.

   Note that because -> can be defined only as a member function, it is specified without parameters. The object associated with its invocation is passed as the implicit argument.

12. In case of the predefined operators [ ], *, and -> the following equivalences hold:

expression	is equivalent to
p->x	(*p).x
*(p+i)	p[i]

   p is a pointer to a class with a member *x*, and *i* is an integer. If operators [ ], *, and -> are overloaded, then these equivalences must be reestablished explicitly by the programmer with appropriate definitions, if desired.

13. Relationships between overloaded operators are not automatically established. For example, if ++ is overloaded for type *complex* to increment the real part of *complex* values by 1.0, then

   a++

   where *a* is of type *complex*, will not automatically be equivalent to

   a += 1.0

   Such relationships exist *a priori* only for the predefined operators. To establish the above relationship between the ++ and += operators for *complex* values, both operators must be overloaded appropriately.

14. Overloaded operators cannot have default arguments.

2. EXAMPLES

Unlike in most languages, array subscripting, function calls and pointer dereferencing are operators in C++. I will now show you an example illustrating the overloading of the array subscripting and function call operators. Consider class *ivec* which implements integer vectors (one-dimensional arrays) (file *ivec.h*):

```
class ivec {
    int *p;
    int l, h;
public:
    ivec(int low, int high);
    ~ivec();
    int& operator [](int i);
    int& operator ()(int i);
};
```

ivec vector sizes can be specified dynamically (they need not be compile-time constants as in case of C++ arrays). *ivec* overloads the subscript operator to perform array bounds checking for *ivec* objects. The function call operator is overloaded to provide a FORTRAN-like notation for accessing array elements.

The subscript and function call operators return a reference to the "subscripted" element so that the subscripted expression can be used on the left side of an assignment operator.

The bodies of the member functions of class *ivec* are (file *ivec.cpd*)

```
   #include <iostream.h>
   #include <stdlib.h>
   #include "ivec.h"
   ivec::ivec(int low, int high)
 5 {
       l = low; h = high;
       p = new int[high-low+1];
   }
   ivec::~ivec()
10 {
       delete [] p;
   }
   int& ivec::operator [](int i)
   {
15     if (i < l || i > h) {
           cerr << "subscript " << i;
           cerr << " out of bounds" << endl;
           exit(1);
       }
20     return p[i-l];
   }
   int& ivec::operator ()(int i)
   {
       return (*this)[i];
25 }
```

Here are examples illustrating the use of class *ivec*:

```
ivec v(-32, 212);
...
v(32) = 0;
v(212) = 100;
...
cout << v[212];
```

3. EXERCISES

1. What are the advantages of overloading operators and functions?

2. How does C++ determine which one of the overloaded functions is being called?

Chapter 11

INPUT / OUTPUT

Input/output facilities are provided by means of predefined classes that are defined as part of standard C++. The bodies of the functions belonging to these classes are stored in the standard C++ library which is automatically loaded and linked with C++ programs.

1. STREAM HEADER FILE iostream.h

Header file *iostream.h* contains all the declarations and definitions required for using the standard input and output stream facilities. It contains the the declarations of the four standard streams: *cin* (standard input), *cout* (buffered standard output), *cerr* (unbuffered standard error), and *clog* (buffered standard error). We have already seen examples of streams *cin*, *cout*, and *cerr*. Stream *clog* is like stream *cerr* except that output written to *clog* is collected in a buffer (like the output written to *cout*) and then physically output when the buffer is filled, when the program terminates, or when the user explicitly asks for the stream to be "flushed."

Header file *iostream.h* also contains the declarations of the classes that implement the streams and define the stream operations. Stream input and output operations, as illustrated by the examples shown in previous chapters, are denoted by the operators >> and <<, respectively. These operators are defined *a priori* for reading and writing values of the predefined types. In "stream" terminology, reading a value from a stream is called "extraction" (input) and writing a value to a stream is called "insertion" (output).

2. INPUT

The standard input stream *cin* is an object of class *istream_withassign*, which is derived from class *istream*. Class *istream_withassign* defines one additional operator: the assignment operator for input streams. The stream input operations (including the overloaded declarations of >>) are themselves specified by class *istream*. We will therefore focus our discussion on class *istream*. Class *istream* has the following specification:

```
class istream : virtual public ios {
  ...
public:
  ...
  // read characters into an array up to delim char
  istream& get(signed char*,int n,char delim = '\n');
  istream& get(unsigned char*,int n,char delim = '\n');
  istream& read(signed char*, int n);
  istream& read(unsigned char*, int n);

  // read characters into an array up to delim char
  istream& getline(signed char*,int n,char delim='\n');
  istream& getline(unsigned char*,int n,char delim='\n');

  // read a single character
  istream& get(unsigned char&);
  istream& get(signed char&);
  int get();

  int peek();  // return next char without reading it
  istream& putback(char); // push back char into input

  istream& seekg(streampos);
  istream& seekg(streamoff, seek_dir);
  streampos tellg();

  // Formatted reads
  istream& operator >>(signed char*);
  istream& operator >>(unsigned char*);
  istream& operator >>(unsigned char&);
  istream& operator >>(signed char&);
  istream& operator >>(short&);
  istream& operator >>(int&);
  istream& operator >>(long&);
  istream& operator >>(unsigned short&);
  istream& operator >>(unsigned int&);
  istream& operator >>(unsigned long&);
  istream& operator >>(float&);
  istream& operator >>(double&);
  istream& operator >>(long double&);

  istream& operator >>(istream& (*)(istream&));
  istream& operator >>(ios& (*)(ios&));
};
```

The first two *get* member functions (lines 6-7) read at most $n-1$ characters into the array specified by the first argument.[1] The *get* functions (lines 6-7) may read less than $n-1$ characters if they encounter a new line or a user specified delimiter character (specified as the third argument). The delimiting character is not read; it is left in the input stream. A terminating null character is added after the characters read and stored in the array specified by the first argument).

The two *read* functions (lines 8-9) read up to n characters. Unlike the *get* functions, the *read* functions do not add a terminating null character at the end of the array.

The two *getline* functions (lines 12-13) are similar to the two *get* functions except that they read the delimiting character from the input stream and store it in the array.

Here is an example illustrating the use of function *getline*:

```
char line[MAX_LINE];
...
cin.getline(name, MAX_LINE);
```

Function *getline* will read at most *MAX_LINE*-1 characters. It always appends the null character (`'\0'`) after the characters read by it. The default line termination character is the new-line character. An alternative line termination character can be specified explicitly as the third argument:

```
cin.getline(name, MAX_LINE, '\r');
```

Literal `'\r'` denotes the carriage-return character.

The three *get* functions (16-18) read a single character. The first two *get* functions return the input stream associated with their invocation as their result, while the third *get* function returns the character read as its result. In case of an end of file, this *get* function returns −1.

Here is an example illustrating the use of function *get* to read characters, one at a time, from the input:

---

1. The first argument is actually a pointer that refers to the beginning of the array. A pointer to the first element of an array can be treated as an array name. An array name can also be treated as a pointer to the first element, but an array name cannot be assigned a new value.

   Note that a parameter name need not be specified in a function prototype. The name can also be omitted in the function definition, but in such a case it will not be possible to refer to the parameter in the function body.

```
#include <iostream.h>
int c;
...
while ((c = cin.get()) !=EOF) {
    ...
}
```

Function *peek* (line 20) returns the value of the next character in the input stream without reading it (taking it out of the input stream). In case of an end of file, *peek* returns −1. Function *putback* (line 20) is used to put the last character actually read from the input stream back to the input stream. The character put back will be read by the next input operation.

Functions *seekg* and *tellg* (line 23-25) are used for reading input from specified positions in a stream instead of reading input sequentially from the input stream. For more details about such input, please refer to the library reference manual of your C++ compiler.

The input operator >> is predefined to read values of a variety of types such as *char, char* *, short, int, float,* and *double* (lines 28-40). Operator >> returns without doing anything if it finds the associated input stream in an "error" state. One such state is the end-of-file.

Operator >> reads strings when its right operand is of type *char* * or *unsigned char* *. >> reads characters from the input stream until it encounters a whitespace character; then >> appends a terminating null character (`'\0'`) at the end of the string. Here is an example:

```
char name[MAX];
...
cin >> name;
```

The stream operator >> always returns the input stream (its left operand) as its result. This allows successive input operations that extract values from the same stream to be combined into a single statement. For example, the two input statements in the following code

```
#include <iostream.h>
...
int x; float y;
...
cin >> x;
cin >> y;
...
```

can be combined into the following single statement

```
...
cin >> x >> y;
...
```

White spaces are treated as delimiters by operator >>. It skips over white spaces[2] to find the next input item even when reading characters, strings, and lines. If spaces are not to be ignored, then member functions *get*, *read*, and *getline* functions should be used instead of >>.

Input manipulators are functions that alter the state of an input stream. For example, one input manipulator of interest is *ws*. It extracts leading white spaces. The input operator >> is overloaded to handle manipulators (lines 42-43) Manipulators are discussed in Section 4.

3. OUTPUT STREAMS

The output streams *cout*, *cerr*, and *clog* are objects of class *ostream_withassign*, which is derived from class *ostream*. Class *ostream_withassign* defines one additional operator: an assignment operator for output streams. The stream input operations (including the overloaded declarations of <<) are themselves specified by class *istream*. We will therefore focus our discussion on class *istream*.

---

2. A "white space" character refers to one of the following characters: space, form-feed, new-line, carriage return, horizontal tab, or vertical tab characters.

The output stream class *ostream* is specified as

```
class ostream : virtual public ios {
    ...
public:
    ...
    // write characters + strings
    ostream& put(char);
    ostream& write(const signed char*, int n);
    ostream& write(const unsigned char*, int n);

    // set/read stream pointer position for output
    ostream& seekp(streampos);
    ostream& seekp(streamoff, seek_dir);
    streampos tellp();

    // formatted writes
    ostream& operator <<(signed char);
    ostream& operator <<(unsigned char);

    ostream& operator <<(short);
    ostream& operator <<(unsigned short);
    ostream& operator <<(int);
    ostream& operator <<(unsigned int);
    ostream& operator <<(long);
    ostream& operator <<(unsigned long);
    ostream& operator <<(float);
    ostream& operator <<(double);
    ostream& operator <<(long double);

    ostream& operator <<(const signed char*);
    ostream& operator <<(const unsigned char*);

    // stream state changers which apply manipulator
    // functions such as endl and flush to ostreams
    ostream& operator <<(ostream& (*)(ostream&));
    ostream& operator <<(ios& (*)(ios&));
};
```

Function *put* (line 6) is used for writing characters. Function *write* (line 7) writes *n* characters starting at the location pointed to (or the array denoted) by the first argument.

Functions *seekp* and *tellp* (line 11-13) are used for writing output at specified positions in a stream instead of writing output sequentially to the output stream. For more details about such output, please refer to the library reference manual of your C++ compiler.

The output operator << is overloaded (lines 16-20) to print values of a variety of predefined types such as *char, char *, short, int, float,* and *double.* Operator << returns without doing anything if the associated output stream is, at the outset, in an error state; << always returns the output stream.

Here are examples illustrating the use of the output operator <<:

```
#include <iostream.h>
...
int x = 4; float y = 3.5;
...
cout << "x = ";
cout << x;
cout << ", y = ";
cout << y;
cout << endl;
...
```

The above statements print the line

```
x = 4, y = 3.5
```

Statement

```
cout << endl;
```

prints a new-line character; it is equivalent to the statement

```
cout << '\n';
```

Note that *endl* is a manipulator function (discussed later).

Because the output operator << always returns the output stream as its result, the above output statements can be combined into a single output statement:

```
cout << "x = " << x << ", y = " << y << endl;
```

A *char* variable used as a small integer *cannot* be printed as

```
char c;
...
cout << c;
```

because C++ invokes the definition of << with a *char* parameter. To print the integer value stored in a *char* variable, the variable must be cast to an *int* before printing, e.g.,

```
cout << (int) c;
```

to ensure that C++ invokes the definition of << with a *int* parameter.

Output manipulators are functions that alter the state of an output stream. For example, one output manipulator of interest is *endl*. It writes a new-line to the output stream and "flushes" the stream. The output operator << is overloaded to handle manipulators (lines 34-35). Manipulators are discussed in the next section.

Class *ostream* defines many other output facilities which are not shown here, such as member functions for controlling the output format. For details, refer to the library reference manual of your C++ compiler.

4. MANIPULATORS

Functions that change the state of a stream are called "manipulators." Manipulators can be specified as (right) operands of the stream input/output operators. An appropriate operator definition is invoked to apply the manipulator on the specified stream (left operand). The manipulator is applied by calling the manipulator with the stream as its argument.

Here are some of the standard manipulators specified by C++:

1. *ws*: skip white spaces.
2. *endl*: write a new-line character and flush the output stream.
3. *ends*: write the null character to terminate the string.
4. *flush*: flush the output stream.

Here are examples illustrating the use of the manipulators:

1. White space characters in the input can be skipped until the first non-white space character as follows:

    ```
    cin >> ws;
    ```

    Note that a reference to a function name such as *ws*, yields a pointer to the function.

2. A new-line character can be inserted into the standard output stream as follows:

    ```
    cout << endl;
    ```

3. The standard output stream *cout* can be flushed as follows:

    ```
    cout << flush;
    ```

5. STREAM STATES

The state of a stream can be examined to determine the stream state, that is, to determine whether the stream is in a "good" state or whether it is in an error state. The stream state can be examined using the operations of class *ios*, which is the base class of the stream types *istream* and *ostream*. Thus members of class *ios* can be referenced through objects of types derived from *ios*. In particular, they can be referenced in conjunction with the standard streams *cin*, *cout*, *cerr*, and *clog*.

Class *ios* provides the following member functions and operators for querying the stream state, and for determining whether or not the last stream operation was successful:

1. Function *eof*: returns a non-zero value if the last operation on the specified stream encountered the end-of-file; otherwise, *eof* returns zero. For example, the following *while* loop executes as long as there is more input:

```
while (!cin.eof()) {
    ...
}
```

2. Function *fail*: returns a non-zero value if the last operation on the specified stream failed or if *bad* returns a non-zero value; otherwise, *fail* returns zero.

3. Function *bad*: returns a non-zero value if an error occurred during the last operation on the specified stream; otherwise, *bad* returns zero. The "bad" state is like the "fail" state, but worse − in some cases the stream may have been corrupted and characters may have been lost.

4. Function *good*: returns a non-zero value if there is no problem with the specified stream, e.g., the last stream operation executed without any problem; otherwise, *good* returns zero.

5. Operator *!*: operator with the same semantics as *fail*. Operator *!* can be used as

```
if (!cout)
    failure;
```

6. Operator *operator void**: conversion operator that returns a zero if the last stream operation failed; otherwise, this conversion operator returns a non-zero value. Here is an example illustrating the use of *operator void**, which is invoked automatically:

```
if (cin >> c)
    ...
else
    failure;
```

The input stream *cin*, which is returned by the >> operator as its result, is converted to zero or to a non-zero value by the coercion function *operator void**; this value is used as the condition of the *if* statement.

A stream operation applied to a stream not in the "good" state is a "no-op" or a null operation − it will have no effect on the stream state.

6. EXTENDING THE STREAM INPUT/OUTPUT LIBRARY

The input and output operators >> and << can be overloaded to read and print values of user-defined types. In this section, we will overload << for printing *ivec* (integer vector) values, and overload >> and << for reading and printing *complex* values.

6.1 INPUT/OUTPUT OF COMPLEX VALUES

Suppose we want to extend the stream input/output operators >> and << to handle input and output *complex* values. For example, it should be possible to write the following code:

```
...
complex c;
...
cin >> c; //read a complex value from standard input
...
cout << c; //write a complex value to standard output
```

Declaring operators >> and << as members of the class *complex* will not work because then C++ will require that the left-hand arguments of >> and << be *complex* values. As shown above, the left-hand values for the operators >> and << are of type *istream_withassign* and *ostream_withassign*, respectively. This use conforms to the manner in which the operators >> and << are used for input/output of the predefined types such as *int* and *float*. Declaring these operators as friends solves the problem.

Here is the modified version of class *complex*:

```
     class complex {
          float r, i;
     public:
          complex(float a = 0, float b = 0);
 5        float real();
          float imag();
          complex operator +(complex a);
          complex operator -(complex a);
          complex operator *(complex a);
10        complex operator /(complex a);
          int operator ==(complex a);
          friend ostream& operator <<(ostream& os, complex& c);
          friend istream& operator >>(istream& is, complex& c);
     };
```

The bodies of the overloaded input/output functions are

```
     #include <iostream.h>
     #include "complex3.h"
          ...
     ostream& operator <<(ostream& os, complex& c)
 5   {
          cout << c.r << " " << c.i;
          return os;
     }
     istream& operator >>(istream& is, complex& c)
10   {
          cin >> c.r >> c.i;
          return is;
     }
```

The overloaded versions of the operators >> and << operate on streams of types *istream* and *ostream*, respectively. These types match the stream types *istream_withassign* and *ostream_withassign* which are derived from them.

Operands (arguments) of the operators >> and << are passed by reference. These operators return references to the input and output streams (references are denoted by the operator &). Passing the stream parameters by reference ensures that the values returned by these operators are the same stream objects passed to them as arguments and not copies of these objects. Returning a reference to a stream allows multiple output operations to be specified in one statement, as illustrated in the following code:

```
...
complex c, d;
...
cout << c << "+" << d << "=" << c+d;
...
```

The output prints as expected because all invocations of << write to the same
output stream and not to copies of the output stream objects. It is important that
the output stream be passed by reference to operator << and that it return a
reference to this stream to ensure that all output operations refer to the same
stream. Passing the stream by value and returning the stream value as a result
will result in output being performed on copies of the output stream variable.
Each copy will have its own buffer and stream pointer; as a result the output will
not print in the order expected, but only when the individual buffers are
"flushed."

Program output is typically "buffered" or stored in memory and then written or
flushed to the output device when the buffer is full, when the program completes
execution, when certain characters such as new-line characters are output, and so
on. Buffering allows blocks of characters, instead of single characters, to be sent
to the output device. Writing to output devices such as printers and disks is
typically slow. Writing blocks of characters to an output device is usually much
faster than writing one character at a time.

Here is the version of the *complex* calculator program that uses the overloaded
definitions of the >> and << operators:

```
     #include <iostream.h>
     #include "complex3.h"
     int main()
     {
5        complex a, b, r; char opr;
         for(;;) {
             cout << "Enter first complex number: ";
             cin >> a;
             cout << "Enter operator: "; cin >> opr;
10           cout << "Enter second complex number: ";
             cin >> b;
             switch (opr) {
             case '+':
                 r = a+b; break;
15           case '-':
                 r = a-b; break;
             case '*':
                 r = a*b; break;
             case '/':
20               r = a/b; break;
             default:
                 cerr << "Bad operator!" << endl;
             }
             cout << "Result is: " << r << endl;
25       }
     }
```

This program is smaller and more elegant than the version shown in Chapter 8, which does not use the overloaded definitions of the input/output operators.

6.2 PRINTING VECTORS

Consider the following class *ivec*, which we saw in Chapter 10, that implements integer vectors (file *ivec.h*):

```
class ivec {
    int *p;
    int l, h;
public:
    ivec(int low, int high);
    ~ivec();
    int& operator [](int i);
    int& operator ()(int i);
};
```

Operator << cannot be overloaded to print *ivec* values because class *ivec* provides no way of determining the lower and upper bounds of an *ivec* object. Consequently, *ivec* must be modified in one of the following ways so that << can be overloaded to print *ivec* arrays:

1.   << is declared as a member function.

2.   << is declared as a *friend* function.

3.   *l* and *h* are made *public* members.

4.   *lo* and *hi* are defined as *public* member functions.

The first two choices will not help in defining the input operation for *ivec* objects. The third alternative breaks encapsulation – the user can erroneously or maliciously change the values of *l* and *h*. However, these members can be made *const public* members, but that will require changing the constructor. We will therefore use alternative 4 and will declare *lo* and *hi* as *inline* member functions. Here is the specification of the integer vector class, now called *ivecn* (file *ivecn.h*):

```
class ivecn {
    int *p;
    int l, h;
public:
    ivecn(int low, int high);
    ~ivecn();
    inline int lo() { return l; }
    inline int hi() { return h; }
    int& operator [](int i);
    int& operator ()(int i);
};
```

Aside from the member functions *lo* and *hi*, the bodies of the other member functions are the same as before.

Here is the prototype of the operator << overloaded to print objects of type *ivecn* (file *ivecnp.h*):

```
ostream& operator <<(ostream& out, ivecn& v);
```

The body of operator << is (file *ivecnp.cpp*)

```
   #include "ivecn.h"
   #include "ivecnp.h"
   ostream& operator <<(ostream& out, ivecn& v)
   {
5      for (int i = v.lo(); i < v.hi(); i++)
           out << v[i] << ' ';
       return out << endl;
   }
```

7. DEFINING NEW STREAMS

Files can be associated with streams by using the following classes, which are
defined in the header file *fstream.h*:

```
     ...
     class ifstream : public fstreambase, public istream {
       ...
     public:
  5    ifstream();
       ifstream(char *,int=ios::in,int=filebuf::openprot);
       void open(char *,int=ios::in,int=filebuf::openprot);
       void close();
       ...
 10  };

     class ofstream : public fstreambase, public ostream {
       ...
     public:
 15    ofstream();
       ofstream(char *,int=ios::out,int=filebuf::openprot);
       void open(char *,int=ios::out,int=filebuf::openprot);
       void close();
       ...
 20  };

     class fstream : public fstreambase, public iostream {
       ...
     public:
 25    fstream();
       fstream(char *, int, int = filebuf::openprot);
       void open(char *, int, int = filebuf::openprot);
       void close();
       ...
 30  };
     ...
```

Class *ifstream* is used for defining input streams, class *ofstream* is used for defining output streams, and class *fstream* is used for defining input/output streams (which can be used for both input and output). A file can be associated with a stream object by supplying initial values to ensure that the second constructor (in each class) is invoked. Alternatively, the stream object can be declared without supplying any initial values, which invokes the first constructor (in each class), and then associated with a file by calling member function *open*. The association between a file and a stream object can be broken by calling member function *close*.

The following code shows an example of a user-defined stream:

```
     #include <stdlib.h>
     #include <iostream.h>
     #include <fstream.h>
     int main()
5    {
         ...
         ofstream result("test.out", ios::out);
         if (!result) {
             cerr << "error, cannot associated file "
10               << "test.output with output stream" << endl;
             exit(1);
         }
         ...
         result << "Test Results." << endl;
15       ...
     }
```

The statement

```
ofstream result("test.out", ios::out);
```

defines *result* as an output stream and associates it with the file *test.out*.

Defining an input/output stream is similar. For example, *io* can be defined as an input/output stream and associated with the file *test.io* as follows:

```
fstream io("test.io", ios::in | ios::out);
```

Operator !, which is a member of the indirect base class *ios* of the classes *ifstream*, *ofstream*, and *fstream*,[3] can be used to determine whether or not the stream was created successfully, for example,

```
if (!io)
    error("could not open file test.io");
```

8. ADDITIONAL FACILITIES

The C++ stream library is quite elaborate. It provides many facilities that have not been discussed here. For example, the stream library provides

1. functions for performing random input/output,

---

3. *ios* is a base class of *ostream* which, in turn, is a base class of *ofstream*.

2. classes *ostrstream* and *istrstream* for performing "in core" format conversions much like those done using the functions *sprintf* and *sscanf*, and

3. facilities for format control.

For more details, refer to the library reference manual of your C++ compiler.

Chapter 12

A LARGE EXAMPLE

We will write a "cross reference generator", which is a program that selects words (identifiers in programs) from the input file and prints them in sorted order along with the numbers of the lines in which they appear. Line numbers will be printed beside each word; they must also be in sorted order. The cross reference generator should work both with English text and with computer programs. Consider, for example, the following C++ program:

```
#include <iostream.h>
int main()
{
    cout << "Hello Programmer!" << endl;
    cout << "Welcome to the World of C++!" << endl;
}
```

The cross reference generator produces the folllowing output for this program:

```
C          5
Hello      4
Programmer         4
Welcome            5
World      5
cout       4       5
endl       4       5
h          1
include            1
int        2
iostream           1
main       2
of         5
the        5
to         5
void       2
```

Words are defined as character sequences that begin with a letter and are followed by one or more letters, digits, or underscores; the character sequence is terminated by a white space.

The cross reference generator program will be structured as follows: the main function will read words and store them and the line numbers in which they appear in an "ordered binary tree" data structure. The tree data structure, explained below, is an efficient technique for storing and printing items in sorted order.

Words will be read from input by calling function *word* that has the prototype (file *word.h*):

```
int word(istream& in, char s[], int max, int& lineno);
```

Function *word* has four parameters:

1. *in*: the name of the input stream;

2. *s*: the array in which the word read from input will be stored;

3. *max*: the size of the array *s* (the largest word that can be stored in *s* will be *max*−1; the last element of *s* will be used to store the null character); and

4. *lineno*: the variable in which the line number on which the word occurs.

Arguments corresponding to *s* and *lineno* will be passed by reference to allow *word* to return values to the calling function by storing them in *s* and *lineno*. Remember that arrays are, by default, passed by reference.

Here is the body of function *word* (file *word.cpp*):

```
#include <ctype.h>
#include <iostream.h>
#include "word.h"
int word(istream& in, char s[], int max, int & lineno)
    //max == sizeof(s); returns EOF at the end of input
{
    static int line = 1; int c, i = 0;

    do {
        if (isalpha(c = in.get())) {
            s[i++] = c;
            while(i<max-1&&(isalnum(c=in.get())||c=='_'))
                s[i++] = c;
            s[i] = '\0';
            lineno = line;
            if (c == '\n')
                line++;
            return 1;
        }
        else if (c == '\n')
            line++;
    } while (c != EOF);
    return EOF;
}
```

Function *word* reads words from input by reading characters one at a time and then assembling the appropriate characters to form a word. Member function *get* of class *istream* is used to read characters from the input (lines 10 and 12) instead of the operator >>. This is because >> treats white space characters such as spaces and new-lines as delimiters and skips them. As far as function *word* is concerned, the treatment of spaces is fine, but the treatment of new-line characters is inappropriate because *word* needs to track the line numbers on which the words appear. In contrast to >>, member function *get* returns each character in the input and lets the calling program decide what to do with the character.

Function *word* remembers the current line number by storing it in the *static* local variable *line* (see lines 7 and 14) so as to preserve its value across function calls. Such *static* variables retain their values across function calls. Variable *line* is initialized to one before the program begins execution.

When function *word* is called, it gets a character from the input and checks it to see whether or not it is a letter (line 9). If it is a letter, then this is the beginning of a word and *word* attempts to read the rest of the word (lines 10-18). If the first character read was not a letter (line 9), then *word* checks to see if it is a new-line character, in which case it increments *lineno* by 1. *word* continues with the loop to find the beginning of a word provided the value of *c*, which contains the character returned by *istream* : :*get* (line 9), is not *EOF* (line 21). *EOF* signals the end of data,

Function *word* stores the characters making up a word in the array *s* as long as there is space in the array.

Words read from the input are stored in an "ordered binary" tree because this data structure makes it efficient to look up a word that has appeared before and to print the words in sorted order. A binary tree is like a list except that each element of the tree has two successor (next) nodes. One successor is called the "left" successor and the other successor is called the "right" successor. In an ordered binary tree, the data item stored at a left successor node has a "value" less than the data item stored at the node. Similarly, the data item stored at a right successor node has a "value" greater than the data item stored at the node.

With each word in the binary tree is kept an "ordered" list of the line numbers identifying the lines containing the word. An ordered list is like an ordinary list except that the list is kept so that the data items appear in some order, say increasing order.

In this program we use two different strategies for storing line numbers and words: ordered lists and ordered binary trees. Lists are storage-wise more efficient than binary trees because each list node has only one successor, which means that each list node uses storage for only one pointer. A binary tree must, on the other hand, make provision for two pointers.

It is typically more efficient to add and lookup arbitrary items in a binary tree. However, we will use an ordered list for storing line numbers because the line numbers appear in non decreasing order. This means that they can be simply appended to the end of the list. Also, lookups to determine whether or not the line number is already in the list are not necessary. We just keep duplicate line numbers.

To see what an ordered binary tree looks like, consider the words (formed as per the rules described above) in the following two lines:

```
#include <iostream.h>
int main(void)
```

The tree constructed by the cross reference program will look as follows (the order in which the words are read from the input determines the "shape" of the ordered binary tree):

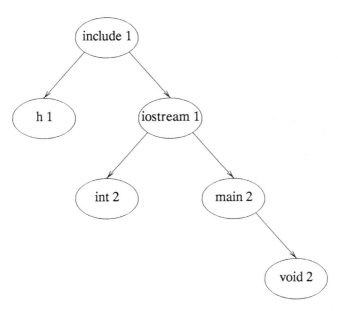

Suppose that the next input word is *cout*. This word will be inserted as the left successor of *h*. Whether one word is "less than" (precedes) another word depends upon the ordering implemented by the C++ string comparison function *strcmp*.

The numbers next to the words in the tree are the numbers of lines on which the words appear. As it happens, in the above input each word occurs only on one line.

We will now discuss the class types used for the cross reference generator. List elements are of the class type *node*[1] (file *node.h*):

---

1. Members of class types specified using the keyword *struct*, instead of the keyword *class*, are *public* members by default.

```
   #include <stdio.h>
   struct node {
       int x;
       node *next;
5      node(int a) { x = a; next = NULL; }
   };
```

Instead of using an object of type *node* to point to the list, we will define another type *list* to point to the "head" of the list. The list head will be an object of type *list* that has pointers to both the first and last elements of list. The pointer to the first element is used for printing the line numbers; the pointer to the last element is used for appending a line number to the list.

Here is the specification of the list head class *list* (file *listx.h*):

```
   #include "node.h"

   class list {
       node *first, *last; //pointers to list elements
5  public:
       list(int a);
       ~list();
       void append(int a);
       void print();
10 };
```

Class *list* provides functions for appending elements to the list and printing the list. The bodies of these functions are defined as follows (file *listx.cpp*):

```
     #include <iostream.h>
     #include "listx.h"

     list::list(int a)
 5   {
         first = last = new node(a);
     }
     list::~list()
     {
10       node *p = first, *q;
         while (p != NULL) {
             q = p->next;
             delete p;
             p = q;
15       }
     }
     void list::append(int a)
     {
         node *pn = new node(a);
20       last->next = pn;
         last = pn;
     }
     void list::print()
     {
25       for (node *pn = first; pn != NULL; pn = pn->next)
             cout << '\t' << pn->x;
     }
```

The list destructor (lines 8-16) frees all elements of the list (of type *node*) when
the list head (of type *list*) is deleted. Notice that the pointer to the next element
stored in a node, say p, is saved in variable q (line 11) before deleting p (line 12).

Class *tree*, which implements the ordered binary tree that stores the input words,
is specified as (file *tree.h*)

```
  #include "listx.h"
  class tree {
      char *name;
      tree *left, *right;
5     list *lines;
  public:
      tree(char *s, int n);
      ˜tree();
      void find_or_add(char *s, int line);
10    void print();
  };
```

Each *tree* object has four data components:

1. *name*: points to the word stored at the node,

2. *left*: points to the subtree that contains words that are less than the word pointed to by *name*,

3. *right*: points to the subtree that contains words that are greater than or equal to the word pointed to by *name*, and

4. *lines*: points to the list containing the line numbers of the lines that contain the word pointed to by *name*.

The constructor for class *tree* (line 7) takes as arguments the first word to be inserted into the tree and the line number on which it appears. Member function *find_or_add* (line 9) is used to store words and their line numbers in the tree.

The bodies of the *tree* member functions are (file *tree.cpp*)

```
     #include <iostream.h>
     #include <string.h>
     #include "tree.h"
     tree::tree(char *s, int n)
5    {
         name = new char[strlen(s)+1];
         strcpy(name, s);
         left = right = 0;
         lines = new list(n);
10   }
     tree::~tree()
     {
         if (left != NULL)
             delete left;
15       if (right != NULL)
             delete right;
     };
     void tree::find_or_add(char *s, int line)
     {
20       tree **t;
         int cmp;
         if ((cmp = strcmp(s, name)) == 0) {
             lines->append(line);
             return;
25       }
         t = cmp < 0 ? &left : &right;
         if (*t == NULL)
             *t = new tree(s, line);
         else
30           (*t)->find_or_add(s, line);
     }
     void tree::print()
     {
         if (left != NULL)
35           left->print();
         cout << name << " ";
         lines->print();
         cout << endl;
         if (right != NULL)
40           right->print();
     }
```

The prototypes of the string manipulation functions are stored in the standard header file *string.h* (line 2). Specifically, it contains the prototypes of the string copy function *strcpy* (used in line 7) and the string comparison function *strcmp* (used in line 22). The string comparison function returns –1, 0, or 1 depending upon whether its first argument is less than, equal to, or greater than its second argument.

The *tree* destructor (lines 11-17) first deletes the left subtree and then its right subtree. It is called automatically when function *main* deletes the "root" (first element) of the tree to perform clean up.

Member function *find_or_add* (lines 18-31) first determines whether or not *s*, the word to be added, is in the tree (implying that the word was encountered previously). If *s* is in the tree, then *find_or_add* simply appends the number *line* to the associated line number list and returns (lines 22-25). Otherwise, it determines whether *s* should be inserted in the left subtree or the right subtree (line 26). If the subtree in which *s* should be inserted is null, then *find_or_add* creates a new *tree* object and makes this object be the subtree (lines 27-28). If the subtree exists, then *find_or_add* calls itself recursively to add the word to the subtree (line 30).

Note that variable *t* is declared as a

> *pointer to a pointer to a tree object*

(line 20). On line 26, *t* is assigned the address either of *left* or of *right*. As a result, **t* refers to *left* or to *right*. This allows us to use **t* to denote either the member *left* or the member *right* (and not just their values), which means that we can use it to assign a value either to *left* or to *right*.

The *tree print* function (lines 32-41) operates as follows:

1. It first prints the words in the tree by recursively printing the words and the associated line numbers in the left subtree (lines 34-35) of the *tree* object.

2. Then it prints the word stored in the object itself and the associated line numbers (lines 36-38).

3. Finally, it prints the words in the right subtree (lines 39-40).

The *main* function is the application "driver." It calls the rest of the program components to make things happen. Here is the body of function *main* (file *xref.cpp*):

```
   #include <iostream.h>
   #include "tree.h"
   #include "word.h"
   const int MAX = 80;
5
   int main()
   {
       char wrd[MAX];
       int line;
10     tree *root = NULL;

       while (word(cin, wrd, MAX, line) != EOF) {
           if (root == NULL)
               root = new tree(wrd, line);
15         else root->find_or_add(wrd, line);
       }
       root->print();
       delete root;
   }
```

Function *main* gets words and the numbers of the lines containing them by calling function *word*; it then adds these words and their line numbers in the ordered tree and in the appropriate lists by calling function *find_or_add*. After the input file has been exhausted, the words in the binary tree are printed.

Chapter 13

TEMPLATES

The C++ facilities we have discussed so far allow only classes or functions to be defined with fixed types of components and parameters. For example, suppose we want to define a class that can be used to implement vectors of arbitrary element types, a function that sorts an array of any type, or a function that swaps two variables of the same, but arbitrary, type. We can define a class for each vector type, a sort function for each type of array, and a swap function for each variable type. But this is too much work, especially since the definitions of the above class and functions will be similar except for the types of some components, parameters, and variables.

To address the above issue, C++ provides a facility, called "templates", that allows users to define functions and classes that are "parameterized" with types [Stroustrup 1988; Ellis & Stroustrup 1990]. In other words, templates allow functions and classes to have types as arguments. Templates can be used, for example, to define one template vector class parameterized with the element type, and one sort and one function for the different vector and element types. Another example of a template class is a *list* template with the list element type as its parameter. This template class can be used for defining a list of *int* elements, a list of *employee* elements, a list of *node* elements, and so on. Member functions with the appropriate result and parameter types automatically become available to operate on such lists.

1. TEMPLATE DECLARATIONS AND DEFINITIONS

Templates are used to define classes and functions with parameters that are typically types. Templates are used for generating ordinary classes and functions.

Template arguments can be type names which match template "type variable" parameters; they can also be function names, character strings, and constant expressions that match the corresponding template parameters. A type variable template parameter is denoted as

`class` *identifier*

Other template parameters are declared as in ordinary functions.

1.1 FUNCTION TEMPLATES

A function template specifies an infinite set of overloaded functions. Function templates have the form

```
template <template-parameter-declarations> function-declaration-or-definition
```

As an example, consider the declaration of the function template *min* (file *tmin.h*):

```
template<class T> T min(const T a, const T b);
```

min is specified as a function template with one template parameter *T* and two ordinary parameters *a* and *b*. Notice that the template parameter can be used in the function declaration (and the definition) just like a type name.

Here is the definition of *min* (file *tmin.cpp*):

```
template<class T> T min(const T a, const T b)
{
    return a < b ? a : b;
}
```

Template arguments are not explicitly specified when calling a function template. Instead, C++ examines calls to function templates and uses overloading rules to determine which template function to call. If necessary, C++ will generate an appropriate function from the template. A function generated from a function template is called a "template function."

Here are examples of calls to the function template *min*:

```
#include "tmin.h"
int i, j, k;
double u, v, w;
char a, b, c;
...
k = min(i, j);
w = min(u, v);
c = min(a, b);
```

These three calls to *min* will cause C++ to generate three template functions with the following prototypes:

```
int min(const int a, const int b);
char min(const char a, const char b);
double min(const double a, const double b);
```

Consider the following two calls to the function template *min* that can cause problems:

```
...
class address {
    ...
};
address x, y;
int i;
char a;
...
x = min(x, y);
i = min(i, a);
...
```

The first call to *min* will result in an error if the less than operator, which is used in the body of *min*, is not defined for class *address*. The second call results in an error because C++ will not generate a template function of the form

```
int min(const int a, const char b);
```

from the function template *min*, nor will it implicitly cast the second argument to an *int* and generate a call to the function template:

```
int min(const int a, const int b);
```

However, this problem does not arise if the user explicitly defines a function with the above prototype.

Function templates can be overloaded with ordinary functions or with additional function templates.

Function template definitions are needed to generate template functions, but only function template declarations are needed to generate calls to template functions.

1.2 CLASS TEMPLATES

Class template specifications have the form

```
template <template-parameter-declarations> class name {
    ...
};
```

As an example, consider the following specification of the template class *queue*:

```
template<class elem, int size> class queue {
    int size;
    ...
public:
    queue(int n);
    int empty();
    ...
};
```

The template class *queue* has two template parameters: a type variable *elem* which specifies the queue element type and *size* which specifies the queue size.

Here are some variable definitions illustrating the use of the template class *queue*:

```
queue<int, 1024> a;
queue<char, 512> b;
queue<char, 1024> c;
queue<char, 512*2> d;
```

Two template class names refer to the same class only if the templates names are identical and their arguments have identical values. Consequently, only variables *c* and *d* have the same types.

A template constructor definition has the form

template<*template-parameter-declarations*>
        class-name<*template-parameters*>::*class-name* (*parameter-declarations*
{
    ...
}

As an example, here is the skeleton of the constructor of the template class *queue*:

```
template<class elem,int size>
        queue<elem,size>::queue(int n)
{
    ...
}
```

Destructor definitions are like constructor definitions.

A template member function definition has the form

```
template<template-parameter-declarations> result-type
    class-name<template-parameters>::member-fun.-name (parameter-declarations)
{
    ...
}
```

As an example, here is the skeleton of member function *empty* of the template class *queue*:

```
template<class elem, int size>
                    int queue(elem, size)::empty()
{
    ...
}
```

2. EXAMPLES

I will show you two examples: one illustrating a function template and the other illustrating a template class.

2.1 FUNCTION TEMPLATE SWAP

We will write a function template *tswap* that exchanges two variables of any type (file *tswap.h*):

```
template<class T> void tswap(T& a, T& b);
```

Here is the body of *tswap* (file *tswap.cpp*):

```
template<class T> void tswap(T& a, T& b)
{
    T tmp = a;
    a = b;
    b = tmp;
}
```

The C++ compiler will generate an "instance" of *tswap* with the right parameter types, if necessary, for each call to *tswap*. Both arguments in each call to *tswap* must have arguments of the same type. If the arguments are of a class type, then

1. this type must either have no constructor or there must be a constructor that does not take any arguments (so that the declaration of *tmp* works correctly), and

2. assignment must be defined, either by default or explicitly, for this type (so that the exchange can take place).

2.2 TEMPLATE CLASS STACK

To illustrate the use of template classes, we will define a template class for stacks. This template will be based on class *stack* that was defined in Chapter 2.

Here is the specification of the stack template (file *tstack.h*):

```
   template<class T> class stack {
       int max;
       int sp;
       T *stk;
5  public:
       stack(int size);
       ˜stack();
       int push(T& a);
       int pop();
10     T& top();
       int empty();
       int full();
   };
```

The prefix

```
template<class T>
```

indicates that the *stack* template is parameterized with one type parameter *T*.

The stack elements are now passed by reference in function member *push* instead of by value as in the original class *stack*. And member function *top* returns a reference. Passing objects by reference will minimize copying, which can be significant if the stack elements are large objects.

Here are the bodies of the *stack* template member functions:

```
   #include "tstack.h"
   template<class T> stack<T>::stack(int size)
   {
       max = size; stk = new T[size]; sp = 0;
5  }
   template<class T> stack<T>::~stack()
   {
       delete [] stk;
   }
10 template<class T> int stack<T>::push(T& a)
   {
       if (sp < max) {
           stk[sp++] = a; return 1;
       }
15     else
           return 0;
   }
   template<class T> int stack<T>::pop()
   {
20     if (sp > 0) {
           sp--; return 1;
       }
       else
           return 0;
25 }
   template<class T> T& stack<T>::top()
   {
       return stk[sp-1];
   }
30 template<class T> int stack<T>::empty()
   {
       return sp == 0;
   }
   template<class T> int stack<T>::full()
35 {
       return sp == max;
   }
```

Here are examples illustrating the use of template classes:

```
stack<int> istk;
stack<float> fstk;
stack<employee> estk, *pestk;
```

stack < *int* >, *stack* < *float* >, and *stack* < *employee* > are template classes. Bodies of their member functions will be automatically generated.

Note that template class names can be used wherever ordinary class names can be used.

3. EXERCISE

1. Class *ivec*, defined in Chapter 10, implements integer vectors. Using this class as the basis, define a class template *vec* that can be used to declare arrays of any type.

Chapter 14

VARIABLE ARGUMENT FUNCTIONS

C++ provides facilities for writing functions such as the C++ library function *printf* (see Chapter 16) which can be called with a variable number of arguments. Ellipses are used to denote the variable arguments in the function prototype and in the header of the function body. For example, here is the prototype of function *printf* that accepts a variable number of arguments to be printed according to the format specified in the string *fmt*:

```
int printf(const char *fmt ...);
```

The types and number of arguments that follow the first argument are not specified. However, in the body of *print* it must be possible to determine the types and the total number of arguments supplied in a call to *printf*. Typically, this information is extracted from the initial arguments of such a function. In case of *printf*, the information is extracted from the first argument which specifies the format of the items to be printed.

Here is an example of a call to function *printf*:

```
#include <stdio.h> //contains prototype of printf
int act; float bal;
...
printf("The balance in account %d is %f\n", act, bal);
```

The items beginning with % in the first argument, called format specifiers, indicate how the arguments that follow are to be printed. The number of format specifiers tells us how many arguments will follow and the letter following the % tells us about the argument type (d for integer and f for float).

Here is the general form of the prototype of a function that accepts a variable number of arguments (denoted by the ellipsis):

result-type   function-name (parameter-declarations , parameter-declaration ...) ;

The last explicitly specified parameter is significant; it is used as a "handle" for accessing the variable arguments. If the ellipsis is not preceded by an explicitly specified parameter, then the variable arguments cannot be accessed. Moreover, this parameter must be declared in the header of the function body; it is not sufficient to simply list its type.

Parameters corresponding to the variable arguments are accessed in the function body by using the following type and routines defined in the standard header file *stdarg.h*:

1. *va_list*: type for holding the variable arguments.

2. *va_start*: macro which must be called before accessing the first of the variable arguments; it has the prototype

    ```
    int va_start(va_list ap, last_parameter);
    ```

    va_start initializes parameter *ap* to point to the first element of a list whose elements refer to the variable arguments.

3. *va_arg*: macro for accessing the values, one at a time, of the variable arguments; it has the prototype

    ```
    type va_arg(va_list ap, type);
    ```

    va_arg returns the next argument (of type *type*) from the list referenced by *ap*; *va_arg* also updates *ap* to point to the next argument.

4. *va_end*: function which is called to indicate that accessing of the parameters corresponding to the variable arguments has been completed; it has the prototype

    ```
    int va_end(va_list ap);
    ```

    va_end must be called before returning from the function that accepts the variable arguments.

C++ converts an argument when there is no corresponding parameter (the argument matches the ellipsis) as follows:

1. *float* arguments are converted to *double*.

2. *char*, *short*, enumeration arguments are converted to *int*.

1. EXAMPLE

We will write a function *max* that computes the largest of its variable number of arguments, all of which will be of type *double*. Here is the prototype of function *max* (file *max.h*):

```
double max(int n, ...);
```

The first argument of *max* is a special one: it specifies the number of the (remaining) arguments from which the maximum is to be computed.

Since the types of the variable parameters have not been specified, C++ will apply the standard conversion rules to the specified parameters.

Here is the body of the function *max* (file *max.cpp*):

```
   #include <stdlib.h>
   #include <stdarg.h>
   #include <iostream.h>
   #include "max.h"
 5 double max(int n, ...)
   {
       va_list args;
       double large, temp;

10     if (n <= 0) {
           cerr << "max: error, n must be > 0" << endl;
           exit(1);
       }
       va_start(args, n);
15     large = va_arg(args, double);
       for (int i = 1; i < n; i++) {
           temp = va_arg(args, double);
           large = temp > large ? temp : large;
       }
20     va_end(args);
       return large;
   }
```

args is defined as a variable of type *va_list* (line 7) and it is initialized to point to the variable arguments with the call (line 14)

```
va_start(args, a);
```

a is the parameter immediately preceding the ellipsis. The variable arguments, of type *double*, are accessed one at a time, by calling *va_arg* (lines 15 and 17):

```
va_arg(args, double)
```

Accessing the variable argument is terminated by calling *va_end* (line 22).

Here are examples of *max* function calls:

```
max1 = max(5, a, b, c, d, e);
max2= max(4, v, w, x, y, z);
```

a, *b*, *c*, *d*, *e v*, *w*, *x*, *y*, and *z* are all expressions of type *double*. The second call specifies that four arguments will follow the first argument, but in fact five arguments have been given. Typically, giving extra arguments will not be harmful, but giving fewer than the number of arguments expected may cause the program to fail.

The output of the following call

```
cout << max(4, 1.0, 2.0, -22.0, 4.0);
```

is 4.0, but that of

```
cout << max(4, 1, 2, -22, 4);
```

is 0 which is garbage. The garbage output is produced because *max* expects arguments of type *double* but we have called it with arguments of type *int*. C++ cannot perform this conversion because the parameter types are not specified explicitly.

2. EXERCISES

1. Give examples of some functions that would be more appropriate if they accept a variable number of arguments.

2. Write a function *print* that prints a variable number of arguments of type *int*.

Chapter 15

PREPROCESSOR

The term "C++ compiler" informally refers to two components: the C++ preprocessor and the "real" C++ compiler. The C++ preprocessor processes a C++ program before it is passed on to the real C++ compiler for compilation. In conformance with existing use, we shall use the phrase "C++ compiler" to refer both to the pair "C++ preprocessor and the real C++ compiler" and to just the "real C++ compiler." The meaning should be clear from the context.

The C++ preprocessor transforms a C++ program as specified by the preprocessor instructions in the program. The preprocessor instructions (such as the *#include* instruction, which we have seen several times) begin with the # character which must be the first non-white-space character on a line.

The C++ preprocessor provides facilities for

- macro definitions,
- text inclusion, and
- conditional compilation.

After a C++ program has been processed by the C++ preprocessor, it must be valid C++ code. Otherwise, the C++ compiler will flag errors.

1. MACRO DEFINITIONS

A macro definition is used to associate a string with an identifier. Every occurrence in the program of such an identifier is replaced by the associated string.

By convention, upper-case letters are used for user-defined macro names (C++ implementations do not adhere to this convention for pre-defined macros).

1.1 CONSTANT DEFINITIONS

The C++ preprocessor macro facility can be used to define constants:

#define *constant-name constant-expression*

It is important to note that as far as the C++ preprocessor is concerned, *constant-expression* is simply a string. It is therefore the programmer's responsibility to ensure that *constant-expression* is a valid C++ expression. Otherwise, the C++ compiler will flag an error when it process the program after the C++ preprocessor has transformed the program.

Some examples of constant definitions are

```
#define M 64
#define N 16
#define MAX (M*2)
#define MONTHS 12
```

Here are three examples illustrating uses of the above definitions:

```
char a[M][N];
float sales[MONTHS];
int x[MAX];
```

Before the above code is compiled, it will be transformed by the C++ preprocessor to the code shown below:

```
char a[64][16];
float sales[12];
int x[64*2];
```

1.2 STRING DEFINITIONS

String definitions, which are similar to constant definitions, are used to give symbolic names to string constants and as abbreviations for C++ source code:

#define *string-name sequence-of-characters*

Two example definitions are

```
#define get(c) cin >> c
#define putline(s) cout << s << endl
```

The preprocessor transforms the macro call

```
get(c)
```

to the code

```
cin >> c
```

and the expression

```
putline(name)
```

to the expression

```
cout << name << endl
```

2. FILE INCLUSION

Typically, C++ declarations such as function prototypes used in source files are kept in header files. The contents of these header files are then included in the source files by using the C++ preprocessor *#include* instruction, which has the following two forms:

```
#include "file-name"
#include <file-name>
```

file-name specifies the file to be included. Angle brackets are typically used to specify standard header files while double quotes are used to specify user header files. The only difference between the two forms of the *#include* instruction is that when the file name is specified using quotes, the C++ preprocessor looks for the specified file in the current directory before looking for the file in standard or user-specified directories.[1]

The second form of the *#include* instruction (with the file name in angle brackets) does not look for the file in the current directory; it looks for the file in standard directories and in user-specified directories.

A path name (a file name with directory information), can be given instead of a simple file name. In MS-DOS, backslashes are used to separate components of the path name while slashes are used in UNIX systems. Many MS-DOS C++ compilers will accept both slashes and backslashes in the path name. For example, the path name can be specified as

```
/business/screen.h
```

or as

---

1. Users can specify additional "include" directories to be searched for "include" files as command-line options when invoking the C++ compiler.

```
\business\screen.h
```

#include instruction can be nested, that is, the included file can itself contain *#include* instructions.

3. CONDITIONAL COMPILATION

Conditional compilation is used to specify default macro definitions, to generate different versions of the same program, and to avoid multiple file inclusions. The C++ preprocessor allows conditional compilation to be based on the value of a constant expression and whether or not a symbol has been defined.

3.1 CONDITIONAL COMPILATION BASED ON THE VALUE OF CONSTANT EXPRESSIONS

The *#if* instruction is used for conditionally compiling code based on the value of a constant expression. This instruction has the forms

```
#if  constant-expression
        true-alternative-text
#endif
```

```
#if  constant-expression
        true-alternative-text
#else
        false-alternative-text
#endif
```

The preprocessor (like C++) treats a non-zero value as true and a zero as false. The text in each alternative can be preprocessor instructions, valid C++ instructions, or simply arbitrary characters

The preprocessor operator *defined* can be used to determine whether or not an identifier has been previously defined using the *#define* instruction.

3.2 CONDITIONAL COMPILATION BASED ON SYMBOL DEFINITION

The *#ifdef* and *#ifndef* instructions are used to conditionally compile code depending upon whether or not the specified identifier has been defined. The *#ifdef* instruction has the forms

```
#ifdef identifier
     true-alternative-text
#endif
```

```
#ifdef identifier
     true-alternative-text
#else
     false-alternative-text
#endif
```

The *#ifndef* instruction is similar to the *#ifdef* instruction, but it does the reverse. Instead of checking to see if a identifier has been defined, it checks to see if the identifier has *not* been defined.

The *#ifdef* and *#ifndef* instructions can be used to provide default constant (or default macro) definitions. For example, if an array size has not been explicitly specified, then a default size can be used:

```
#ifndef MAX_SIZE
#define MAX_SIZE 128
#endif
```

If identifier *MAX_SIZE* has been defined before the above instructions are encountered, then it will not be given a new value; otherwise, it will be defined to have the value 128.

As another example of conditional compilation, suppose you are writing a C++ program that contains machine-dependent code for the IBM and Apple^{TM} computers. Only code appropriate to one of these computers can be compiled as follows:

```
#ifdef IBM
     code for IBM computer
#endif
#ifdef APPLE
     code for Apple computer
#endif
```

To compile code for an IBM computer, a header file, which will be included by all functions containing code to the two different computers, should define the identifier *IBM*:

```
#define IBM 1
```

When compiling code for Apple computers, this definition should be replaced by a definition of the identifier *APPLE*.

4. AVOIDING MULTIPLE FILE INCLUSIONS

Conditional compilation is often used to avoid multiple inclusions of header files as a result of nested *#include* statements. Consider, as an example, a file *accounts.cpp* that includes two header files *screen.h* and *window.h*:

```
#include "screen.h"
#include "window.h"
```

If the header file *screen.h* also includes *window.h*, then the resulting effect is to include *window.h* twice in *accounts.cpp* leading to some items being defined twice. Such definitions will be flagged as errors by the C++ compiler.

Inclusion of *window.h* twice can be avoided by using conditional compilation to define a "shield" as follows:

1. Associate an identifier with each header file which, if defined, will indicate that the header file has been included.

2. Write code to conditionally include a header file only if the associated identifier has not been defined.

Suppose, for example, that identifiers *SCREEN* and *WINDOW* are associated with the header files *screen.h* and *window.h*. Using the above paradigm, file *window.h* is included in *screen.h* as follows:

```
#ifndef WINDOW
#define WINDOW 1
#include "window.h"
#endif
...
```

Files *window.h* and *screen.h* are included in *accounts.cpp* as follows:

```
#ifndef SCREEN
#define SCREEN 1
#include "screen.h"
#endif

#ifndef WINDOW
#define WINDOW 1
#include "window.h"
#endif
...
```

The inclusion of *window.h* in *screen.h* will not take place because *WINDOW* will have been defined after *screen.h* has been included.

Chapter 16
LIBRARY FACILITIES

C++ provides many facilities as library functions and library classes. Each C++ compiler is expected to supply these facilities as part of its standard environment. The difference in providing facilities as "part of the language syntax" or by putting them in the standard "library" concerns mostly the language designer and implementor. As far as the user is concerned, it does not matter how the facilities are provided. In either case, the facilities will be part of the language definition.

We have already discussed the stream input/output library facilities. In this chapter, we will discuss the standard functions provided by C++. These standard C++ functions are functions that C++ "inherits" from C.

C++ compilers typically also provide many other library classes and functions, such as those for graphics, tasking, complex arithmetic, and list manipulation. For details, please refer to the library reference manual of your C++ compiler.

1. USING THE LIBRARIES

C++ library functions and macros will be described in three steps:

1. An *#include* statement will be given that includes the appropriate header file. The *#include* statement must be appear in the program prior to any references to the library function or macro.

2. A prototype for the function (in case of macros an equivalent function prototype) is given. This prototype (or the appropriate definition in case of macros) is contained in the header file specified by the *#include* statement.

3. An informal description of the function semantics.

Commonly used C++ library facilities, such as the stream input/output facilities, and character and string processing functions, are stored in the standard C++ library. This library is automatically linked ("combined") with C++ object files to produce an executable program. Other libraries, if required, must be explicitly specified to produce an executable program.

To produce an executable program (a *.exe* file on MS-DOS systems and a *a.out* file on UNIX systems), the C++ compiler first determines which functions are used in the program, but not defined in the program. The compiler then looks for the definitions of these functions in the standard C++ library and in other libraries that have been explicitly specified by the programmer.

Functions whose definitions are found in the C++ libraries are automatically loaded and linked with the C++ program. If there are functions which are referenced in a C++ program, but which are not defined in it, and these functions are also not in the specified libraries, then the C++ compiler will flag an error.

1.1 STANDARD HEADER FILES

Each C++ compiler provides a set of standard header files which contain the prototypes of the library functions, macro definitions, and related type and constant definitions. Using the library facilities in general requires that the program include the appropriate header files. The header file to be included when you use a library facility is specified in the description of the facility.

Including a standard header file more than once is harmless. Standard header file inclusion is "idempotent"; in other words, the effect of including a header file more than once in the same file is equivalent to including it once. However, multiple inclusions of user-defined header files are not automatically idempotent. Their inclusion can be made idempotent by protecting the contents of each header file with a "shield" which ensures that only the first inclusion of the header file has any effect (see Chapter 15).

Each C++ implementation provides many standard header files, including the following often-used header files:

header file	contains declarations/definitions for
ctype.h	Character classification macros.
float.h	Floating-point limits.
fstream.h	Facilities for defining streams.
iostream.h	Stream input/output facilities.
limits.h	Integral limits.
math.h	Mathematical functions.
new.h	Function *operator new*, which is called by the storage allocator *new* to allocate storage, and function *set_new_handler*, which changes the behavior of *operator new*.
setjmp.h	Non-local jump routines.
signal.h	Signal handling facilities.
stdarg.h	Facilities for accessing the parameters of functions that accept a variable number of arguments.
stddef.h	Types such as *size_t* (type of value returned by *sizeof*), and constants such as *NULL* and the declaration of the external variable *errno*.
stdio.h	Input/output facilities (inherited from C).
stdlib.h	Types such as *size_t*, constants such as *NULL*, utility functions, and the declaration of the external variable *errno*.
string.h	String and memory functions such as *strlen*, *strcpy*, and *memmove*.

The header file to be included when using a library facility will be specified in the description of the facility.

2. STANDARD FUNCTIONS

The standard functions are grouped into categories such as character, strings, input/output, math, etc. We will now discuss these functions.

2.1 CHARACTER

Character processing functions are of two kinds: *classification* and *conversion*.

2.1.1 CLASSIFICATION The specification of the character classification functions has the form

```
#include <ctype.h>
int istest(int c);
```

istest returns 1 if character parameter *c* satisfies the test; otherwise, it returns zero.

2.1.2 CONVERSION The character classification functions defined are

function	test
isalnum	letter or digit
isalpha	letter
iscntrl	control character
isdigit	digit
isgraph	printing character (except a space)
islower	lower-case letter
isprint	printing character (including a space)
ispunct	punctuation character
isspace	space, carriage-return, form-feed, new-line, horizontal, or vertical-tab character
isupper	upper-case letter
isxdigit	hexadecimal digit

The specification of the character conversion functions has the form

```
#include <ctype.h>
int totype(int c);
```

If function *totype* can perform the conversion, it returns the converted character; otherwise, it returns *c*.

There are two character conversion functions:

function	conversion
tolower	lower case
toupper	upper case

2.2 MATH

2.2.1 ACOS: ARC COSINE

```
#include <math.h>
double acos(double x);
```

acos returns the arc cosine of *x*.

2.2.2 ASIN: ARC SINE

```
#include <math.h>
double asin(double x);
```

asin returns the arc sine of *x*.

2.2.3 ATAN: ARC TAN

```
#include <math.h>
double atan(double x);
```

atan returns the arc tangent of *x*.

2.2.4 ATAN2: ARC TAN

```
#include <math.h>
double atan2(double y, double x);
```

atan2 returns the arc tangent of y/x.

2.2.5 COS: COSINE

```
#include <math.h>
double cos(double x);
```

cos returns the cosine of its parameter *x*.

2.2.6 SIN: SINE

```
#include <math.h>
double sin(double x);
```

cos returns the sine of its parameter *x*.

2.2.7 TAN: TANGENT

```
#include <math.h>
double tan(double x);
```

tan returns the tangent of its parameter *x*.

2.2.8 COSH: HYPERBOLIC COSINE

```
#include <math.h>
double cosh(double x);
```

cosh returns the hyperbolic cosine of its parameter *x*.

2.2.9 SINH: HYPERBOLIC SINE

```
#include <math.h>
double sinh(double x);
```

sinh returns the hyperbolic sine of its parameter x.

2.2.10 TANH: HYPERBOLIC TAN

```
#include <math.h>
double tanh(double x);
```

tanh returns the hyperbolic tangent of its parameter x.

2.2.11 EXP: EXPONENTIATION

```
#include <math.h>
double exp(double x);
```

exp returns e^x.

2.2.12 FREXP: SPLIT DOUBLE VALUE INTO FRACTION AND EXPONENT

```
#include <math.h>
double frexp(double v, int *xp);
```

frexp returns the fractional part of parameter v and stores the exponent of v in the integer referenced by *xp*.

2.2.13 LDEXP: COMBINE FRACTION AND EXPONENT INTO A DOUBLE

```
#include <math.h>
double ldexp(double v, int x);
```

ldexp returns the *double* formed by combining the fractional part v and the exponent x.

2.2.14 LOG: NATURAL LOGARITHM

```
#include <math.h>
double log(double x);
```

log returns the natural logarithm of its parameter x.

2.2.15 LOG10: BASE 10 LOGARITHM

```
#include <math.h>
double log10(double x);
```

log10 returns the base 10 logarithm of its parameter x.

2.2.16 MODF: SPLIT DOUBLE VALUE

```
#include <math.h>
double modf(double x, double *ip);
```

modf splits *x* into an integer part that is stored in the object referenced by *ip* and returns the fractional part.

2.2.17 POW: RAISE TO A POWER

```
#include <math.h>
double pow(double x, double y);
```

pow returns x^y.

2.2.18 SQRT: SQUARE ROOT

```
#include <math.h>
double sqrt(double x);
```

sqrt returns the square root of its parameter *x*.

2.2.19 CEIL: CEILING

```
#include <math.h>
double ceil(double x);
```

ceil returns the next smallest integer greater than its parameter *x*.

2.2.20 FLOOR: FLOOR

```
#include <math.h>
double floor(double x);
```

floor returns the next largest integer smaller than its parameter *x*.

2.2.21 FMOD: FLOATING-POINT MODULUS

```
#include <math.h>
double fmod(double x, double y);
```

fmod returns the fractional part of the result of dividing *x* by *y*.

2.3 NON-LOCAL JUMPS

2.3.1 SETJMP: SAVE ENVIRONMENT FOR LONG JUMP

```
#include <setjmp.h>
int setjmp(jmp_buf env);
```

Macro *setjmp* saves the program environment at the point of the call in the buffer *env* and returns zero. Calling *longjmp* with the environment saved using *setjmp* causes *setjmp* to return with a non-zero value.

2.3.2 LONGJMP: RESTORE SAVED ENVIRONMENT

```
#include <setjmp.h>
void longjmp(jmp_buf env, int v);
```

longjmp restores the program environment *env* saved by a *setjmp* call. The program then continues as if this *setjmp* call had returned the value *v*.

2.4 SIGNAL HANDLING

C++ supports several signals, e.g.,

signal	condition
SIGABRT	abnormal termination
SIGFPE	zero divide or overflow
SIGILL	illegal instruction
SIGINT	interrupt
SIGSEGV	illegal memory reference
SIGTERM	termination signal

For a complete list, please refer to the library reference manual of your C++ compiler.

2.4.1 SIGNAL: SET UP A SIGNAL HANDLER

```
#include <signal.h>
void (*signal(int sig, void (*sigfun)(int))) (int);
```

signal sets up the signal handler. Upon the occurrence of the signal *sig*, function *sigfun* is called with *sig* as its argument. *signal* returns the old signal handler (*SIG_ERR* in case of an error). Two special pre-defined signal handler functions are *SIG_IGN* (ignore signal) and *SIG_DFL* (take default action).

2.4.2 RAISE: GENERATE A SIGNAL

```
#include <signal.h>
int raise(int sig);
```

raise generates the signal *sig*. If successful, *raise* returns zero; otherwise, it returns a non-zero value.

2.5 INPUT/OUTPUT

Header file *stdio.h* contains the declarations and definitions necessary for using the standard input/output facilities. The following constants are defined in the header file *stdio.h*:

stdin	Standard input stream.
stdout	Standard output stream.
stderr	Standard error stream.
EOF	End-of-file value (−1).
FILE *	Type used to declare objects that refer to files.
NULL	The null pointer.

2.5.1 REMOVE: DELETE A FILE

```
#include <stdio.h>
int remove(const char *filename);
```

remove deletes the specified file. If successful *remove* returns zero; otherwise, it returns a non-zero value.

2.5.2 RENAME: CHANGE FILE NAME

```
#include <stdio.h>
int rename(const char *old, const char *new);
```

rename changes the name of a file from the one referenced by *old* to that referenced by *new*. If successful, *rename* returns zero; otherwise, it returns a non-zero value.

2.5.3 TMPFILE: CREATE A TEMPORARY FILE

```
#include <stdio.h>
FILE *tmpfile(void);
```

tmpfile creates a temporary file and returns a pointer to the file or, in case of an error, the null pointer.

2.5.4 TMPNAM: GENERATE UNIQUE FILE NAME

```
#include <stdio.h>
char *tmpnam(char *fname)
```

tmpnam returns a pointer to a unique file name generated by it. If *fname* is not null, then *tmpnam* stores the file name in the array referenced by *fname*, which is returned as the result.

2.5.5 FCLOSE: CLOSE STREAM

```
#include <stdio.h>
int fclose(FILE *stream)
```

fclose flushes and closes the specified stream. If successful, *fclose* returns zero; otherwise, it returns *EOF*.

2.5.6 FFLUSH: FLUSH OUTPUT BUFFER

```
#include <stdio.h>
int fflush (FILE *stream);
```

fflush flushes the specified stream by printing the output collected in the associated buffer. If successful, *fflush* returns zero; otherwise, it returns *EOF*.

2.5.7 FOPEN: OPEN A FILE

```
#include <stdio.h>
FILE *fopen(const char *fname, const char *mode);
```

fopen opens the file with the name referenced by *fname* as a stream and returns a pointer to the stream. In case of an error, *fopen* returns the null pointer.

Argument *mode* has the following semantics:

mode	effect
"r"	Open existing file for reading.
"w"	Create a new file or open an existing file for writing and mark it as empty.
"a"	Create a new file or open an existing file for writing in append mode.
"rb"	Open a binary file for reading.
"wb"	Create a new binary file or open an existing binary file for writing and mark the file as empty.
"ab"	Create a new binary file or open an existing binary file for writing in append mode.
"r+"	Open an existing file for update with the file pointer positioned at the beginning of the file.
"w+"	Create a new file or open an existing file for updating and mark it as empty.
"a+"	Create a new file or open an existing file for updating in append mode.
"r+b"	Open an existing binary file for update starting from the beginning of the file.
"w+b"	Create a new binary file or open an existing binary file for updating and mark the file as empty.
"a+b"	Create a new binary file or open an existing binary file for updating in append mode.

Read and write operations for update files must be separated by calls to functions *rewind* or *fseek*.

2.5.8 FREOPEN: REOPEN A FILE

```
#include <stdio.h>
FILE *freopen(const char *fname,
              const char *mode, FILE *stream);
```

freopen closes the specified file, and then opens and associates it with the specified stream using the specified mode. If *freopen* is successful, then it returns *stream*; otherwise it returns *NULL*.

2.5.9 SETBUF: SET BUFFERING

```
#include <stdio.h>
void setbuf(FILE *stream, char *buf);
```

Calling *setbuf* is equivalent to the call

```
setvbuf(stream, buf, _IOFBF, BUFSIZE);
```

If *buf* is the null pointer, then calling *setbuf* is equivalent to the call

```
setvbuf(stream, NULL, _IONBF, 0);
```

2.5.10 SETVBUF: SET BUFFERING

```
#include <stdio.h>
int setvbuf(FILE *stream, char *buf, int mode, size_t size)
```

setvbuf is called to specify stream buffering. If *mode* is equal to

- *_IOFBF* then input/output will be fully buffered;
- *_IOLBF* then input/output will be line buffered;
- *_IONBF* then input/output will not be buffered.

If *buf* is not a null pointer, then the array referenced by *buf* (size equal to *size*) will be used for buffering instead of a buffer allocated by *setvbuf*.

2.5.11 FPRINTF: WRITE FORMATTED OUTPUT TO A FILE

```
#include <stdio.h>
int fprintf(FILE *stream, const char *fmt ...);
```

fprintf is similar to function *printf* except that it can be used to write to any stream.

2.5.12 FSCANF: READ FORMATTED INPUT FROM A FILE

```
#include <stdio.h>
int fscanf(FILE *stream, const char *fmt ...);
```

fscanf is similar to function *scanf* except that it can be used to read input from any stream.

2.5.13 PRINTF: WRITE FORMATTED OUTPUT TO STDOUT

```
#include <stdio.h>
int printf(const char *fmt ...);
```

printf is used for writing formatted text to the standard output stream. The print format is specified by the string referenced by *fmt*, which contains text to be printed and the conversion specifications (print formats). The conversion specifications also act as place holders for the arguments.

Each conversion specification begins with the percent character and has the form

%FlagsWidthPrecisionType

Items *Flags*, *Width*, and *Precision* are optional and may be omitted. Note that two percent characters must be given to print a single percent character.

The optional *Flags* is a sequence of characters that modify the format specified by the other components:

flag	effect
–	Left justify the item.
+	Print a leading sign (normally only a minus is printed).
space	Like plus, but a space is printed instead of a leading plus.
#	Prefix numbers printed in octal and hexadecimal format with a 0, 0x, or 0X.
0	Use leading zeros, instead of blanks, for padding.

The optional *Width* is a non-negative integer that specifies the minimum field width of the item to be printed.

The optional *Precision* consists of a decimal point followed by an optional integer (zero if omitted) whose meaning depends upon the value of *Type* in the item format:

1. For integer formats (*d*, *o*, *u*, *x*, and *X*), *Precision* specifies the minimum number of digits to be printed.

2. For the floating-point format (*f*) and for the scientific formats (*e* and *E*), *Precision* specifies the number of fractional digits.

3. For the floating/scientific format (*g*), *Precision* specifies the maximum number of significant digits.

4. For the string format (*s*), *Precision* specifies the maximum number of characters to be printed.

The *Type* component specifies the actual conversion necessary to print the corresponding argument. The conversion is specified by one of the characters listed below. Note that to print *long* (*short*) arguments, the conversion character for printing integers should be preceded by the letter *l* (*h*); for *long double* arguments, the conversion character for printing *double* values should be preceded by the letter *L*:

conversion	effect
c	Print a character.
d	Print a decimal integer.
e	Print a double-precision value (in scientific notation).
E	Same as the conversion character *e* except that the exponent is preceded by an *E* instead of an *e*.
f	Print a double-precision value.
g	Print a double-precision value in either *e* or *f* format as appropriate; the *e* format is used for very large or very small values.
o	Print an octal number.
s	Print a string.
u	Print an unsigned integer.
x	Print a hexadecimal integer.

printf returns the number of characters that are printed. If unsuccessful, it returns a negative value.

2.5.14 SCANF: READ FORMATTED INPUT FROM STDIN

```
#include <stdio.h>
int scanf(const char *fmt ...);
```

scanf reads data from the standard input stream as specified by the format string *fmt*; this data is stored in variables whose addresses are given as arguments following the format string. The format string contains four classes of items:

1. White space characters which cause input to be read up to the first non-white space character in the input.

2. Format items which specify the data format and act as place holders for the pointer arguments, which specify where data is to be stored.

3. Any other character which is not part of a conversion specification must be matched by an identical character in the input.

4. Pairs of percent characters to match a single percent character in the input.

Each conversion specification is of the form

%*WidthType*

The optional asterisk specifies a suppressed conversion. No argument is given for such an item.

Format item component *Width*, which is a non-zero unsigned decimal integer, specifies the maximum field width for the data item.

The *Type* component specifies the actual conversion necessary when reading the corresponding input item. The conversion is specified by one of the following characters:

conversion	effect
c	Read a character.
d	Read a decimal integer.
f	Read a double-precision value (using *e*, *E*, or *g* is identical to using *f*).
o	Read an octal number.
s	Read a string; a white space terminates the string.
u	Read an unsigned integer.
x	Read a hexadecimal integer.

To read *long* (*short*) arguments, the conversion character for reading integers should be preceded by the letter *l* (*h*); to read *long double* arguments, the conversion character for reading floating-point values should be preceded by the letter *L*:

If successful, *scanf* returns the number of items read and stored in the addresses specified by the arguments following the format string; otherwise, *scanf* returns a negative value.

2.5.15 SPRINTF: WRITE FORMATTED OUTPUT TO A STRING

```
#include <stdio.h>
int sprintf(char *s, const char * fmt ...);
```

sprintf is similar to *printf* with one exception: *sprintf* writes to a string (specified by the parameter *s*). A terminating null character is added at the end of string *s*.

2.5.16 SSCANF: READ FORMATTED INPUT FROM A STRING

```
#include <stdio.h>
int sscanf(const char *s, const char *fmt ...);
```

sscanf is similar to function *scanf* with one exception: *sscanf* reads data from a string (specified by the parameter *s*).

2.5.17 VFPRINTF: WRITE FORMATTED OUTPUT TO A STRING

```
#include <stdio.h>
int vfprintf(FILE *stream, const char *fmt, va_list arg);
```

vfprintf is similar to function *fprintf* with one exception: the variable argument list denoted by the ellipsis is replaced by the parameter *arg*, which must have been initialized properly by calling macro *va_start*.

2.5.18 VPRINTF: WRITE FORMATTED OUTPUT TO A FILE

```
#include <stdio.h>
int vprintf(const char *fmt, va_list arg);
```

vprintf is similar to function *vfprintf* except that it writes to standard output.

2.5.19 VSPRINTF: WRITE FORMATTED OUTPUT TO A FILE

```
#include <stdio.h>
int vsprintf(char *s, const char *fmt, va_list arg);
```

vsprintf is similar to function *vfprintf* except that it writes to the string *s*.

2.5.20 FGETC: GET A CHARACTER FROM A FILE *fgetc* is the function version of macro *getc*:

```
#include <stdio.h>
int fgetc(FILE *stream);
```

fgetc returns the next character from the specified stream. If *fgetc* encounters the end-of-file, then it returns *EOF*.

2.5.21 FGETS: GET A STRING FROM A FILE

```
#include <stdio.h>
char *fgets(char *s, int n, FILE *stream);
```

fgets reads characters from the specified stream and stores them in the array referenced by *s*. Characters are read until an end-of-file or until a new-line character is encountered, or *n-1* characters have been read. A terminating null character is then added at the end of the array. Note that the new-line character is stored in the string.

fgets returns *s* as its result unless an immediate end-of-file is encountered or an error occurs, in which case *fgets* returns the null pointer *NULL*.

2.5.22 FPUTC: WRITE A CHARACTER TO A FILE *fputc* is the function version of macro *putc*:

```
#include <stdio.h>
int fputc(int c, FILE *stream);
```

fputc writes the character *c* to the specified stream. If successful, *fputc* returns *c*; otherwise, it returns *EOF*.

2.5.23 FPUTS: WRITE A STRING TO A FILE

```
#include <stdio.h>
int fputs(const char *s, FILE *stream);
```

fputs writes string *s*, which must be terminated by a null character, to the specified stream. The null character is not written. If an error occurs, *fputs* returns *EOF*; otherwise, it returns a non-negative value.

2.5.24 GETC: GET A CHARACTER FROM A FILE *getc* is the macro version of function *fgetc*:

```
#include <stdio.h>
int getc(FILE *stream);
```

Macro *getc* returns the next character from the specified stream unless an end-of-file is encountered, in which case it returns *EOF*.

2.5.25 GETCHAR: GET A CHARACTER FROM STDIN *getchar* is the macro version of function *fgetchar*:

```
#include <stdio.h>
int getchar(void);
```

getchar returns the next character from the standard input unless an end-of-file is encountered, in which case it returns *EOF*.

2.5.26 GETS: GET A STRING FROM STDIN

```
#include <stdio.h>
char *gets(char *s);
```

gets reads characters from standard input and stores them in the array referenced by *s*. Characters are read until an end-of-file or a new-line character is encountered; the new-line character is replaced by a terminating null character.

gets returns *s* as its result unless an immediate end-of-file is encountered or an error occurs, in which case it returns the null pointer *NULL*.

2.5.27 PUTC: WRITE A CHARACTER TO A FILE *putc* is the macro version of function *fputc*:

```
#include <stdio.h>
int putc(char c, FILE *stream);
```

putc writes character *c* to the specified stream and returns *c*. In case of an error, *putc* returns *EOF*.

2.5.28 PUTCHAR: WRITE A CHARACTER TO STDOUT

```
#include <stdio.h>
int putchar(char c);
```

putchar writes character *c* to the standard output.

2.5.29 PUTS: WRITE STRING TO STDOUT

```
#include <stdio.h>
int puts(char *s);
```

puts writes string *s* to the standard output and then prints the new-line character. If an error occurs, *puts* returns *EOF*; otherwise, it returns a non-negative value.

2.5.30 UNGETC: PUSH A CHARACTER BACK INTO THE INPUT FILE

```
#include <stdio.h>
int ungetc(char c, FILE *stream);
```

ungetc puts the character *c* back on to the specified stream. *c* will be the character first read by the next input operation. If successful, function *ungetc* will return *c*; otherwise, it will return *EOF*.

2.5.31 FREAD: READ BLOCKS FROM A FILE

```
#include <stdio.h>
int fread(void *p, size_t size, size_t n, FILE *stream);
```

fread reads up to *n* elements, each *size_t* bytes long, from the specified stream, and stores them in the array referenced by *p*. *fread* returns the number of elements read successfully.

2.5.32 FWRITE: WRITE BLOCKS TO A FILE

```
#include <stdio.h>
int fwrite(const void *p, size_t size,
           size_t n, FILE *stream);
```

fwrite writes *n* elements, each *size_t* bytes long, starting at the array referenced by *p*, to the specified stream. *fwrite* returns the number of elements written successfully.

2.5.33 FGETPOS: GET FILE POSITION

```
#include <stdio.h>
int fgetpos(FILE *stream, fpos_t *pos);
```

fgetpos stores the current file position of the specified stream in the object referenced by *pos*. If successful, *getpos* returns zero; otherwise, it returns a non-zero value.

2.5.34 FSEEK: MOVE TO SPECIFIED FILE POSITION

```
#include <stdio.h>
int fseek(FILE *stream, long int offset, int whence);
```

fseek moves the file position indicator associated with the specified stream:

```
switch whence {
case SEEK_SET:
```
    move by `offset` *characters relative to the beginning of the file;*
```
    break;
case SEEK_CUR:
```
    move by `offset` *characters relative to its current position;*
```
    break;
case SEEK_END:
```
    move by `offset` *characters relative to the end-of-file;*
```
}
```

If successful, *fseek* returns zero; otherwise, it returns a non-zero value.

2.5.35 FSETPOS: SET FILE POSITION

```
#include <stdio.h>
int fsetpos(FILE *stream, const fpos_t *pos);
```

fsetpos sets the file position indicator associated with the specified stream to the value referenced by *pos*. This value must have been obtained by calling *getpos* on the specified stream. If unsuccessful, *fsetpos* returns zero; otherwise, it returns a non-zero value.

2.5.36 FTELL: GET CURRENT FILE POSITION

```
#include <stdio.h>
long int ftell(FILE *stream);
```

ftell returns the position of the file position indicator associated with the specified stream; if unsuccessful, *ftell* returns −1.

2.5.37 REWIND: RESET A FILE

```
#include <stdio.h>
void rewind(FILE *stream);
```

rewind resets the file position indicator of the specified stream to the beginning of the stream.

2.5.38 CLEARERR: CLEAR ERROR AND EOF INDICATION

```
#include <stdio.h>
void clearerr(FILE *stream);
```

clearerr clears the error and the end-of-file conditions associated with the specified stream.

2.5.39 FEOF: END-OF-FILE CHECK

```
#include <stdio.h>
int feof(FILE *stream);
```

feof returns a non-zero value if an end-of-file is encountered while reading from the specified stream; otherwise, it returns zero.

2.5.40 FERROR: ERROR CHECK

```
#include <stdio.h>
int ferror(FILE *stream);
```

ferror returns a non-zero value if an error is encountered while reading from or writing to the specified stream; otherwise, it returns zero.

2.5.41 PERROR: PRINT ERROR MESSAGE

```
#include <stdio.h>
void perror(int errno);
```

perror prints an error message consisting of the string *s* followed by a string describing the error indicated by *errno*.

2.6 GENERAL UTILITY

Only the commonly used functions in this library are described here.

2.6.1 RAND: RANDOM NUMBER

```
#include <stdlib.h>
int rand(void);
```

rand returns a random number between zero and *RAND_MAX*, which is defined in *stdlib.h*.

2.6.2 SRAND: SET SEED FOR RANDOM NUMBER GENERATOR RAND

```
#include <stdlib.h>
void srand(unsigned int seed);
```

srand sets the seed for the random numbers generated by *rand*. The default seed used is one.

2.6.3 CALLOC: ALLOCATE & CLEAR MEMORY

```
#include <stdlib.h>
void *calloc(size_t n, size_t size);
```

calloc allocates storage for an array of *n* elements of size *size*; all bits of the allocated storage are set to zero. If storage can be allocated, *calloc* returns a pointer to the beginning of the allocated storage; otherwise, it returns the null pointer *NULL*.

2.6.4 MALLOC: ALLOCATE MEMORY

```
#include <stdlib.h>
void *malloc(size_t size);
```

malloc allocates a block of memory of size *size* bytes. If successful, *malloc* returns a pointer to the allocated block; otherwise, it returns the null pointer *NULL*.

2.6.5 REALLOC: REALLOCATE MEMORY

```
#include <stdlib.h>
void *realloc(void *ptr, size_t size);
```

realloc takes a pointer to a previously allocated memory block and changes its size as specified while preserving its contents (up to the specified size).

2.6.6 FREE: FREE MEMORY

```
#include <stdlib.h>
void free(void *ptr);
```

free deallocates a previously allocated memory block referenced by *ptr*.

2.6.7 ABORT: RAISE ABORT SIGNAL

```
#include <stdlib.h>
void abort(void);
```

abort raises the signal *SIGABRT* and the program terminates regardless of whether or not a handler is specified for *SIGABRT*.

2.6.8 EXIT: TERMINATE PROGRAM

```
#include <stdlib.h>
void exit(int status);
```

exit terminates the program; the value *status* is returned to the environment. Successful program execution is indicated by calling *exit* with zero or with *EXIT_SUCCESS*; failure is indicated by calling *exit* with *EXIT_FAILURE*.

2.6.9 GETENV: GET AN ENVIRONMENT VARIABLE

```
#include <stdlib.h>
char *getenv(const char *s);
```

getenv searches the environment for a string that matches the string referenced by *s*. If successful, *getenv* returns the string associated with the matched string; otherwise, it returns a null pointer.

2.6.10 SYSTEM: EXECUTE OPERATING SYSTEM COMMAND

```
#include <stdlib.h>
int system(char *cmd);
```

system executes the operating system command specified by the string *cmd*; it returns an implementation-dependent value.

2.6.11 BSEARCH: BINARY SEARCH

```
#include <stdlib.h>
int *bsearch(const void *key, const void *base,
             size_t n, size_t size,
             int (*cmp)(const void *, const void *));
```

bsearch searches the array *base*, which has at least *n* elements of the specified size, for the object referenced by *key*. The array must be sorted in increasing order according to the comparison function *cmp*, which returns an integer greater than, equal to, or less than zero, depending upon whether the object referenced by *key* is less than, equal to, or greater than an array element. If *bsearch* finds a match, then it returns the address of the array element matched; otherwise, it returns the null pointer.

2.6.12 QSORT: QUICKSORT AN ARRAY

```
#include <stdlib.h>
int qsort(void *base, size_t n, size_t size
          int (*cmp)(const void *, const void *));
```

qsort sorts the array *base*, which must have *n* elements each of size *size*. The array is sorted in increasing order according to the comparison function *cmp*, which returns an integer greater than, equal to, or less than zero depending upon whether its first argument is less than, equal to or greater than its second argument.

2.6.13 ABS: ABSOLUTE VALUE

```
#include <stdlib.h>
int abs(int x);
```

abs returns the absolute value of *x*.

2.6.14 DIV: INTEGER DIVIDE

```
#include <stdlib.h>
div_t div(int num, int denom);
```

div returns a value of type

```
typedef struct div_t {
    int quot;
    int rem;
} div_t;
```

that contains the quotient and remainder of dividing *num* by *denom*.

2.6.15 LABS: LONG INTEGER ABSOLUTE VALUE

```
#include <stdlib.h>
long int labs(long int x);
```

labs returns the absolute value of *x* (like *abs* except that it is used for *long int* values).

2.6.16 LDIV: LONG INTEGER DIVIDE

```
#include <stdlib.h>
ldiv_t ldiv(long int num, long int denom);
```

ldiv returns a structure of type

```
typedef struct ldiv_t {
    long quot;
    long rem;
} ldiv_t;
```

that contains the quotient and remainder of dividing *num* by *denom* (like *div* except that it is used for *long int* values).

2.7 STRING MANIPULATION

Only the commonly used string manipulation functions are described here.

2.7.1 STRCPY: COPY STRING

```
#include <string.h>
char *strcpy(char *d, const char *s);
```

strcpy copies the string referenced by *s* to the array referenced by *d* and returns *d*.

2.7.2 STRNCPY: COPY n CHARACTERS OF STRING

```
#include <string.h>
char *strncpy(char *d, const char *s, size_t n):
```

strncpy copies *n* characters from string pointed by *s* to the array referenced by *d* and returns *d*. If *n* is greater than *strlen(s)*, then null characters are appended to *d* until a total of *n* characters have been copied.

2.7.3 STRCAT: CONCATENATE STRINGS

```
#include <string.h>
char *strcat(char *d, const char *s);
```

strcat appends a copy of the string referenced by *s* to the end of the string referenced by *d*. The terminating null character in the string referenced by *d* is overwritten with characters from the string referenced by *s* and a new terminating null character is added after the appended characters. *strcat* returns the value of *d*.

2.7.4 STRNCAT: CONCATENATE n CHARACTERS

```
#include <string.h>
char *strncat(char *d, char *const s, size_t n);
```

strncat appends the first *n* characters from the string referenced by *s* to the end of the string referenced by *d*. The terminating null character in the string referenced by *d* is overwritten with characters from the string referenced by *s* and a new terminating null character is added following the characters appended. If *n* is greater than *strlen(s)*, then *strncat(d, s, n)* is equivalent to *strcat(d, s)*. *strncat* returns the value of *d*.

2.7.5 STRCMP: COMPARE TWO STRINGS

```
#include <string.h>
int strcmp(const char *a, const char *b);
```

strcmp returns a negative, a zero, or a positive integer value depending upon whether the string referenced by *a* is lexicographically less than, equal to, or greater than the string referenced by *b*.

2.7.6 STRNCMP: COMPARE UP TO n CHARACTERS OF TWO STRINGS

```
#include <string.h>
int strncmp(const char *a, const char *b, size_t n);
```

strncmp is the same as *strcmp* except that it compares at most the first *n* characters of the two strings.

2.7.7 STRCHR: SEARCH FOR THE FIRST OCCURRENCE OF A CHARACTER

```
#include <string.h>
char *strchr(const char *s, int c);
```

strchr returns a pointer to the first occurrence of *c* provided the string referenced by *s* contains *c*; otherwise, it returns the null pointer *NULL*.

2.7.8 STRCSPN: MEASURE SPAN (COUNT NUMBER) OF CHARACTERS NOT IN SET

```
#include <string.h>
size_t strcspn(const char *a, const char *b);
```

strcspn returns the number of leading characters in the string referenced by *a* that are not in the character set specified by the string referenced by *b*.

2.7.9 STRPBRK: FIND BREAK CHARACTER

```
#include <string.h>
char *strpbrk(const char *a, const char *b);
```

strpbrk returns a pointer to the first character in the string referenced by *a* that belongs to the character set specified by the break string referenced by *b*; in the absence of such a character, *strpbrk* returns the null pointer *NULL*.

2.7.10 STRRCHR: SEARCH FOR THE LAST OCCURRENCE OF A CHARACTER

```
#include <string.h>
char *strrchr(const char *s, int c);
```

strrchr is the same as *strchr* except that it returns a pointer to the last occurrence of *c* in the string referenced by *s*.

2.7.11 STRSPN: MEASURE SPAN (COUNT NUMBER) OF CHARACTERS IN SET

```
#include <string.h>
int strspn(const char *a, const char *b);
```

strspn returns the number of leading characters of the string referenced by *a* that are members of the character set specified by the string referenced by *b*.

2.7.12 STRSTR: FIND SUBSTRING

```
#include <string.h>
int strstr(const char *a, const char *b);
```

strstr returns a pointer to the first substring in the string referenced by *a* that matches the string *b*. If there is no such string, then *strstr* returns the null pointer *NULL*.

2.7.13 STRTOK: GET A TOKEN

```
#include <string.h>
char *strtok(char *a, const char *b);
```

strtok extracts "tokens" from the string referenced by *a* ; this string is treated as a list of tokens separated by the characters in the string referenced by *b*. To get tokens from a string referenced by *y* with the separators specified in the string referenced by *y*, *strtok* is first called with arguments *x* and *y*, and then called repeatedly with the null pointer *NULL* as its first argument and *y* still as its second argument. Each time *strtok* will return a pointer to the next token from the string referenced by *x*. Upon reaching the end of the string referenced by *x*, *strtok* returns the null pointer.

2.7.14 STRLEN: STRING LENGTH

```
#include <string.h>
int strlen(const char *s);
```

strlen returns the length of the string referenced by *s*.

BIBLIOGRAPHY

Ellis, M. A. and B. Stroustrup 1990. *The Annotated C++ Reference Manual*. Addison-Wesley.

Kernighan, B. W. and D. M. Ritchie 1989. *The C Programming Language (Second Edition)*. Prentice Hall.

Skinner, M. T. 1992. *The Advanced C++ Book*. Silicon Press.

Stroustrup, B. 1986. *The C++ Programming Language*. Addison-Wesley.

Stroustrup, Bjarne 1988. Parameterized Types for C++. *USENIX C++ Conference Proceedings*, Denver, CO.

Stroustrup, Bjarne 1991. *The C++ Programming Language* (Second Edition). Addison-Wesley.

INDEX